OVERTURNING
WRONGFUL
CONVICTIONS

SCIENCE SERVING JUSTICE

ELIZABETH A. MURRAY, PHD

Author Dedication: This book is dedicated to all individuals who have
been falsely accused within the legal system, particularly those whose
charges resulted in wrongful conviction and who may be currently
serving an undeserved sentence. Great tribute is due to the members of
exoneration organizations who devote their time to free the innocent.
I also want to honor all police officers, attorneys, judges, jurors, and my
fellow forensic scientists, whose good work leads to findings of truth and
justice.

Twenty-First Century Books
A division of Lerner Publishing Group, Inc.
241 First Avenue North
Minneapolis, MN 55401 USA

For updated reading levels and more information, look up this title at
www.lernerbooks.com.

Main body text set in Adobe Caslon Pro 11/15
Typeface proved by Adobe Systems

Library of Congress Cataloging-in-Publication Data

Murray, Elizabeth A.
    Overturning wrongful convictions : science serving justice / by Elizabeth A.
Murray, PhD.
      pages   cm
    Includes bibliographical references and index.
    ISBN 978-1-4677-2513-2 (lib. bdg. : alk. paper)
    ISBN 978-1-4677-6307-3 (EB pdf)
    1. Crime analysis—United States—Juvenile literature. 2. Vindication—Unit-
ed States—Juvenile literature. I. Title.
    HV7936.C88M87 2015
    364—dc23   2014017225

Manufactured in the United States of America
1 – VI – 12/31/14

CONTENTS

INTRODUCTION **HOW COULD THIS HAPPEN?** • 5

CHAPTER ONE **ENTERING THE CRIMINAL JUSTICE SYSTEM** • 13

CHAPTER TWO **THE PATH TO EXONERATION** • 25

CHAPTER THREE **EVIDENCE WORKING FOR CHANGE** • 37

CHAPTER FOUR **CAN YOU BELIEVE YOUR EYES?** • 51

CHAPTER FIVE **GOOD COP, BAD COP** • 59

CHAPTER SIX **BAD SCIENCE** • 67

CHAPTER SEVEN **PAYING FOR LIES** • 75

CHAPTER EIGHT **POOR LAWYERING AND UNJUST JUSTICES** • 81

CHAPTER NINE **WHERE DO WE GO FROM HERE?** • 89

EXONERATION PROFILES • 104
SOURCE NOTES • 108
SELECTED BIBLIOGRAPHY • 111
FOR FURTHER INFORMATION • 113
INDEX • 116

"It is better that ten guilty persons escape, than one innocent suffer."

—Sir William Blackstone, English jurist, judge, and politician, 1765

HOW COULD THIS HAPPEN?

On the night of April 19, 1989, members of a group of more than thirty teenagers stormed through New York City's Central Park committing robberies and assaults. One of the victims of attack was twenty-eight-year-old investment banker Trisha Meili, who was out jogging. Around 9:30 p.m., Meili was brutally raped, beaten, and left for dead in a clump of bushes at the edge of the woods. She had been tied up with her own shirt. More than four hours later, when police officers and paramedics arrived on the scene, they determined that Meili was in a coma due to massive blood loss. In addition, her skull had been fractured to the point that her left eye was hanging out of its socket. Twelve days later, Meili came out of her coma. She had survived the brutal attack but remembered nothing about it. Authorities promised to find those responsible for the vicious assault on this bright, successful young woman.

On the night of the attack itself, police had rounded up some of the more than thirty teenagers in Central Park. Of those teens, the police ultimately settled on five fourteen- to sixteen-year-old suspects as the assailants in Meili's attack. Some of the youths had a history of problems at school. Others came from broken homes, and one was hearing impaired and developmentally challenged. All were from Harlem, an impoverished neighborhood of New York with a large minority population. None of the five teens had ever been in trouble with the law before.

The situation was racially charged from the outset. Meili was white, four of the suspects were black, and one was Hispanic. Normal police guidelines in cases involving juveniles call for withholding the identity of underage suspects from the public at the outset of an investigation. This practice is also the law in many US states. Yet, in the Meili case, authorities released the names of the five teens. The media then published their photographs and addresses before police had formally arrested and charged them. The suspects, who became known as the Central Park Five, were Antron McCray, Kevin Richardson, Yusef Salaam, Raymond Santana, and Korey (sometimes spelled Khorey or Kharey) Wise.

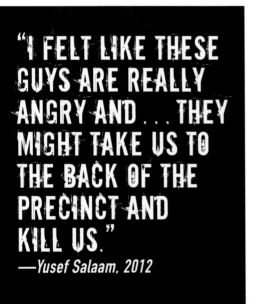

"I FELT LIKE THESE GUYS ARE REALLY ANGRY AND . . . THEY MIGHT TAKE US TO THE BACK OF THE PRECINCT AND KILL US."
—Yusef Salaam, 2012

During police questioning, authorities separated the boys. Throughout many hours of individual police interrogation, officers falsely told each teen that the others had blamed him. Four of the five suspects confessed on videotape to the attack, at the same time minimizing their own involvement. Yusef Salaam said of his questioning by police, "The tone was very, very scary. I felt like these guys are really angry and, you know what, they might take us to the back of the precinct and kill us." Salaam was the only one to refuse to sign a confession. All the same, officers wrote down an admission they assigned to him, and the other four teens pointed to him in their confessions. Within the next few weeks, however, all four teens changed their stories, saying they had made false admissions under extreme pressure from police.

WHAT DID THE EVIDENCE REVEAL?

Crime scene photos showed an 18-inch-wide (45.7 centimeter) trail of bloodstain and flattened grass between the lane where Meili had been knocked down and the bushes where she was discovered. The narrow trail did not suggest multiple attackers in a group effort to drag her into the brush. Investigators did not find the victim's blood on any of the suspects. Not a single witness to any events observed in the park that night could identify any of the five teens. The DNA profile from Meili's rape matched none of the young men. Although hairs found on one suspect were similar to the victim's hair, no physical evidence positively tied any of the teens to the crime.

Even so, all five juveniles were brought to trial and convicted in 1990. Among their various convictions for the attack on Meili were rape, assault, sexual abuse, and attempted murder. The confessions of guilt seemed to outweigh all other considerations. Each teen received the maximum sentence allowable based on age, ranging from five to fifteen years behind bars. Korey Wise, sixteen years old when the attack occurred, was tried as an adult and served the longest sentence. The names of each of the Central Park Five were also entered into New York's registry of criminal sex offenders.

When his punishment was announced, Kevin Richardson turned to his family and said, "Don't worry. The truth will come out. I'll never stop fighting. I never did this crime."

The guilty verdicts divided the nation. Some Americans celebrated the decision as a victory and praised police and prosecutors. Others were outraged, believing justice had not been served. Calvin O. Butts III, a local leader in Harlem stated, "The presumption of innocence was lost in the rush to judgment. People are not saying they forgive the crime. They're not saying they don't have compassion for that woman. All they're saying is, there is a considerable amount, an overwhelming amount, of reasonable doubt." C. Vernon Mason and William Kunstler, attorneys for Antron McCray and Yusef Salaam, claimed that the case had been built on racial prejudice and amounted to nothing more than a "legal lynching." Jurors later admitted that at least one of the defendants didn't have a good lawyer to argue his case.

THE EAST SIDE RAPIST

Twelve years later, in 2002, one of Wise's fellow prison inmates, Matias Reyes, approached him. After their conversation, Reyes requested to speak with authorities. Reyes confessed that, as a seventeen-year-old, he had been Meili's sole attacker. Known as the East Side Rapist for the part of New York in which he committed his crimes, Reyes was serving a long sentence. He had been convicted for five other rapes committed around the same period as the Central Park case and for the murder of a pregnant woman just two months after the attack on Meili. Authorities had not compared the DNA from Meili's case to the DNA from a rape that had occurred just two days earlier and in the same neighborhood. If they had, the testing would have quickly shown that Meili was also one of the victims of the East Side Rapist. Reyes's DNA had been sampled before he went to prison. However, authorities did not compare it to the DNA from Meili's attack until after he confessed.

Forensic testing showed that Reyes's DNA profile was a match to the semen found on Meili's sock. As a result of the DNA evidence, District Attorney Robert Morgenthau requested a hearing before the New York State Supreme Court in which he recommended the court vacate (reverse) the 1990 convictions of the Central Park Five and dismiss the criminal charges against the teens. All guilty verdicts against the five young men from 1990 were vacated in late 2002.

SERVING SOMEONE ELSE'S TIME

What makes up for the years of freedom the Central Park Five lost? What can erase the suffering of the men's families and the damage to their reputations? How can the harsh realities of prison life ever be forgotten? Santana has said about his fellow prisoners, "In the beginning it was very hard because they perceived me as . . . a rapist [who had] committed one of the most heinous crimes in New York State history. My faith was gone, and I didn't know what to do." Regarding the tension and violence of prison life, McCray said, "It's real hectic in there, people dying over cigarettes. It was real crazy." Wise was unable to attend his father's funeral or grieve along with his family. He said, "When I heard that my dad had passed, it was hurting."

In 2012 the documentary film *The Central Park Five* returned the case to public attention. About the film, Yusef Salaam said, "It wasn't a popular thing to be one of us . . . [but the documentary] really gave us our lives back." In the summer of 2014, twenty-five years after the attack on Trisha Meili, the Central Park Five agreed to settle their lawsuit against the City of New York for $40 million.

The men known as the Central Park Five at the New York premiere of the 2012 documentary **The Central Park Five,** *a film about their experiences of wrongful conviction.* **From left to right:** *Antron McCray, Raymond Santana, Kevin Richardson, Yusef Salaam, and Korey Wise.*

EXONERATION

In the decades between 1989—when the Central Park Five were first accused—and mid-2014, more than 1,400 convicted people in the United States have been cleared of guilty verdicts in a process known as exoneration. Many of these individuals were serving time after being convicted of serious crimes, such as rape and murder, that they did not commit. Each of these stories of unjust incarceration involves a tragic loss of dignity and liberty. Each story of exoneration involves righting a terrible injustice.

It is impossible to know how many innocent people are sitting in prison at this moment. Studies suggest that around 2 to 5 percent of all US inmates did not commit the crimes for which they were convicted. That translates to approximately 40,000 to 100,000 people currently unjustly behind bars in the United States alone. This statistic also means that the vast majority of people in prison do belong there.

The focus of most attempts to exonerate people who have been falsely convicted is on the worst offenses, such as murder and rape. These crimes carry the stiffest sentences, sometimes including the death penalty. For that reason, the majority of innocent people who have been convicted of less serious crimes will never be cleared.

"Anger is not a trait I was born with. It began in prison, and it grows each day. . . . For most of my life I took pride in being easygoing, slow to react, and naturally calm. But I have changed. . . . I wake up each morning to prison bars. . . . As soon as I open my eyes, I am mad. . . . I am so angry that complete madness cannot be far away."

—Calvin C. Johnson Jr., wrongfully convicted inmate (since exonerated), circa 1993

CHAPTER ONE
ENTERING THE CRIMINAL JUSTICE SYSTEM

Convictions and exonerations take place within the criminal portion of the US jurisprudence (legal) system. Criminal cases are those in which a person has broken a law. Civil cases involve disputes between people or institutions. Only in criminal cases do juries or judges decide guilt and innocence. The US legal system is based on the presumption that people are innocent in criminal matters until a judge or jury finds them guilty, based on evidence presented in the courtroom. In a criminal case, the responsibility to establish guilt—known as the burden of proof—lies with the government (local, state, or federal). Attorneys known as prosecutors represent the position of the government in these cases. The accused individual, known during the legal case as the defendant, is represented by one or more lawyers.

The location of a crime determines its jurisdiction, or the level of government with legal authority to prosecute the matter. This authority typically lies with a state. The county within the state where the crime took place undertakes the prosecution. If the crime occurs on federal property or the crime scene boundaries cross state lines, the federal government will prosecute the case. In some instances, jurisdictions will make agreements about which one will undertake the prosecution. In the United States, regardless of jurisdiction, the US Constitution protects the rights of individuals even before trial, such as during questioning or arrest by the police. The Constitution also specifies that any person charged with a crime is entitled to a speedy and fair trial. The guilt of that individual must be established beyond any reasonable doubt on the part of the judge or jury who hears the case.

ARREST AND CHARGES

An arrest by a police officer or a federal agent is the first step toward a criminal court case. Arrests can take place at the scene of a crime. They can also occur during questioning at police headquarters or after officers reach a logical conclusion that a person likely committed an offense. An arrest can also occur after a grand jury agrees, based on a review of information, that an arrest should be made. For example, following a murder, officers might seek and obtain legal permission to search a suspect's home. There, the police might find evidence such as blood on some of the suspect's clothing. Investigators would then present their findings to a judge or grand jury. If the judge or jury agrees that the evidence points strongly to the suspect's involvement in the killing, a warrant (legal authorization) would be issued for that person's arrest.

Officers can only make arrests if they have probable cause (strong suspicions they can later support before the court) to detain the suspect. A person cannot be arrested based only on mild suspicion. Probable cause is present when an officer witnesses an offense as it unfolds or if compelling circumstances lead the officer to believe a person broke the law. For example, a police officer might happen to observe a man with a duffel bag running from the scene of a bank robbery and thus consider him a likely suspect in the crime. If the officer is able to stop the man, the officer has the right to question him. (Police have the legal authority to question anyone, whether witness or suspect, at any time.) If, during questioning, the officer begins to believe the man is guilty of the robbery, or finds a large amount of cash in the duffel bag (which can be searched if the police have probable cause), the officer can make an arrest on the spot.

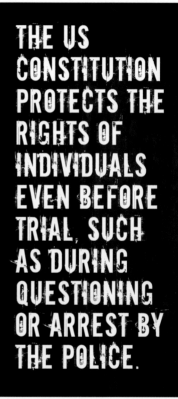

THE US CONSTITUTION PROTECTS THE RIGHTS OF INDIVIDUALS EVEN BEFORE TRIAL, SUCH AS DURING QUESTIONING OR ARREST BY THE POLICE.

The arrested person is then booked at a police station. There, officers take the suspect's fingerprints, obtain personal information (name, age, and physical features), and take a photographic mug shot. Police will also conduct a background check on the subject. Officers will collect and inventory any personal property with the suspect at the time, and the person will be placed in a holding cell.

Next, a court hearing takes place to formally announce the official charges against an accused individual. At that point, a judge or magistrate will decide, based on the crime and the arrested person's background, if the suspect will be held in jail.

RIGHTS AND RESPONSIBILITIES

Parts of the US Constitution's Bill of Rights protect individuals from unfair treatment in the legal process. Some of the provisions outline certain rights of people who find themselves in police custody in the United States. Other sections protect individuals from a police search of their body, vehicle, or home without a warrant, except in extreme emergencies where evidence may be destroyed or lives are at risk. (A pat-down procedure, during which police check for concealed weapons, is allowed.)

In the 1960s, the US Supreme Court established the Miranda warning. It not only protects citizens from unjust treatment but also ensures that information given legally to police may be used later in court. The police are required by law to read this warning out loud to an arrested suspect before interrogation. They must also do their best to ensure the person understands the warning. After an arrest, any information that comes from an interview in which the warning was not read cannot be used as evidence in court.

The Miranda warning typically includes the following: A person may remain silent and does not have to answer police questions. If a person does tell police anything after being read the Miranda warning, that information can later be used in court. The suspect is entitled to speak with a lawyer and have an attorney present during all police questioning. If the suspect cannot afford an attorney, the jurisdiction will provide one at no expense. If a person agrees to talk to police without an attorney, he or she can stop answering questions at any time.

The Miranda warning is named for Ernesto Miranda (above). In 1966 the US Supreme Court ruled that Miranda's right to protect himself during police questioning had been violated. This decision confirmed that officers must verbally inform suspects in police custody of their rights under the Fifth Amendment to the US Constitution.

Should a person choose not to reply to police questioning, the decision must be shared with the officers out loud. Unless placed under arrest, a person does have the right to leave the scene of questioning. To avoid danger or false accusations, individuals should never run from police. Nor should they deliberately interfere with the official duties or responsibilities of officers. If individuals believe their constitutional rights have been abused, they can turn to organizations such as the American Civil Liberties Union for help.

The judge may allow the person to put up bail money instead, releasing that person until trial. If the accused cannot afford a lawyer, a public defender (who works for or is paid by the government) will be assigned to handle the defendant's case. All courtroom hearings are recorded by a court reporter, typically through computer transcription or audiotape.

GUILTY OR NOT GUILTY?

The arraignment is a hearing before a judge or magistrate at which the accused, in consultation with his or her attorney, enters a plea regarding the charges. If the person pleads guilty at arraignment, the court accepts the plea. The next step may be a pre-sentencing hearing. For less serious offenses, punishment may range from community service to a fine, depending on the jurisdiction. More serious cases can lead to significant prison time. In states that allow capital punishment, the death penalty may be the sentence for the most severe offenses. However, in some jurisdictions, the accused is not permitted to plead guilty in death penalty cases. Such cases must be heard by a jury or judge for a final verdict.

Defendants have the constitutional right to remain silent throughout any or all of the legal process. If this occurs, a judge must enter a plea of not guilty on behalf of the defendant. If the accused pleads not guilty in any offense, he or she has the right to full court proceedings. The defendant can choose to have a judge hear the case or instead request a jury trial under the supervision of a judge.

In actuality, only about 10 percent of all criminal cases go to trial. Most often, the two opposing sides make a plea bargain. In a plea bargain, the accused can plead guilty, perhaps to a lesser charge than the original, and accept a lesser sentence than might be received after a guilty verdict at trial. Lawyers for the defense and the prosecution may also negotiate these deals when they believe their position will be hard to prove. The prosecuting attorneys who represent the jurisdiction trying the case may agree to a deal with the defense lawyers. This is sometimes a way to avoid putting the victim through a difficult public trial. On the other hand, the prosecutor can refuse to bargain with the defense. Some courts do not allow plea deals in offenses such as sex crimes against minors. In some jurisdictions, a judge must approve any bargain. In some cases, a living victim or the grieving relatives of a deceased victim must agree to any plea negotiation.

If a person pleads not guilty, and a plea deal is not made, the next step may be a preliminary or evidentiary hearing. This is sometimes called a probable cause hearing. At this hearing, prosecuting attorneys present evidence to a judge or a grand jury. They review the evidence to determine whether there is enough proof to move forward with full prosecution of the case. Grand jury hearings are not open to the public or to the defense and do not involve a judge.

If the judge or grand jury decides the evidence presented is sufficient, a trial is scheduled. At this point, the assigned trial judge sets the ground rules for the case's courtroom proceedings. The prosecution and defense can request that the judge allow witness or expert testimony at the trial. The defendant's attorney can ask for a change of venue, moving the trial to a different location. In a new setting, the local community from which jurors would be selected may have less access to information about the case. The defense attorney can also ask the judge to exclude information about the defendant's prior criminal history or other prejudicial evidence at the trial. The judge makes these and all other decisions about the pending court proceedings. According to pre-trial rules of discovery, each side must share its evidence with the opposing attorneys. They must also reveal the testimony they plan to present. This allows both the prosecution and the defense to plan their case.

THE TRIAL

Defendants may choose to have their case heard before a judge or jury, depending on the charges and the jurisdiction. Defense attorneys may advise a client to choose a jury trial if they believe the general public will be more sympathetic. In particularly gruesome crimes, defendants may opt to have a judge hear the case. A seasoned judge may be less shocked by the offense and perhaps give a less harsh punishment than a jury might recommend.

Unless the defense agrees that a judge will hear the case, a courtroom trial begins with jury selection. The number of jurors varies by jurisdiction. Typically twelve are selected, along with one or two alternates to fill in if one of the original jurors cannot serve. During jury selection, the defense and prosecuting attorneys take turns asking potential jurors their opinions about matters related to the case. They also ask the jury candidates to talk about what they may already know or think about the situation. Both the defense and the prosecution are looking for jurors who will be sympathetic to their case. For this reason, the attorneys are legally allowed to dismiss a certain number of prospective jurors for any reason.

At the start of trial, the prosecution is the first to make an opening statement. The prosecuting attorney will introduce the government's view of how and why the crime took place. The defense attorney usually follows with an opening statement but does not have to do so. In some situations, the defense may prefer to wait until the prosecution finishes presenting all of its case. In an opening statement, the defense attorney will explain that his or her client is not responsible for the crime and why. The attorney may also provide alternate theories about what occurred. The point is to put doubt in the mind of the jurors about the prosecution's claims.

Witnesses called by the prosecution provide a range of testimony. This includes statements by any eyewitnesses, police officers, forensic scientists, or other experts. The goal of the testimony is to present a chain of events regarding the crime. The prosecution asks its witnesses to discuss the physical evidence, how it was obtained, and what it means to the case. The defense can choose to cross-examine those witnesses to try to discredit them or to challenge the evidence they presented. The prosecution can then engage in redirect examination. In this questioning, prosecution witnesses can be asked to clarify or modify statements based on issues that came up on cross-examination.

In the United States, a defendant is considered innocent until the prosecution proves its case. For this reason, the defense does not have to call a single witness or present any evidence. In addition, the defendant has a constitutional right not to testify. Typically, the defense attorney will call witnesses to help support the defendant's case. These may include eyewitnesses and perhaps expert witnesses with opinions that differ from those of the prosecution. If called, any defense witnesses may be cross-examined by the prosecution. This can be followed by redirect questioning by the defendant's attorney. During closing arguments in the case, the prosecution goes first, summing up its position. The defense then gets to argue, aiming to establish doubt in the minds of the judge or jury. The prosecution gets the last word during closing arguments because it has the burden of proving guilt.

THE VERDICT

At the end of a jury trial, the judge gives instructions to the jury about how they must conduct deliberations. The judge reminds jurors that a guilty plea can only be rendered if the jury members agree that the prosecution has proved its case beyond a reasonable doubt. The judge explains the complexities of that principle. Reasonable doubt is more than an assumption that the defendant is probably guilty. However, reasonable doubt is neither absolute certainty nor proof beyond all doubt in the minds of the jurors.

After the judge's instructions, jurors go to a private room to deliberate and render a verdict. The jury typically must reach a unanimous decision on a verdict. If they cannot, they are considered a deadlocked or hung jury, and the judge will declare a mistrial. If that happens, the prosecution can decide to try the case again, engage in plea bargaining, or dismiss the charges against the accused. However, if the verdict is a unanimous not guilty, the defendant is freed. The same applies if the case is heard by a judge who renders a not guilty verdict. The prosecution cannot request another trial.

With a guilty verdict, a judge presides over a sentencing hearing. There, the accused, the victim, or relatives and friends of either may make statements. The law sets forth what punishments a judge can choose for any given charge. Some serious crimes have a mandatory sentence. Typically, however, the judge will make a decision based on the evidence presented at trial. The judge will also review a pre-sentencing report about the convicted person's background and past offenses. The judge will consider the extent of harm inflicted on the victim and whether the accused shows remorse. If the defendant is convicted of multiple charges in a single case, the judge can decide whether the prison terms for each will be served concurrently (at the same time) or consecutively (back to back). When the death penalty is an option, the jury may have a role in making the sentencing decision. In some instances, judges with more experience with the death penalty will conduct a special hearing.

THE APPEALS PROCESS

Guilty verdicts may be appealed to a higher court if the defense believes a legal error was committed at any point in the history of the case. The basis for an appeal may involve improper police procedures during interrogation, search, or arrest. Defense attorneys may believe the judge made mistakes during the preliminary hearings or in the pre-trial motions. Either the defense or the prosecution may appeal the sentence given for a conviction. By law, a notice to appeal must be filed quickly after the conclusion of a trial. Often an attorney who specializes in appeals will take over the process. The party that is appealing (whether it is the defense or prosecution) is referred to as the appellant.

The United States has three layers of courts. The first layer includes the trial courts where cases are initially heard (also known as district courts, except in New York State, where they are called supreme courts). The next are the appellate courts where appeals are heard (also known as circuit courts). The last layer includes supreme courts, the courts of last resort. Appeals move up through the system to higher courts. The United States has twelve regional circuit appellate courts, which hear appeals for given groups of states, and one in the District of Columbia. If all else fails, some appeals move up to the US Supreme Court—the highest court in the United States—for a final decision. This entire process can take many years.

The appeal isn't another trial. It is a review of the relevant records, testimony, and evidence by a panel of three judges in the higher court to which the appeal is made. To start the appeal process, the defendant's appeals attorney provides a summary, known as a brief, to cover the main arguments for reversing the original court's decision. At an appeal, the prosecution can also present its reasons for allowing the original verdict or sentence to stand.

Appeals are rarely successful, however. This is true even in cases where the person who has been convicted and sentenced is actually innocent. Furthermore, during the appeals process, the appellant must serve any of the prison time originally sentenced. If the punishment was the death penalty, however, the execution remains on hold until all possible appeals have been heard.

"The common themes that run through these cases [of wrongful conviction]—from global problems like poverty and racial issues to criminal justice issues . . . cannot be ignored and continue to plague our criminal justice system."

—The Innocence Project, n. d.

CHAPTER TWO

THE PATH TO EXONERATION

Verdicts have been questioned, challenged, and appealed throughout legal history. At present, most US states have one or more organizations dedicated to overturning false convictions. Many of these agencies are at university schools of law or criminal justice. Others are within the offices of public defenders. Some organizations take cases from across the nation. Others do not. Some have specific requirements or restrictions. For example, an agency might only take a case if the prisoner has more than a certain number of years left to serve in the sentence. Others limit the types of crimes they will consider. These groups are not devoted to cases in which people admit to their crime, even if the prisoner claims a killing was somehow justified. All groups require that the people requesting services are truly innocent of the crimes for which they were convicted.

Exoneration organizations typically do not work with those who are still suspects in criminal investigations. They work only with people who allege they have been falsely convicted by a judge or jury. Most agencies do not accept cases until all standard appeals of the conviction have been exhausted. Some exoneration groups require that physical evidence, such as DNA samples, be available for scientific analysis to help prove the person not guilty. Other organizations will accept more difficult cases in which those claiming innocence are challenging legal procedures or subjective evidence, such as eyewitness testimony.

The general process for seeking assistance begins with writing to an exoneration organization to explain the facts of a case. Some of the larger agencies have applications for assistance on their websites. This paperwork requests specific facts about the case, the conviction, and the sentence. It also asks about any new evidence that has surfaced since the trial. Review panels at the agencies evaluate this information, and their legal experts examine the issues. They conduct additional research to determine whether the case meets the organization's specific guidelines. It may take months to review the application. Once an agency accepts a case, the organization is neither the defense nor the prosecution. It is an advocate, or amicus curiae ("friend of the court"), that files an amicus brief to the appellate court. This brief is a document covering arguments and evidence for the convict's innocence.

THE INNOCENCE PROJECT

The Innocence Project is one of the first major organizations to be founded with the sole purpose of exonerating those falsely convicted. Attorneys Barry C. Scheck and Peter J. Neufeld launched the project in 1992 at the Benjamin N. Cardozo School of Law at Yeshiva University in New York. The group's interest partly stemmed from the unreliability of eyewitness testimony and related misidentifications. Its exonerations also grew from the increasing availability of forensic DNA testing to give more solid evidence of guilt or innocence. In 2004 the Innocence Project

Peter Neufeld (left) and Barry Scheck (right) founded the Innocence Project in 1992. They serve as codirectors of the project and have written several books on the topic of wrongful convictions.

became an independent nonprofit organization. The professors and students of the Cardozo School of Law are still extensively involved in each case the agency reviews and accepts.

The Innocence Project will take cases from most US states. Its current focus is on convictions in which physical evidence exists that can be tested for DNA. The organization receives more than three thousand requests each year, and the amount of time the Innocence Project is involved can last from one to ten years. As a result, the project can only accept a small number of inquiries. The attorneys and law students who work on these cases do so at no charge. Working in this way is known as pro bono publico work, a term that means "for the public good."

Most clients cannot afford the high financial costs of proving their innocence. The Innocence Project relies on donations from individuals, corporations, and foundations to pay for DNA analysis, court expenses, and any necessary travel. DNA testing costs about $1,000 per sample, and a single case may require analysis of several pieces of evidence. If a private lab performs these DNA tests, average costs for a single case can be as high as $8,500. To keep costs down, government-run labs perform some of the DNA tests for the project, often at little or no expense. According to Innocence Project data as of 2014, DNA testing exonerated 317 falsely convicted people in the United States—including eighteen who were on death row. The average time those individuals had spent behind bars before being cleared was more than thirteen years. The Innocence Project was involved in more than half of those DNA exonerations.

DNA EVIDENCE

DNA technology, based on genetic research at Leicester University in the United Kingdom, was first used in a criminal investigation in a 1986 offense. In that case, DNA comparison data exonerated Richard Buckland, a British man who had confessed to a rape and a murder he did not commit. The following year, the same technology was used to identify the real perpetrator, Colin Pitchfork.

Prior to the development of DNA testing, forensic scientists relied on serology, which is the study of bodily fluids and the various proteins they contain. Serological methods test a variety of genetically determined proteins, including those that determine a person's blood type. Some individuals also display blood proteins in other body fluids, such as saliva or semen. Serology allows for limited forensic testing on all body fluid samples. However, the proteins found in them are not unique to a single person. For example, the four major blood types (A, B, AB, and O) are shared by large groups of people. Therefore, those proteins, whether found in blood or semen, can only be properly used to exclude a suspect if that person does not have the same blood-type protein as found in a crime scene sample.

In some past criminal cases, however, serological testing was misused in forensics. It was also misrepresented to juries, resulting in wrongful convictions. Beginning in 1986, however, DNA testing allowed definitive identification of a person from body fluids and other tissues. It also permitted the reanalysis of biological samples, such as blood or semen stains, that had been stored from old crimes.

Forensic scientists can test the DNA of a living or deceased person by taking cells from the person's body. Early in DNA technology, scientists collected blood or other tissue samples. As methods improved, swabbing the inside of a person's cheek became a standard way of collecting cells for DNA testing from living individuals. In a lab, the genetic material is then extracted from either the nucleus or the mitochondria of the sample cells.

Investigators can also analyze genetic material from blood, hair, semen, saliva, skin cells, bones, and other body tissues that are found on evidence. This profile can then be compared to the DNA from known individuals (such as the suspect or the victim) to look for matches. When forensic DNA technology was first used, it required a sample of blood or semen about the size of a US quarter coin. By the 1990s, much smaller samples could be tested,

DNA

Deoxyribonucleic acid, or DNA, is a molecule that is contained in two places inside a cell—in the nucleus and in organelles known as mitochondria. Nuclear DNA comes from both of a person's parents. The mother contributes 50 percent and the father the other 50 percent. Mitochondrial DNA is inherited only from a person's mother and is identical in every direct descendant along a person's female genetic lineage. Nuclear DNA, however, is unique to each person, except for identical twins, who share the same DNA at birth.

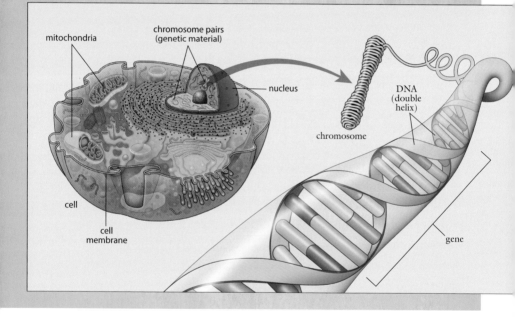

as long as they were visible. In the twenty-first century, fewer than ten cells can produce a genetic profile, including from skin cells left behind by just touching a surface.

All humans share 99.9 percent of their nuclear DNA in common. Technologies allow scientists to compare the small amount of genetic variation among people. Using chemical enzymes that act like molecular scissors, scientists can cut the variable regions of DNA into fragments. They then use a technique called electrophoresis to apply an electric current that separates those fragments by size. From there, scientists can see the resulting patterns of variation that are unique to each person. Mitochondrial DNA is tested in the same way. However, mitochondria are inherited solely from a person's mother, so all persons in a maternal line share the same mitochondrial DNA profile.

All US states require some convicted felons, such as all sex offenders, to provide a DNA sample. The sample is then tested. The encoded profile is kept in a national database for police and other legal authorities to consult for comparisons. In 2013 police began to take DNA samples from anyone arrested with probable cause for a serious crime. These DNA samples and records have the potential to solve old cases, as well as to become the basis for future exonerations.

CENTER ON WRONGFUL CONVICTIONS

Another major institution that re-examines guilty verdicts is the Center on Wrongful Convictions (CWC) at Northwestern University in Chicago, Illinois. This organization arose after the university's law school hosted a national conference in 1998 for people who had been sentenced to execution but were later exonerated. The meeting organizers wanted to use those cases to better inform the public about wrongful convictions, especially with regard to death penalty issues. Based partly on this conference and on related work, the state of Illinois abolished capital punishment in 2011. The CWC receives about 2,400 requests for assistance each year from inmates across the country.

GUILT OR INNOCENCE?

Exoneration agencies require that those who request assistance be factually innocent. All the same, statistics from the Innocence Project's DNA analyses show that people requesting testing are nearly as likely to be guilty as not guilty. Over a five-year study, DNA testing showed innocence in 43 percent of submitted cases and guilt in about 42 percent of the cases. Testing results were inconclusive in about 15 percent of requests. In more than 40 percent of those cases in which DNA did prove innocence, the same test identified the person who was actually guilty of the crime. Thus, through their work, exoneration organizations are potentially preventing perpetrators from committing other crimes, which benefits all of society.

The center's three-part mission is to represent, research, and reform. Like the Innocence Project, the CWC represents clients seeking to exonerate wrongful convictions and researches the issues that cause unjust guilty verdicts. This includes problems with unreliable eyewitness testimony and untruthful testimony from witnesses in the courtroom. It also considers cases involving poor legal representation by convicts' attorneys and misconduct on the part of police officers or forensic scientists. Like other exoneration organizations, the CWC uses the results of its studies to attempt to improve police procedures, forensic science techniques, and court processes. The center hopes to reform the system to help avoid future miscarriages of justice.

MICHIGAN INNOCENCE CLINIC

The vast majority of serious felony cases lack crime scene evidence containing biological material from which DNA can be extracted. The Michigan Innocence Clinic (MIC) at the University of

Michigan Law School in Ann Arbor was established in 2009 with a specific focus on exactly these types of cases. Wrongful convictions in non-DNA cases typically hinge on faulty eyewitness testimony, inaccurate science, or unjust legal processes. The MIC was founded on the belief that the many convictions later overturned by DNA evidence suggest unjust convictions must also exist in similar numbers in criminal cases lacking DNA evidence.

As of 2014, the MIC had taken on only eighteen requests from convicts. Seven of those people were exonerated without DNA testing. These are among the more difficult cases to reinvestigate. They involve appeals based on grounds less convincing than what DNA or fingerprint evidence can provide. As with the Innocence Project and the CWC, law students are heavily involved in the work of the MIC.

A NATIONAL DATABASE OF EXONERATIONS

In May 2012, the CWC and the MIC cofounded the National Registry of Exonerations (NRE). This database contains all known exonerations in the United States since 1989. These cases include all persons completely cleared of their charges using new evidence. By mid-2014, the NRE had listed more than 1,400 such cases. They include cases of assault, child abuse, kidnapping, arson, robbery, burglary, theft, drug possession or sale, gun possession or sale, forgery, fraud, tax evasion, traffic offense, and other crimes.

A Federal Bureau of Investigation (FBI) report found that in one year (2012) nearly 70 percent of all US arrests were of white Americans and 28 percent were black Americans. This statistic shows that black Americans—who make up about 13 percent of the US population—are arrested at higher rates than their overall representation in the nation's population. By contrast, white

Americans make up approximately 78 percent of the population and are arrested in much more proportionate measure. The NRE shows that almost half (46 percent) of the 1,325 people exonerated between 1989 and March 2014 were black Americans. These data suggest that false convictions following arrests are also higher in that racial group. Statistics from the Innocence Project show that about 70 percent of their exonerations involved individuals who are black, Hispanic, or Asian.

THE NRE SHOWS THAT ALMOST HALF (46 PERCENT) OF THE 1,325 PEOPLE EXONERATED BETWEEN 1989 AND MARCH 2014 WERE BLACK AMERICANS.

The FBI also reports that nearly 75 percent of arrested individuals were males. In the NRE data, males account for 92 percent of the exonerations. Studies show that males are more likely than females to commit the types of serious and violent crimes considered by exoneration agencies.

WORLDWIDE INVOLVEMENT

Some exoneration organizations across the globe have banded together to form the Innocence Network. Its aim is to provide free legal aid and investigative services to those who claim to have been wrongfully convicted. The Innocence Network also promotes research about the causes of unjust convictions and works toward reforms. The organization launched in 2000 with ten participating exoneration groups, including the Innocence Project. By 2014 the Innocence Network numbered sixty-five separate agencies. A majority (56) of them are based in the United States or its territories. The other nine are in Australia, Canada, France, Ireland, Italy, the Netherlands, New Zealand, South Africa, and the United Kingdom.

All exoneration groups, whether in the United States or abroad, use science in the service of justice. Criminal justice studies use the behavioral sciences, such as psychology, sociology, criminology, and police science. Forensic sciences involve biology, chemistry, physics, technology, and medicine as applied to evidence of crime. Exoneration organizations also study jurisprudence and the philosophy of law in their search for improved justice and for reform of faulty laws and legal processes.

"We have thousands of innocent people in prison in this country right now. . . . And if we don't hurry, if we don't hustle, if we don't raise money, if we don't get them out, eventually—soon—we will know in this nation, by clear DNA evidence, that we have killed an innocent man."

—John Grisham, author of *The Innocent Man* and member of the board of directors of the Innocence Project, 2008

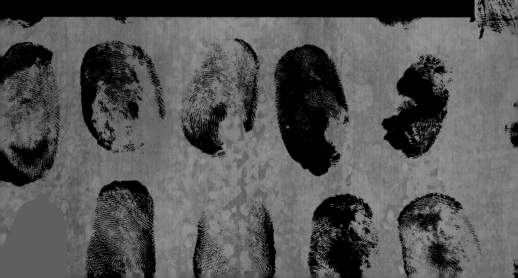

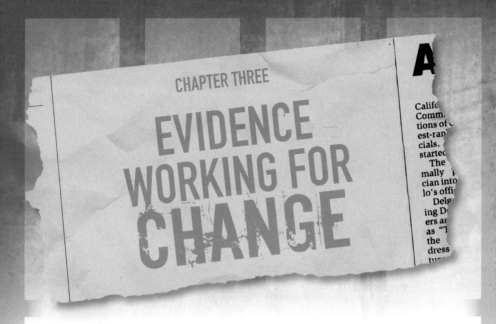

CHAPTER THREE

EVIDENCE WORKING FOR CHANGE

Calif
Comm
tions of
est-ran
cials.
started
The
mally
cian into
lo's offi
Del
ing D
ers ar
as "1
the
dress

One of the guiding concepts in forensic science is that every contact leaves a trace. Set forth by French police scientist Dr. Edmond Locard about a century ago, Locard's Exchange Principle states that wherever we go and whatever we do, we leave a trail of evidence, whether we can see it or not. We also take evidence away from every interaction. In forensic terms, this means that no criminal can completely clean up all signs of a crime, and no person truly disappears without a trace. The challenge for investigators is to find that trace and to link it to a suspect.

At a crime scene, the clues left behind are sometimes obvious, such as a wall covered in blood spatter or bullet casings littering the floor. But in other cases, only minute amounts of matter—or trace evidence—is left behind or taken away. This material includes hair, skin cells, fingerprints, clothing or carpet fibers, and soil particles or plant matter on shoes or clothing.

Police, crime scene investigators, and forensic scientists must collect and treat any evidence, large or small, as if it may someday wind up in court. Most evidence does not. In many instances, the case never goes to trial or the material turns out not to be relevant to the case. Evidence may be used in court years or even decades after the crime. For this reason, officials must carefully document a chain of custody to make sure evidence holds its legal value. Materials must be securely handled and stored. The whereabouts of evidence at all points and the names of everyone who has dealt with, collected, stored, or analyzed the evidence must be carefully recorded. If suspicions arise at any point that the evidence was tampered with or that an unauthorized person has handled it, that item cannot be used in court. Improper handling of evidence or a broken chain of custody should be recognized by a judge or automatically challenged by attorneys.

THE EVIDENCE RULES

In court, evidence can include physical items such as a knife, a bloodstained jacket, rope, bones, crime scene photos, or scientific reports about fingerprint analysis or DNA testing. Evidence also includes the testimony of witnesses, law enforcement officers, and forensic experts. The purpose of all evidence presented at trial is to help the judge or jury reach a decision about the defendant's guilt or innocence. However, legal rules govern whether evidence is admissible. A case's judge determines whether or not evidence will be considered.

Rules of evidence indicate that to be admitted into court, physical items and testimony must be relevant to the case. They must also be useful in proving something about the charges under examination. For instance, if a man suspected of burglarizing a home has a gun in his car when he is caught, the presence of that gun does not establish his guilt in the burglary. The gun would not be considered as evidence unless the man used it during the burglary. The man could be charged with a separate gun offense, however. Unless the prosecuting attorney is able to clearly connect the gun to the theft—such as that it was among the stolen items— the judge would not allow the jury to hear about the gun during a trial related to the burglary charges.

In the United States, any physical evidence that makes its way to court must have been obtained by the guidelines set forth in the US Constitution. That includes the requirement of a legally executed search warrant to take evidence from private property, including the property of a suspected criminal. To do otherwise violates a person's constitutionally guaranteed right to privacy. In some cases, police are under time pressure to arrest a suspect. This may be to ensure that others are not harmed or that key evidence is not lost or destroyed. When police have probable cause that someone is guilty of a specific offense, officers are legally allowed to perform an emergency search and seizure of relevant items. If the defense later challenges probable cause, and the judge agrees,

ANY PHYSICAL EVIDENCE THAT MAKES ITS WAY TO COURT MUST HAVE BEEN OBTAINED BY....A LEGALLY EXECUTED SEARCH WARRANT TO TAKE EVIDENCE FROM PRIVATE PROPERTY, INCLUDING THE PROPERTY OF A SUSPECTED CRIMINAL.

any evidence obtained from the emergency search will not be admissible in court.

In addition, to be admitted as evidence in a court case, materials or testimony cannot unfairly prejudice the jury. For instance, information about a defendant's prior convictions is typically not permitted at trial. Such information would likely taint the opinions of the jury. Considering other crimes in the defendant's past may cause jurors to think, "Once a criminal, always a criminal." This reaction goes against American jurisprudence, which holds that a person is innocent until proven guilty in each and every case. Prior convictions may be considered during sentencing, but only after a judge or jury concludes guilt in the case.

Testimony given at trial also cannot be hearsay, or observations from someone who was not an eyewitness (or ear-witness) to the crime. For example, if a witness was present at a scene and heard the defendant threaten another person, the witness can tell the courtroom what he or she heard.

> INFORMATION ABOUT...PRIOR CONVICTIONS IS TYPICALLY NOT PERMITTED AT TRIAL.... CONSIDERING OTHER CRIMES IN THE DEFENDANT'S PAST MAY CAUSE JURORS TO THINK, "ONCE A CRIMINAL, ALWAYS A CRIMINAL."

However, witnesses may not state what they heard from anyone other than the defendant. The accused's spouse, physician, psychologist, lawyer, or clergy member cannot be forced to testify in court about anything the defendant may have told them. Communications in these types of relationships are considered privileged matters. The US Constitution protects the conversations between people and their most trusted confidants to preserve key social bonds. In some cases, however, a judge may make exceptions to this rule about privileged communications.

SCIENCE IN THE COURTROOM

Scientific evidence, such as expert testimony about DNA results, hair analysis, or a bite-mark pattern, is governed by its own set of rules in court. By law, scientific evidence presented in a courtroom cannot be based on experimental procedures or practices. Instead, the techniques and technologies of forensic science—or any other type of science used in court—must be generally accepted as worthy by the majority of scientists in that field. This has come to mean that such tests and methods have already been published in scientific literature after having first been examined and approved by other scientists. Valid research must be conducted using standards known as controls to make sure results are accurate. Any statistical error with any method or technique must be reported and explained to the jury.

The prosecution and the defense in a criminal case may call on any scientific expert or knowledgeable authority to testify at trial. Although those witnesses may disagree in their opinions, the methods they use to reach their conclusions must still meet all legal standards. Before such persons may speak about evidence or scientific analysis to the judge or jury, however, the court must approve a witness's expertise. Typically, the judge does this by examining an expert's resumé or by asking the expert directly about his or her credentials. The court will also determine the relevance of expert witness testimony and whether the testimony will aid the jury in making their verdict. The court can do this ahead of time at pre-trial evidentiary hearings or by an examination of the expert's scientific reports. The judge can also do this at trial. If the judge decides the testimony does not meet the rules of evidence, it cannot be used at trial.

DIRECT AND CIRCUMSTANTIAL EVIDENCE

All forensic evidence is categorized as either direct or circumstantial. Both types are acceptable in court as long as they meet legal standards. They must be relevant to the case and have the potential to prove something. They must also have been collected through constitutional means.

Eyewitness testimony, such as when a witness says, "I saw her stab that man," is direct evidence in a criminal trial. The judge or jury does not have to draw a conclusion from direct testimony. They need only to accept it as true or false. All physical findings—such as DNA, fingerprints, hairs and fur, fibers, and shoeprints—are considered circumstantial evidence. Such evidence cannot definitively prove that a person committed an offense. It can only show that the suspect could have been at the scene. From circumstantial evidence, the judge or jury must draw a conclusion about the case. They often must combine multiple conclusions to develop what they believe to be a logical explanation of events that occurred during the crime.

Some traces, such as hairs and fibers, are types of circumstantial evidence that can be easily transferred from one person, pet, or object to another. They can give the false impression that the person to whom the evidence was transferred was present at a crime scene when, in fact, they may not have been. Other types of evidence, including fingerprints, are much more difficult to transfer from one place to another. All the same, they can only show that a person—or something that person touched—was present at a crime scene. They do not prove that the individual is guilty of any offense committed there.

Additionally, many items—known as class evidence—are common to a wide range of people or types of clothing. They are not distinctive enough to be tied to a single person. This can include trace evidence such as hair or more obvious evidence such as a shoeprint. For example, the color and microscopic appearance of hair can be very similar from one person to another. Clothing fibers and shoes are mass-produced. Such evidence can therefore be assigned only to a class (large grouping) of like or identical materials rather than to one specific person.

Rarely, evidence such as clothing, paper, or glass can be positively linked to a source. An example is when a tear or break from one piece can be perfectly matched, like a puzzle piece, to its adjacent piece. Occasionally, unique damage, wear, or debris on objects such as shoes or tires can also provide a confident link to crime scene evidence. Such added features can turn class evidence into individuating, or unique, evidence. Individuating evidence makes for compelling evidence in a courtroom. This information is still circumstantial, however, because the judge or jury must draw a conclusion about the case from it.

Investigators sometimes find hairs or fibers at a crime scene that appear to match known sample hairs or fibers from a suspect. In such cases, the most a reputable forensic scientist can usually say is that those items are consistent with—though not necessarily an exact match to—hair or fibers belonging to the accused. It is up to the judge or jury to draw a conclusion from that circumstantial information. On the other hand, DNA and fingerprints are

CAN DNA LEAD TO THE WRONG MAN?

In the summer of 2008, a forty-year-old teacher named Genai Coleman was killed in a suburb of Atlanta, Georgia. She had been waiting to pick up her teenage daughter at a transit station. A man approached her vehicle, shot her in the chest, and stole her car, leaving her body behind the station. Witnesses provided a description of the man. A surveillance camera from a nearby gas station also captured video of a man matching the reports. When authorities later located the stolen car, they found a cigarette butt under the driver's seat. Authorities tested saliva on the cigarette stub for DNA. They compared the results to profiles in a DNA database of persons convicted of felonies. The sample matched a man with a prior drug conviction. His name was Donald Smith.

The odds that the DNA test results were incorrect were ten billion to one. So when police apprehended Donald Smith in early 2010, they did not believe him when he said he hadn't committed the crime. Officers showed him the surveillance footage. To their surprise, Donald told them the man in the video was his identical twin brother, Ronald. He also stated that if the images were shown to the rest of the Smith family, they would confirm his claim, which they did.

Additional support for Ronald's guilt came from fingerprints found in the stolen car. Identical twins share the same DNA profile, but they do not share the same fingerprint ridge patterns. Records from Ronald Smith's cell phone usage also placed him in the vicinity where Coleman's vehicle had been abandoned. On the basis of this evidence, Ronald was arrested, charged, and brought to trial. Initially, Ronald admitted to shooting Coleman, but at trial, Ronald attempted to blame Donald. He said his own fingerprints were in the car because he had tried to help Donald clean the vehicle after the carjacking. Jurors did not believe this claim and found Ronald Smith guilty of killing Coleman. He was sentenced by the judge to spend the rest of his life in prison.

distinctive enough to be considered individuating evidence. Both, however, are still considered circumstantial because neither DNA nor fingerprints can prove on their own that the person to whom they belong is guilty of a particular crime. Only the judge or jury assigned to hear a case can make that determination as they consider other aspects of the case.

EYEWITNESS TESTIMONY

The testimony of an eyewitness is considered direct evidence because the judge or jury does not need additional information to draw a conclusion from what is stated. The statement supports a claim on its own. The listener either believes or doesn't believe what the witness says. However, people are not always honest. Eyewitnesses can also make honest mistakes, especially when asked during questioning to recall a traumatic event, such as a rape or killing.

RESEARCH HAS LONG SUGGESTED THAT EYEWITNESS OBSERVATIONS CAN BE PRONE TO SERIOUS ERROR.

Research has long suggested that eyewitness observations can be prone to serious error. Such mistakes can result in legal injustice. In 1908, for example, the German American psychologist Dr. Hugo Münsterberg wrote a landmark book entitled *On the Witness Stand: Essays on Psychology and Crime* in which he discussed how memory can fail in a person's retelling of events. He also wrote about how emotions can cloud an individual's recollection and discussed the errors eyewitnesses make when identifying suspects. In 1932 law professor Edwin Borchard of Yale Law School wrote *Convicting the Innocent,* a book about his study of false convictions. Borchard determined that eyewitness mistakes in identification of criminals were the greatest contributors to unjust guilty verdicts.

In the 1970s, psychologist Dr. Elizabeth Loftus began conducting rigorous scientific studies. She focused on how easily memory and recall are influenced. Other information and experiences can often change a person's memories. Since then Loftus has written extensively about eyewitness testimony. She has challenged its reliability and has helped to establish that direct evidence may not be straightforward and may depend greatly on circumstances.

EXONERATED: KENNY WATERS

In May 1980, the body of Katharina Reitz Brow was found in her blood-spattered Massachusetts home. Her body had more than thirty stab wounds. Some jewelry, Brow's purse, and $1,800 in cash had been stolen. Scientific testing of the blood at the crime scene showed most of it was type B, Brow's blood type. Police also found some type O blood, which they assumed belonged to the

Kenny Waters (left) and his sister Betty Anne Waters (right) hold hands on the day he was exonerated in 2001. Betty Anne went to law school and became an attorney to help free her brother. Their story was made into the 2010 film **Conviction.** *Betty Anne continues to volunteer for the Innocence Project, which aided her in obtaining her brother's exoneration.*

killer. Authorities eventually settled on twenty-six-year-old Kenny Waters as the prime suspect. He lived next door to Brow and worked at a restaurant she often visited. He also had type O blood. Police arrested Waters for the killing. Based entirely on circumstantial evidence, he was convicted in 1983 and sentenced to life in prison.

The verdict was quickly appealed, but the appeal failed. Kenny's younger sister, Betty Anne Waters, believed in his innocence and said, "Right up until that point, I really thought the system would work. I always thought only guilty people go to jail. Absolutely. That's why I was so shocked." Following that, one court appeal after another was denied.

Looking back on that time, Betty Anne said, "When Kenny was first convicted I would tell people, 'My brother's in prison and he's innocent.' And I would get that look of, 'I feel so sorry for you, Betty Anne, because he's probably guilty.' I could see the look . . . I would have thought the same thing . . . If you're in prison, you're guilty, right? Why would a jury convict you? Why would the system put you there? . . . So that's why I stopped telling people."

A SISTER'S FAITH

When Kenny attempted suicide, resulting in a month in an isolation cell, Betty Anne knew she had to take action. She made him promise not to harm himself again. In exchange for that agreement, Kenny asked her to become a lawyer and help set him free. A high school dropout, Betty Anne got her high school General Equivalency Diploma (GED) and enrolled in the local community college. After graduating with a degree in economics, Betty Anne went on to law school so she could be directly involved in her brother's case. When she learned of a new technology called DNA testing, Betty Anne knew it might be the key to freeing her brother—if the bloodstained evidence from the crime still existed.

Betty Anne Waters became her brother's attorney in 1998 and located the old evidence, including a knife and a piece of a bloodstained curtain. The evidence had been preserved in a courthouse storage area in Boston, Massachusetts. The Innocence Project agreed to take Kenny's case. The agency helped

Betty Anne arrange DNA testing on the bloodstains, which proved her brother's innocence. Kenny was released from prison in 2001, having served eighteen years behind bars for a murder he did not commit. He died in an accidental fall only six months after his release from prison, at forty-seven years of age.

Betty Anne didn't stop there, however. Her review of case documents showed that fingerprint evidence had been used during the original police investigation that led up to her brother's conviction. She was determined to find those records and learn why fingerprint evidence had not been presented in the original court case. Seven years later, Betty Anne got legal permission to search a storage unit belonging to a retired police officer involved in the case. There she found fingerprint evidence and a list of the individuals police had excluded as potential matches. Kenny Waters's name was on that list. The list proved that the police had known all along that Kenny was innocent but had held back that evidence from court. Betty Anne sued Ayer, the Massachusetts town in which Kenny had been convicted. She won her case and was awarded almost three-and-a-half million dollars.

Betty Anne assists the Innocence Project and its causes as a volunteer. She does not practice law, claiming she only went to law school to free her brother. Katharina Brow's murderer has yet to be identified.

"I couldn't believe it when the defense attorney tried to claim this was a case of mistaken identity—that I had been 'stressed' after the assault and couldn't properly identify the man who had been lying on top of me . . . I knew what I'd seen. I would never forget that face. How could I?"

—Jennifer Thompson-Cannino, rape victim and coauthor of *Picking Cotton: Our Memoir of Injustice and Redemption*, 2009

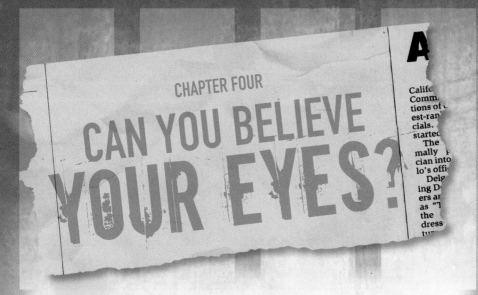

CHAPTER FOUR

CAN YOU BELIEVE YOUR EYES?

Dr. Robert Buckhout, a psychology professor at Brooklyn College in the 1970s, conducted a series of eyewitness experiments using the campus as his laboratory. In one situation, Buckhout arranged a fake assault on a fellow professor in front of almost 150 students. Then he waited seven weeks and showed the witnesses six photos of possible attackers. Forty percent of the students did identify the correct person. Yet 36 percent picked a bystander and 23 percent picked someone who hadn't even been at the scene of the attack. When Buckhout staged a purse snatching, fewer than 15 percent of the fifty-two witnesses chose the correct suspect. These early studies, and many more since, have made it clear that no two people come away from the same experience with an identical memory of it.

The Innocence Project has conducted research on successful DNA exonerations. Their studies have concluded that almost 75 percent of those wrongful convictions were due to faulty eyewitness testimony. Scientific research has revealed that our memories are not like video recorders. We create only an impression of what happened, based partly on how we were feeling at the time.

In creating a memory, a person's mind often adds other elements. These may be pieces of events that occurred at other times during which a person felt similar emotions.

TIME, PLACE, FACE, AND STRESS

Psychologists know that time is a key factor in accurate recall of memory. Memory error rates have been shown to increase within twenty minutes of an event. Experts suggest that only long-term memories—those our brain stores in a different way than casual or fleeting thoughts—can be readily recalled. Short-term memories are events that do not stick in the mind, either because they are of no significance or they do not stand out in some way. For instance, if a person passes you at the door of a convenience store and does nothing to attract your attention, you are very unlikely to recall that person's face or clothing at a later time—even if it turns out that person robbed the store.

Drugs, alcohol, and sensory or mental impairment also affect a person's ability to process and remember events or people clearly. So can factors such as poor lighting, physical distance from the event or person, or viewing point. For example, a person sitting or lying on the ground will often report a standing attacker as taller than the assailant actually is. Those who see a suspect face-on will have better recall than those who see the suspect in profile. People are also more likely to correctly recall the detailed facial features of someone from their own race. This tendency is known as cross-race identification bias. It holds true even for people who are raised in multi-racial environments. The bias reflects the brain's hardwired inability to easily distinguish among faces of those who bear less resemblance to us. Studies have also shown that people whose faces would be considered average are less memorable than those who stand out as very attractive or very unattractive.

Under certain types of stress, such as a sexual assault, the victim's brain may even alter the attacker's face as a psychological defense mechanism. In experimental studies, witnesses who were very forcefully questioned face-to-face for forty minutes misidentified their pushy interrogator almost 70 percent of the time. In a low-pressure version of that test, only 12 percent were unable to recognize the face of the questioner.

When the stress of a confrontation is created by the presence of a weapon, a weapon focus effect is introduced. If a criminal has a gun or a knife, the victim will pay more attention to the weapon than to the face of the person holding it. On the other hand, if something appeals to someone's interests in a very positive way, that person is more likely to recall that item or event. For example, a person who is very interested in cars may remember details of a vehicle more clearly than someone who is not as passionate about cars.

HOW CONFIDENT IS MEMORY?

One person's memory can be tainted by another person's memory. This is one reason witnesses in a trial are not permitted to hear each other's testimony. Younger children and the

WITNESSES WHO WERE VERY FORCEFULLY QUESTIONED FACE-TO-FACE FOR FORTY MINUTES MISIDENTIFIED THEIR PUSHY INTERROGATOR ALMOST 70 PERCENT OF THE TIME.

elderly, in particular, have been shown to have memories that are very easily influenced by suggestion, especially from those in authority. The Innocence Project has reported numerous instances in which witnesses repeatedly changed their descriptions of a suspect. Whether subconsciously or deliberately, the witnesses' new descriptions better matched what they had learned from authorities about the suspect's height, facial hair, or other features since giving their original descriptions. To avoid tainted memory recall, exoneration agencies suggest that police officers should question witnesses individually. They should also avoid suggestive and leading statements or questions. Such an approach can plant ideas into a memory that the witness didn't originally have.

People can also mistrust a first instinct, especially when they don't confidently know the answer to a question. From there—as we might do on a test, for example—we can talk ourselves into an answer, whether it is the correct answer or not. In fact, an eyewitness who is unsure of an identification in a police lineup can actually become more confident in a misidentification over time. A key factor that distinguishes a test from a police lineup, however, is that a typical multiple-choice test has a correct answer among the responses from which we select. The actual criminal may not be among the persons police show to a witness. Many variables affect a person's ability to recall a criminal's face or other aspects associated with a stressful event, leading to confusion and error.

EXONERATED: RONALD COTTON

In 1984 a black male broke into the North Carolina apartment of white college student Jennifer Thompson. While the man was raping her, Thompson consciously tried to memorize every detail of the man's face, body, and clothing. She figured that if she survived, her memories would be her best hope of making the man pay for what he had done to her. After the assault, Thompson carefully described her attacker to

police so they could create a sketch that might help find the rapist. Officers thought her confidence would allow Thompson to pick out the right man from a photo lineup if they could find him.

Officers soon got an anonymous call that led to a man named Ronald Cotton. He worked in the area where the rape had taken place. The police handed his photograph, along with those of five other black men, to Thompson just days after the attack. She quickly pushed away four pictures and studied the remaining two. As Thompson carefully compared the pair of photos for almost five minutes, she became increasingly convinced one of the men was her rapist. She handed Ronald Cotton's photo to police and asked them how she did. They responded that she had done well. This response cemented Thompson's faith that she had chosen the right man.

Police later brought in Cotton and six other black men for a police lineup. He was the only one of the group whose photo had previously been included in the stack Jennifer had viewed. She recognized and chose him. When police again supported Thompson's selection, saying that Cotton was the same person she had identified among the photos, Ronald Cotton's fate was sealed.

At trial, Cotton maintained his innocence. But, based on Thompson's identification of him as her rapist, the jury convicted him, and he was sent to prison. There, Cotton eventually met a new inmate named Bobby Poole, who was also serving time for rape charges. Poole and Cotton looked so similar that guards and other prisoners sometimes mistook the two for each other. Cotton found out that Poole was from the same town in North Carolina where Jennifer Thompson had been raped. Cotton approached Poole and asked if he was responsible for the crime. Poole denied the accusation but later admitted to a fellow prisoner that he was Jennifer Thompson's rapist. Poole was eventually brought to court. There, Thompson swore she had never seen him, still insisting Ronald Cotton was her attacker.

"MY DNA IS NOT GOING TO BE IN THERE"

In 1994, ten years after the rape, Cotton heard about DNA testing and wondered if it might clear him.

A new pro bono attorney, Richard Rosen, had taken an interest in his case in 1992. Rosen expressed concerns about how Cotton's many failed appeals had been handled by other attorneys. Rosen also believed DNA testing would reveal the truth if crime scene samples were still available. However, Rosen warned Cotton that if he had really committed the rape and his DNA was found among the evidence, he would lose any further legal chances to pursue exoneration. Cotton replied, "I promise you I didn't do it. My DNA is not going to be in there." In time DNA testing exonerated Cotton, after eleven years in prison, and proved Bobby Poole was the true rapist.

Jennifer Thompson-Cannino and Ronald Cotton have since become friends. They tour the country, speaking out about the unreliability of eyewitness testimony and other judicial issues. They have written a book together called *Picking Cotton: Our Memoir of Injustice and Redemption.* Thompson's misidentification of Cotton and all it cost him still haunt her. Thompson wrote, "Seeing Ronald Cotton's face in the lineup, and in court, meant that his face eventually just replaced the original image of my attacker.... The standard way eyewitness evidence was collected had failed me, and because of that, I'd failed, too." Cotton is forgiving, believing that Thompson made an honest mistake influenced by flawed police line-up procedures that pushed her to identify him as the perpetrator of the crime.

"He [the policeman] taps his finger on my arm at one point. 'This is where the needle's gonna go in if you don't cooperate . . . . They're gonna send you to death row; you're gonna get executed.' This is going on for hours . . . I don't know what's going on. Everything's spinning."

—Christopher Ochoa, exoneree, speaking about his 1988 interrogation in 2005

CHAPTER FIVE

GOOD COP, BAD COP

Scientific studies highlighting the unreliability of eyewitness testimony have led to changes. They have also suggested improvements in police procedures. One suggested change is that officers show a witness a group of photos or individuals in a lineup one at a time, not all at once. With the one-at-a-time approach, the witness is less likely to compare each person or photo to the others. If the actual suspect is in the lineup, and the eyewitness has good recall, he or she will recognize a person naturally. The officer also has a duty to inform the witness that the actual criminal may not be present in the lineup or photos the witness is reviewing. These improvements can make the witness less likely to feel forced to choose a right answer.

Another reform is the blind lineup. This is a presentation of suspects in which the administrating officer does not know which member of the lineup is the actual suspect. This has been implemented because a police officer can unknowingly (or even intentionally) say things or exhibit body language that may influence the witness's decision. If the witness does pick out a member of the group, the officer should ask about and record the person's level of confidence in his or her choice. That statement would later be relayed to the judge and jury, if the case goes to court.

UNDER PRESSURE

Whether a person is talking with police or testifying on the witness stand in court, a high level of confidence does not automatically indicate truth. People can and do sometimes completely believe something that is untrue. This is different than lying. A victim or an investigating police officer may want very sincerely or feel intense pressure for a criminal to be caught. This can cause them to convince themselves or each other that the guilty party has been identified.

In some cases, questioning by the police can be so intense or hostile that suspects can mix up or begin to doubt their own story. Sometimes police pressure is so great, or the suspect's mind is so troubled, that a suspect confesses to a crime he or she did not commit. People give false confessions for a variety of reasons. These may include attention seeking, poor memory of events due to drugs or mental illness, or to protect a loved one who may be guilty. However, exoneration organizations have concluded that long hours of harsh, misleading, or threatening questions by authorities are the most frequent cause of false admissions of guilt.

A national study on wrongful convictions showed that 84 percent of false confessions happened after more than six hours of questioning. The average length of these grueling interrogations was sixteen hours. After this amount of questioning, most suspects are desperate to escape the situation, and many will confess. Often suspects confess just to buy time and much-needed rest. They tend to believe that the matter will be straightened out and their innocence revealed later in court.

All exoneration cases involving false confessions show that police did not tell the truth to the suspects about key aspects of the crime or misled them about the circumstances of events during questioning. It is not illegal for an officer to lie to a suspect during an interrogation. Lying to a witness or suspect, however, is particularly troublesome when that person is a child or is mentally handicapped. When police lie to vulnerable individuals, especially by telling them they have been abandoned or turned in by someone they trust, such individuals may give up hope. They may stop believing in themselves or think that they can go home after admitting guilt and for these reasons will falsely confess.

Police sometimes falsely tell a suspect they have absolute proof the person committed a crime. They tell the suspect he or she must have blacked out during or after the offense and doesn't remember what took place. This tactic is especially convincing to people with mental illness or drug or alcohol problems and can lead them to confess. In some instances, interrogating officers will suggest to a suspect that things will go easier if he or she admits to involvement in a killing, but that it happened in circumstances other than in cold blood. The idea of conviction for a lesser crime with a lesser punishment can be enough for people under stressful interrogation to admit to things they didn't do. Suspects cannot be told, however, that they will not be charged if they admit to a crime.

LONG HOURS OF HARSH, MISLEADING, OR THREATENING QUESTIONS BY AUTHORITIES ARE THE MOST FREQUENT CAUSE OF FALSE ADMISSIONS OF GUILT.

In a properly conducted police interrogation, questioning is directed solely to get at the truth, not to coerce a suspect into a confession. If a suspect admits guilt, an officer should ask detailed follow-up questions to make sure the suspect's account of what happened closely matches the actual crime. This will help to guard against false confessions.

THE TRUTH ABOUT LIE DETECTORS

So how do authorities uncover the truth? Polygraph machines (so-called lie detectors) and voice analyzers do not uncover lies. They indicate only a person's stress level. Stress does not automatically mean a person is lying. Anyone being questioned by police is under terrible mental pressure. Sometimes suspects who are innocent agree to a lie detector test, believing it will show they are not guilty. Yet they can begin to doubt themselves when police tell them (truthfully or not) they have failed the test. Lie detection technologies are, in fact, so flawed that the results of polygraph tests are inadmissible in most US courts. Some states do allow them, but only if both the defense and the prosecution agree to the results.

One technology, however, is extremely important during all phases of police work. As much as possible, all police procedures— whether lineups, interviews, interrogations, or confessions— should be fully recorded on video. Video recording helps protect the innocent from unacceptable police methods that contribute to false confessions and to wrongful convictions. When law enforcement uses proper processes, such recordings can also be presented in court to aid the prosecution and jury in cases of actual guilt.

EXONERATED: NICOLE HARRIS

Nicole Harris was a twenty-three-year-old woman with a degree in psychology. She worked in a nursing home. She was also the mother of two boys, five-year-old Diante and four-year-old Jaquari. On May 14, 2005, the boys' father, Sta-Von Dancy, woke from a nap in the family's apartment in Chicago, Illinois. He found Jaquari in the bedroom the two boys shared, strangled by an elastic band. The elastic had come

loose from his fitted bed sheet and was wrapped around his neck ten times. Both parents tried to revive Jaquari. They called emergency medical care, which arrived too late. Police found Harris at the chapel in the hospital where her son had been pronounced dead and took her in for an interview.

A death investigator also questioned Diante, the couple's older son, who said that Jaquari liked to play Spider-Man. The boy would jump off his bed using an elastic band as a sort of spider web around his neck. The medical examiner ruled Jaquari's death an accident. Later that same day, however, Harris gave police a videotaped confession in which she admitted to strangling her son with the elastic band because he wouldn't stop crying after being punished. She was charged with first-degree murder. A trial was set for October 2005.

TRUE CONFESSIONS?

Harris informed her lawyer that she was innocent and had endured a grueling police interrogation lasting twenty-seven hours. She said officers physically and verbally abused her, shoving her and calling her a monster. She also said that police deprived her of food, water, and access to a bathroom. They gave her a polygraph test and told her she had failed it. They then coerced her into making a false confession in front of a video camera. The rest of her interrogation was not recorded.

Harris's attorney wanted the judge to allow Diante's statement about his brother's Spider-Man game as evidence. However, the prosecution claimed the boy was too young and gullible to testify. At trial, jurors saw the short video-recorded section of Harris's interrogation in which she confessed. Based primarily on the confession, she was convicted and sentenced to thirty years in prison. Six weeks after her questioning, in July 2005, Illinois law made it mandatory for police interrogations in a homicide investigation to be electronically recorded in their entirety.

Harris presented her case to the Center on Wrongful Convictions, which accepted it. At a post-conviction motion for a new trial, CWC lawyers argued that the judge had ruled incorrectly in dismissing Diante's critical testimony.

They also pointed out that Harris's defense attorney should have put the death investigator who took Diante's original statement on the witness stand. The CWC also claimed that the original trial judge had shifted the burden of proof from the prosecution to the defense. Doing so went against the laws of the state of Illinois and against accepted norms of American jurisprudence.

Ultimately, after several appeals, the Seventh Circuit Court of Appeals in Chicago gave Harris the right to a new trial. She was released in February 2013, after nearly eight years in prison. The prosecution appealed the decision of the Seventh Circuit Court to the US Supreme Court, which refused to hear the case. The prosecuting attorneys dropped the matter and did not seek a new trial. In January 2014, the Chicago court that initially prosecuted Ms. Harris issued a certificate of innocence in her name.

Steve Drizin, the legal director for the CWC, said of cases like Harris's in which there is no biological evidence, "I am hopeful that the [county] and the courts will take a close look at many of those cases in the same way they look at cases where there is DNA evidence because there are many, many more Nicole Harrises out there." As for confessing to a crime she didn't commit, Harris says, "A lot of people may not understand it. I did not understand false confessions either . . . until it happened to me." Harris could have spent the majority of the rest of her life behind bars, but with the help of the Center on Wrongful Convictions, she is a free woman.

"I can still remember looking at the jury in my trial when they heard the scientist testify. That's when I knew it was all over and I was going to prison, probably for the rest of my life. Junk science sent me to prison, but real science proved my innocence. We have to make sure that this doesn't keep happening to other people, that our system relies on solid science."

—Roy Brown, exoneree, speaking about his 1992 trial in 2009

CHAPTER SIX

BAD SCIENCE

Forensic science has proven invaluable in exonerating those who have been wrongfully convicted. However, forensic techniques, or those who misuse them, sometimes can be the reason for incorrect guilty verdicts. For example, Joyce Gilchrist was a forensic scientist with the police department in Oklahoma City, Oklahoma. She had analyzed evidence in thousands of criminal cases between 1980 and 1994. DNA testing later conclusively showed that several people her analysis and testimony had helped convict were, in reality, innocent. Gilchrist's methods included falsifying lab results and perjury (intentional lying on the witness stand). By the time her faulty methods had been exposed, eleven defendants in cases she had worked had been executed. Twelve more were sitting on death row.

Gilchrist had started her career as a forensic chemist. During two decades in the lab, she branched out to analyzing hair, carpet fibers, blood, and other evidence. She eventually became a lab supervisor. As early as 1987, some of Gilchrist's colleagues and a network of defense attorneys complained to authorities about her sloppy work. On several occasions, for example, experts for the defense had alleged in court that Gilchrist was making positive identifications of suspects based on insufficient amounts of circumstantial evidence.

Exoneration organizations, including the Innocence Project, recognized early on that some of Gilchrist's cases had resulted in wrongful convictions. They also knew that her scientific peers were accusing her of malpractice. None of the complaints were taken seriously, however. Gilchrist continued to work in the lab and was known as a very compelling witness for the prosecution. The district attorney's office regularly used her testimony to help obtain convictions, and judges allowed her to take the stand.

After a long career as a forensic scientist with the Oklahoma City Police Department, Joyce Gilchrist (**above**) was dismissed from her job in 2001. She had a history of falsifying evidence and making serious scientific errors in her work.

By 2001 Gilchrist's work had come under increasing scrutiny, and the FBI began to study her casework. In six of the first eight cases it examined, the FBI concluded that Gilchrist had committed scientific errors or had overstated what could be properly concluded from her testing. Follow-up studies discovered Gilchrist had sometimes failed to perform tests that might have cleared the accused. She had also withheld important evidence from the defense. Further investigation showed that some evidence necessary to appeal convictions was mysteriously and improperly missing from her lab. Some of it had even been destroyed.

For this reason, those who were falsely convicted because of her work may never have a chance to clear their guilty verdicts. In all, Gilchrist may have been negligent or deceitful in more than 1,875 instances in the 3,000 cases in which she participated.

WHAT IS GOOD SCIENCE?

Rules of evidence require that judges and juries consider the worth of the scientific evidence attorneys present in court. This helps ensure that "junk science" does not make its way into the courtroom. Good science can be recognized in several ways. Proper science must be developed using the scientific method. This means creating a solid hypothesis and testing the idea using controlled experimentation. An example of a hypothesis might be: If two bullets are fired by the same gun, they will show the same pattern of microscopic marks known as striations. To support the hypothesis, researchers would carry out many repeated experimental trials using bullets fired from the same gun. They would then compare the striations on those bullets to striations on identical bullets fired from different guns. Quality science does not end there. It must then be presented to other scientists for their evaluation and testing. When a group of scientific peers has agreed that a method such as bullet comparison is valid, it is accepted as reliable science. Only then can such methods be properly used to analyze similar forensic evidence in a criminal case.

The FBI began relying solely on DNA as individuating evidence in 1999. However, only 5 to 10 percent of all criminal cases have any DNA-containing biological material to test. For example, cases such as drive-by shootings typically leave no physical trace of the perpetrator at the crime scene. In other offenses, forensic investigators may have used poor evidence collection or storage techniques. Evidence may have been destroyed before its importance was recognized, especially prior to the development of DNA technology. While some of these issues can be addressed with improvements in forensic science, others cannot.

FORENSIC SCIENCE GOES ON TRIAL

As experts learn more or as techniques fail, the standards for judging reliable science can change. For example, many longstanding methods are under increasing scrutiny. They include polygraphs and related lie detection methods, microscopic hair comparisons, bite-mark analyses, burn patterns in arson cases, handwriting examination, and bullet comparisons. In fact, in 2005, the US Congress appointed the National Academy of Sciences (NAS) to thoroughly review forensic science practices. The resulting 350-page NAS report from 2009 concluded that DNA is the only forensic method that can consistently and with a high rate of accuracy connect evidence to a specific person.

Stemming from the NAS report, the FBI began a review in 2013 of more than two thousand of its own cases. The FBI is looking at situations in which microscopic hair comparisons were used to identify and convict suspects between 1985 and 2000. The FBI is using DNA technology to check the accuracy of its hair matches in these old cases. DNA can be extracted from hair shafts, even those that are decades old. The DNA testing will prove whether the microscopic hair matches were correct or not. The FBI will then be able to scientifically document the reliability of microscopic hair comparisons. These types of rigorous tests may shed further doubt on methods formerly considered accurate. If so, they may form the groundwork for future exonerations.

The NAS report also found fault with some areas of forensic

career preparation and training. It also uncovered a lack of established procedures by which forensic scientists are qualified. Some of this is related to the rapid growth of forensic science and technology in the late twentieth century. Many practitioners rose up through the ranks without proper education and competency testing. They got jobs that agencies were desperate to fill. Yet forensic analysts who are not well trained can misinterpret results or boost their conclusions to levels that cannot be scientifically supported. Their testimony can sway jurors, especially those who lack science education. Some jurors may believe that simply because something sounds scientific, it must be accurate.

In addition, the NAS report identified a lack of centralized oversight for forensic labs in the United States. The lack of a single system of lab protocols has led to inconsistencies in forensic analyses. As a remedy, the NAS and the Innocence Project both support the creation of an independent federal institution to conduct research on forensic methods and their reliability. The institution would establish and enforce standards for forensic science, from the crime scene to the courtroom, including all laboratory analyses.

About half of the cases successfully overturned through the intervention of the Innocence Project included faulty forensic science. Any human endeavor is open to error. All forensic testing that relies heavily on subjective, opinion-based interpretation is vulnerable to human bias. This does not mean all forensic methods are wrong or based on bad science. Many experts argue that vague and poorly defined forensic standards—along with poor practitioners seeking fame or to advance their careers—are far more to blame for mistakes than are flawed methods.

EXONERATED: JAMES E. RICHARDSON JR.

James Richardson was outside his father's West Virginia home in May 1989 when he realized a neighbor's house was on fire. He broke down the neighbor's door and saved a three-year-old girl from the burning house. After the fire was extinguished, the body of the child's mother, Kelli Gilfilin, was discovered. She had been tied up, raped, and beaten to death.

At first, thirty-three-year-old Richardson received a hero's praise. But he was quickly arrested and charged with arson, rape, and murder. Three other suspects were dismissed based on forensic serology tests. The investigation centered on Richardson. He was thought to have raped and killed Gilfilin, set the fire to cover the crime, and then staged the rescue of the child.

Two months after the crime, forensic scientist Fred Zain of the West Virginia State Police Crime Lab testified in court. He said that proteins in semen on the victim not only connected Richardson to the crime but also excluded the other three men as suspects. A jury was presented this serological class evidence (which turned out to be false) even though more precise individuating DNA testing was available at the time. They convicted Richardson to life in prison with no chance of parole.

THE CASE AGAINST ZAIN

Ten years later, a different criminal case was building. The states of West Virginia and Texas had brought charges against Zain for allegedly falsifying data. They also charged that Zain did not actually conduct some tests he claimed to have undertaken during a sixteen-year career at various state crime labs. Zain had earned poor grades as he pursued his college chemistry degree and had lied about his credentials. Yet somehow he ended up working on hundreds of cases spanning a dozen states. He had a history of being fired by one agency, only to be hired by another.

In analyzing the semen in Gilfilin's murder, Zain had not even considered or examined the victim's body fluid proteins. The victim's own proteins could have completely masked those of the suspect, making Zain's determination about Richardson's guilt invalid. George Castelle, the chief public defender in Charleston, West Virginia, said Zain's methods amounted to "a blueprint on how to convict an innocent person."

A reinvestigation of Richardson's case also showed that police had not revealed that a bloodstained flashlight had been found at the crime scene. DNA testing showed that the blood on the flashlight belonged neither to Richardson nor to the victim. It belonged to a third person (yet to be identified). Records also showed that the three-year-old witness to her mother's murder had told police that she had seen part of the attack on her mother and that Richardson was not the man who did it. That evidence was not presented at trial.

Following indictments against Zain, Richardson's conviction was set aside in 1996 based on the state's reinvestigation of his case. Richardson was released from prison and assigned to home confinement, pending further investigation. Home confinement ended in 1998, and all charges against him were dropped in 1999. Richardson married and had a son, to whom he gave the middle name Castelle, after the public defender who pursued the allegations against Zain.

In a later legal settlement, the state of West Virginia awarded Richardson two million dollars for his wrongful conviction and for the seven years he had spent in prison. Zain's trial was indefinitely postponed when he developed cancer. He died in 2002. Richardson, a true hero for saving Kelli Gilfilin's three-year-old daughter, died of a heart attack in 2011.

"The history of the snitch is long and inglorious. . . . Their motives, then as now, were unholy. . . . When the criminal justice system offers witnesses incentives to lie, they will."

—Center on Wrongful Convictions, Northwestern University, 2004

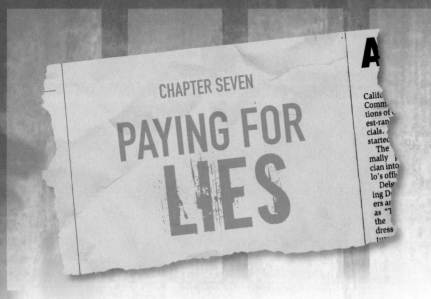

CHAPTER SEVEN

PAYING FOR LIES

Prosecuting attorneys and police commonly rely on giving rewards or incentives for testimony. In exchange for information about a suspect, an imprisoned criminal may be able to receive a reduced sentence or earn other privileges. Sometimes the prosecutor's office pays cash rewards to informants or to others willing to testify in a case. This can encourage people to make false statements about what they've heard. They may also invent phony eyewitness accounts of events.

The informants can include fellow inmates, who often claim that a suspect confessed to them. They may be members of organized crime networks not currently in jail but who want to see a member of a rival gang punished or out of the way. Angry spouses, ex-lovers, estranged family members, or other enemies may also lie about innocent persons just to see them put behind bars. Perjurers can include a co-defendant (someone who has been charged with the same crime). In such cases, one of the defendants may lie to the police, judge, or jury to implicate the other innocent defendant and to remove blame from him or herself. Agreeing to testify against a co-defendant may also be part of a plea bargain.

Overzealous law enforcement officers, eager to obtain a guilty verdict, sometimes feed jailhouse snitches insider information about a case that is not publicly available. These informants may have pending charges of their own for which they want to avoid prosecution. They will agree to testify in court about the information police feed to them as if it was their own knowledge. Jurors tend to view this information, which seems like something only an eyewitness would know, as truthful and therefore compelling.

Statistics from the National Registry of Exonerations show that perjured testimony and false accusations occurred in 56 percent of more than 1,300 recorded exonerations. Perjured testimony is most common in cases involving homicide and child sexual abuse. In the wrongful convictions of homicide cases, 65 percent involved testimony that was later discovered to be false. In some cases, the testimony was found to have been the result of police prompting of witnesses. In 81 percent of exonerated allegations of childhood sexual abuse, victims have changed their stories. They admit that sex abuse did not actually take place but that family members or others in charge of their welfare had pressured or coached them to make a false accusation.

AVOIDING PERJURED TESTIMONY

It is illegal in the United States for a criminal defendant to tamper with the testimony of a witness. This is true whether the tampering is to prevent or to promote testimony. Yet the practice of paying for testimony is widespread among government prosecutors, defense attorneys, and other authorities. Judge Paul J. Kelly Jr. of the US Court of Appeals for the Tenth Circuit said of one appeal, "If justice is perverted when a criminal defendant seeks to buy testimony from a witness, it is no less perverted when the government does so. . . . The judicial process is tainted and justice is cheapened when factual testimony is purchased, whether with leniency or money."

Exoneration organizations recommend that law enforcement agents record any interviews with potential informants in full. This will show that police have not provided details to which the cooperating witness later testifies. Agencies also recommend that jailhouse informants wear a hidden wire (recording device) during pre-arranged conversations with fellow inmates or with other criminals they claim have confessed to crimes. During these secretly recorded conversations, the informant should be directed by authorities to ask questions that capture specific and unique follow-up details about any confession they claim to have heard. Without this proof, testimony related to jailhouse conversations should not be permitted in court. Exoneration agencies also point out that situations involving incentivized testimony are highly suspicious if informant statements are the only evidence, either direct or circumstantial, in a criminal case. A strong, factual case must always include a much wider range of evidence.

Prosecutors are legally required to tell the defense about any deals they have made with witnesses. In addition, exoneration organizations suggest that police report to the judge and jury when any incentives are offered for testimony. This would allow judges and jurors to weigh the source of and potential motives for such information in their decision-making process. Judges are also encouraged to explain the risks and known problems with informant testimony during jury instructions. Perjured testimony—whether rewarded or not—has caused too many innocent individuals to pay for lies with years behind bars.

EXONERATED: ELROY "LUCKY" JONES

In early June 2006, several people outside a drug-infested apartment building in Detroit, Michigan, heard gunshots from inside. As they watched, a man named Matenis Carter ran away from the scene. Another man shoved an AK-47 rifle out of a second-story window in the building and began firing at him. A third man, Cleo McDougal, lay shot to death inside the apartment. Carter was the brother of the victim and denied knowing the shooter. A few days later, however, Carter told police the gunman was Elroy "Lucky" Jones, a twenty-six-year-old man he knew. Jones had a criminal record that included drug convictions and an assault. As a result of Carter's information, Jones was charged with first-degree murder and with other offenses related to the shootout at the apartment building.

At the preliminary hearing, officers brought Jones in before a male eyewitness who lived in the apartment across the street from the murder. Police and prosecutors wanted to see if the eyewitness would identify Jones as the shooter. Jones's mother reported, "I watched the police bring in a young man that was their witness and as soon as he seen my son, he looked, and then he mouthed to the police, 'that's not him.'" Still, the police and prosecutor pressed on with the charges against Jones. At trial, that same witness took the stand for the defense, stating that the man who had been shooting out of the window was not Jones. The witness claimed he was sure the defendant was much larger than the actual gunman. He stated the shooter was small enough to get much of his body out of the apartment window as he was firing the gun. The male witness also testified that a police officer had pressured him during a lineup to say Jones was the gunman.

In addition to questionable eyewitness testimony, physical evidence did not connect Jones to the crime. The only person to say Jones was the shooter was the dead man's brother. All the same, Jones was convicted in late 2006 and was sentenced to life behind bars without parole. An appeal was impossible, however, because someone stole the tapes of the court proceedings from the court reporter's car before she could transcribe them. Unable to assess the information presented at the original court case, the Michigan Court of Appeals reversed Jones's conviction in 2008. By Michigan law, the overturned conviction paved the way for a new trial. At his second trial in 2008, Jones was again convicted and handed a life sentence.

AN INFORMANT PAYS OFF

In 2011, while federal officers were investigating a totally unrelated matter, they interviewed a man who informed them he had driven the real gunman to the Detroit apartment in 2006. This alleged shooter was in prison on drug charges. Detroit police arranged a lineup with the new suspect for some of the original wit-

nesses to the crime. Almost all of them identified the new man as the gunman from the 2006 murder. In fact, one of the witnesses claimed he had identified the man as the killer to authorities in 2006, but at that time they would not listen. After learning of the new information, the police began working to free Jones and to find the real criminal. Deputy Chief David Levalley said, "If we put the wrong person in prison and we find out about it later on, and we don't take the necessary steps to correct that, then our credibility going forward is tarnished."

Based on the new evidence, Jones's attorney filed a motion to overturn his conviction in Michigan's Wayne County Circuit Court. Once again, the court set aside Jones's conviction and ordered another new trial. However, the prosecutor's office decided not to pursue a third trial, and in early 2014, Elroy Jones finally got lucky. He was released from prison, after seven years, with all charges dropped.

"I thought they were there to help . . . I really thought, 'You know what? I'm innocent and there is no way I'm going to prison.' And I didn't worry. All the way through trial I wasn't worried. I wasn't worried until the day they came back and said, 'Guilty.' Then I got worried real fast."

—Peter Rose, exoneree, reflecting on his 1995 trial in 2005

CHAPTER EIGHT

POOR LAWYERING AND UNJUST JUSTICES

Once a criminal suspect has been arrested, he or she has the right to an attorney. But that right doesn't guarantee an outstanding lawyer, or even a satisfactory one. Studies of exonerations have shown that poor legal counsel has often contributed greatly toward wrongful guilty verdicts.

Defense attorneys may fail their clients in various ways. An incompetent lawyer may neglect to thoroughly investigate or present the defendant's story. The attorney may ignore an alibi that would show the accused was nowhere near the scene of the crime. Bad lawyering has also failed to expose faulty science and poor police procedures. Exoneration organizations cite examples of defense attorneys who did not show up for court or who were aslccp or drunk during courtroom proceedings.

Exoneration agency research shows that faulty lawyering often lies in what a defense attorney does not do in a case, rather than what he or she actually does. But it is difficult to uncover and right the wrongs of a poor legal defense, even when an unjust conviction is up for appeal. This is because the standard appeals process is limited to what took place at a previous trial. It is not based on new evidence that may be discovered or that was previously withheld. The appeals attorney or an exoneration agency may want to present new evidence to an appellate court, such as information the trial lawyer neglected in the case. But to do so, an attorney must first submit a legal brief explaining why the new evidence should be permitted after the original trial. The appellate court must then agree to the motion to hear the new evidence before it can be considered.

Prosecuting attorneys who abuse their authority can also contribute to wrongful convictions. In 2013 one federal appeals judge remarked on what he saw as an epidemic of prosecuting attorneys purposely withholding important evidence they know would aid the defense. This is against the rules of discovery in a criminal case. In addition, both prosecutors and defense attorneys sometimes attempt to include court testimony of individuals they know to be lying. Some attorneys also use experts they know are unethical or incompetent. In such cases, an attorney's zeal for winning a case can overcome the obligation to uphold justice. It is up to the judge to try to recognize these tactics and prevent them from tainting the legal case.

ERRORS OF JUDGMENT

Judges are attorneys who, after years of experience (usually as a prosecutor), are appointed or elected to their position. They decide cases brought before a court of law. A good judge is completely familiar with all legal processes. Like anyone else, though, a judge can make mistakes. Judges can also be guilty of official misconduct if they ignore policies and procedures. If a jury is deadlocked, for example—unable to make a decision about guilt or innocence—a judge is legally required to declare a mistrial. This leads to a new trial. However, some judges may tell a deadlocked jury they must continue to deliberate no matter what. Judges may also deny legal motions they know should be granted or hold back evidence that should be allowed.

Judges are not advocates for one side or the other. They are more like referees who must try to avoid all bias and fairly apply the law. Trial judges evaluate evidence and questions of fact. Appellate judges, on the other hand, are experts in examining questions of law. The appeals process is a way to allow other judges to examine and re-evaluate a court case. Appellate judges will look for problems that may have occurred at trial, including judicial errors or bias. Rather than focusing on evidence, appeal courts review how well the law was applied by a previous trial judge when hearing a case. When appellate courts find legal mistakes or negligence, they must reverse or amend the original trial court's decision. The criminal justice system is responsible for identifying patterns of misconduct—such as bias, corruption, or incompetence—and should push to remove unethical or ineffective lawyers and judges from their positions.

> **THE CRIMINAL JUSTICE SYSTEM IS RESPONSIBLE FOR IDENTIFYING PATTERNS OF MISCONDUCT—SUCH AS BIAS, CORRUPTION, OR INCOMPETENCE.**

PREVENTING FUTURE LEGAL MISCONDUCT

The Innocence Project reports that misconduct on the part of the prosecution was behind nearly half of all its cases resulting in exoneration. These included cases in which the prosecution knew of—but concealed—evidence that would have supported the defendant's innocence. But the Innocence Project accepts only cases for which DNA evidence exists. For this reason, its work likely represents only a small fraction of wrongful convictions based on inadequate legal defense.

The types of legal issues that promote wrongful convictions are complex. In many parts of the country, funding is not sufficient to provide salaries for enough highly qualified public defenders to handle the area's caseload. When overworked, lawyers may not have the time to fully study each case and prepare a solid defense. Research also suggests that defense attorneys who are incompetent, prosecutors who engage in misconduct, and judges with track records of mistakes are not routinely removed from office and/or punished for their misdeeds. The same is often true for police who misuse their authority. To reduce the number of wrongful convictions associated with legal errors, exoneration agencies stress the need to address all such issues. They also suggest the need for strict standards of ongoing training to help ensure competence among attorneys and police.

EXONERATED: EARL WASHINGTON JR.

In 1983 twenty-two-year-old Earl Washington Jr. was picked up by police in his Fauquier County, Virginia, neighborhood. He was accused of breaking into the home of Helen Weeks, an elderly woman, earlier that same morning and hitting her with a chair. Police questioned Washington for two days before claiming he had confessed to the attack. He also admitted to five unsolved

Earl Washington Jr. (center) walks with his legal team, Marie Deans (left) and Barry Weinstein (right) on their way to a 2001 press conference after Washington's exoneration. During police interrogation in 1983, he had falsely confessed to rape and murder.

crimes in several nearby areas. He would not be free again until 2001.

At the time, Washington's estimated intelligence quotient (IQ) was 69. The clinical psychologist who

85

tested Washington classified him as having mild mental retardation (now called intellectual disability). Worldwide, an average IQ is around 100, and only 2.2 percent of the population has a score below 70. To be considered competent or fit to stand trial, defendants must be deemed able to understand the nature of the legal charges against them. They must also be able to understand the sentencing they may face. In addition, they must be judged able to assist their attorneys in their own defense. This includes the ability to recall the facts of the case and to testify on their own behalf, if desired. In cases where the judge suspects intellectual disability, the court will order a psychological assessment of a defendant.

Washington was indicted for attacking Weeks, and he later pled guilty in that case. When witnesses in four of the five unresolved crimes to which Washington had confessed did not recognize him, those charges were eventually dropped. The fifth crime, for which Washington had admitted guilt, was the unsolved rape and murder of Rebecca Lynn Williams, a nineteen-year-old mother of three young children. About a year before Washington's arrest, Williams had been stabbed multiple times in nearby Culpepper County, Virginia. Before losing consciousness, the victim had told her husband that one black man had attacked her. During pre-trial hearings in the case, a Culpepper County Circuit Court judge ruled Washington competent to stand trial for the rape-murder. The judge also determined that police had properly taken Washington's confession.

By the time of the trial, both the defense and the prosecution had the psychological report and the full transcript of the police interrogation of Washington. It showed that Washington did not know the rape-murder victim's race or address. He also did not know that she had been raped before being killed. Washington's confession stated that he had stabbed her two or three times. In fact, the autopsy report documented thirty-eight wounds. Washington was only able to identify the apartment where the attack had taken place after police took him there three times and pointed it out to him. In addition, serological protein testing on a semen sample from the crime scene did not match Washington's proteins. The lab report had been altered to falsely suggest the testing was inconclusive.

"THEY DIDN'T PUT ON MUCH OF A CASE"

Washington had a very poor defense attorney who had never tried a death penalty case. The attorney did not build a strong case of innocence for his client despite the wealth of information available to him. For example, he did not present to the jury the forensic psychologist's report of Washington's strong desire to please others, particularly authority figures. Nor did he expose that Washington functioned at what was judged to be the mental level of a ten-year-old child. Instead, the only psychological evaluation presented to the jury came from the prosecution—not the defense. It stated only that Washington was competent to stand trial. Juror Jacob Dodson later

said, "I figured the defense was saying he was guilty, too, because they didn't put on much of a case."

The court case lasted less than five hours, including jury deliberations. The jury found Washington guilty. At the sentencing hearing, he received the death penalty. His defense attorney did not argue against the punishment. The US Supreme Court has since ruled that those with intellectual disability cannot be sentenced to death, as it violates the US Constitution's ban on cruel and unusual punishment.

In a federal appeal, a panel of judges established the lack of proper legal representation in Washington's case. All the same, the panel refused to reverse the conviction. In prison, Washington was only nine days away from death when a last-minute appeal delayed his execution. A concerned fellow death row inmate—Joseph Giarratano—had contacted legal authorities about Washington's case. He instituted a lawsuit on Washington's behalf, citing the lack of proper legal representation. The inmate's actions led to the appeal that postponed Washington's execution and ultimately caused the Innocence Project to accept his case.

In October 1993, new DNA testing showed that the semen found on the victim's body could not have been Washington's. However, the law in Virginia at the time stated that to be considered in a case, new evidence had to be introduced within twenty-one days after trial. (That law has since been repealed based on this case.) So on his last day in office, the governor of Virginia reduced Washington's sentence from execution to life in prison. Six years later, a new governor requested additional DNA testing. Testing took some time, but the improved technology revealed two distinct DNA profiles, neither of which belonged to Washington. The governor pardoned Washington of murder in October 2000. However, he was not freed until more than four months later, when he reached the release date of his sentence for assaulting Weeks. By the time he was finally freed in February 2001, Washington had served more than seventeen years behind bars.

In 2006, using the DNA testing results obtained in 2000, authorities were able to identify and to indict the actual perpetrator of the rape-murder—Kenneth M. Tinsley. He was already in prison for another rape committed after the attack on Williams. (The source of the second DNA profile from the case has still not been identified). Washington and his attorneys filed a lawsuit against the state of Virginia, and he was awarded more than two million dollars in damages in 2006.

WHERE DO WE GO FROM HERE?

The year 2012 marked a milestone in the history of innocence-advocacy organizations. The National Registry of Exonerations reported that, for the first time, police or prosecutors aided in or were actually responsible for initiating more than half (54 percent) of that year's sixty-three overturned convictions. This shift shows the increasing willingness of the legal system to police itself by recognizing and correcting injustice, regardless of its cause. Cooperation from officials, however, is still least likely in exoneration attempts for cases that are highly publicized. It is also unlikely in cases in which the probable legal errors are enormous. Grave mistakes are often the hardest to admit. They can bring even more scrutiny and public disapproval upon the authorities responsible.

The NRE also indicated an increase in 2012 of overturned convictions for those who were innocent but who had actually pled guilty. When the total registry data (from 1989 to 2014) is considered, 11 percent of those exonerated had originally pled guilty to crimes they did not commit. The remaining 89 percent

"There is no way to tell from [past] cases whether we are getting better at avoiding wrongful convictions in the first place. It does seem, however, that we are working harder to identify the mistakes we made years ago and that we are catching more of them. If we are also learning from those tragic errors that have come to light, that would be a big step in the right direction."

—National Registry of Exonerations, 2014

had pled not guilty but were convicted at trial by juries or judges. This increasing trend in overturning convictions of those who had pled guilty is thought to reflect an environment of greater openness. Authorities are more readily re-examining cases where the defendant opted for (or was pressured into) a plea bargain rather than risk a more severe penalty at trial.

EXONERATIONS AND THE DEATH PENALTY

As of 2014, thirty-two states permit the death penalty as a sentencing option. So do the federal government and the US military. Eighteen states and the District of Columbia have abolished it. Only 8 percent of the cases in the NRE are those of convictions that led to death sentences. This is significant, however, since only a small fraction of all guilty verdicts result in a sentence of execution (less than 1/100th of 1 percent). Overall, death sentences have decreased in the United States. In the decade from 1991 to 2000, the average was more than 280 per year. From 2001 to 2010, that average dropped to around 123 per year. Between 2011 and the end of 2013, the average number of death sentences each year in the United States fell to 80. This decrease may be in part because exonerations—especially those in which DNA testing has led to the real perpetrator—have highlighted a range of mistakes. This includes faulty eyewitness testimony, controversial police procedures, flawed forensic science, and other legal errors.

If conducted properly and reported honestly, DNA testing provides the legal system with more accurate identification of criminal perpetrators even before court proceedings. This results in fewer false convictions now than in the past. For this reason, the number of wrongful convictions overturned by DNA testing continues to fall slowly. However, non-DNA exonerations, which

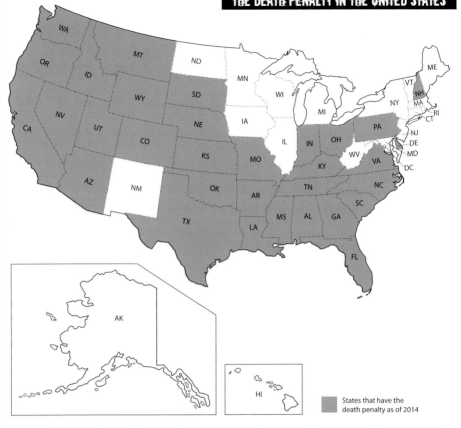

States that have the death penalty as of 2014

This map shows the states that currently have the death penalty and those that do not.

are more difficult to achieve, are on the rise. They will make up the majority of future exonerations because most cases have no biological evidence to test.

A RECORD YEAR

According to the National Registry of Exonerations, 2013 was a record year in the United States. A total of eighty-seven exonerations were recorded by the time the registry's 2013 annual report was finalized. About one-fifth of those were aided by DNA analysis. Nearly one-third involved alleged crimes that never even took place. These were mostly false allegations of sexual assault or drug offenses for which individuals had been framed. One-third of the total exonerations were for crimes other than homicide or rape. Almost half (46 percent) were in murder cases, one of which overturned a death-row sentence.

Nearly half (forty-three) of the convictions overturned in 2013 occurred in just five states: Texas, Illinois, New York, Washington, and California. This may mean some geographic areas are working harder than others to fight injustices or that they are catching up on a larger number of overdue exonerations. It may also be that the likelihood of error is greater overall in states with larger populations and with more legal cases than other, smaller states.

COMPENSATING FOR LOST TIME

Exonerations can be made during a person's lifetime or posthumously, after the wrongfully convicted person is dead. Exonerations clear a person's name, bring the family justice, and help society and the legal system learn from past mistakes. But what about those men and women who finally walk free after years of being wrongfully held in prison? The media captures tearful reunions with family members, attorneys and exoneration organizations receive heartfelt thanks, and a tragic chapter in the lives of those who have been falsely convicted closes.

The lost years can never be reclaimed, however. Of the first 250 exonerations made through DNA testing, 21 percent of the individuals were younger than twenty-one years of age (6 percent were younger than age eighteen). The average age at conviction was twenty-seven; the average age at exoneration was forty-two.

For many people, these are among the most productive years of life. Some exonerated individuals missed the opportunity to get married or have children. Others suffered in prison while their children grew up or loved ones died. Many of the wrongfully convicted individuals were incarcerated during formative career years. They lost out on a chance to enhance their skills and contribute to society.

To help avoid future mistakes in federal criminal cases, as well as to aid the victims of federal crimes, the US Congress overwhelmingly passed the Justice for All Act into law in 2004. Among other things, this legislation provided federal funding for forensic DNA testing in suspected wrongful convictions. It also required preservation of biological evidence, which may hold key DNA, and improved legal services to those charged with capital crimes at both the state and federal levels. The Justice for All Act provided funds for improvements at state and local crime laboratories, including for training and DNA testing.

The law suggested (but did not require) compensation guidelines for those wrongfully convicted of crimes they did not commit. It suggested payment up to $50,000 for each year of wrongful incarceration except in death penalty cases. In those instances, the law suggested compensation of up to $100,000 for every year the person sat on death row. The guidelines only cover exonerated federal crimes. The act recommended, however, that states compensate those who are wrongfully convicted at the state level, particularly when they receive the death penalty as punishment. However, no minimum payments were established, and state courts are free to do as they choose.

As of 2014, more than half the states in the United States have laws that require some compensation for those exonerated.

For various reasons, only about two-thirds of exonerees get damage payments after being cleared of charges. For example, some states put restrictions on who can be compensated. Some states do not allow payments to anyone who contributed to his or her own conviction, whether through a false confession or through a plea bargain. Of those who are compensated, most wait an average of three to four years after exoneration before receiving any funds. This can be a real hardship. Exonerated men and women—like most people who have served time behind bars—typically leave prison with no money. They have few personal possessions, no means of transportation, no employment, and sometimes nowhere to stay.

In addition, almost all states make payments by annual installments only. This requires an exoneree—who has not been used to handling finances while in prison—to carefully manage the funds. If the exonerated person dies, the compensation is typically terminated. Funds often cannot be passed to heirs, even though they too suffered while a loved one was incarcerated. One expert points out that these policies have the most negative impact on elderly or sick prisoners. The policies are also more unfair to those whom the prosecution fights to keep in prison. In the end, the longer an innocent person remains incarcerated, the less likely that person is to be fully compensated, even if an award is made.

MOVING FORWARD TOGETHER

Even if those freed do receive a timely financial settlement, it never rights the wrongs a falsely convicted person has suffered. For this reason, a variety of organizations in the United States help exonerees reintegrate into society. Resurrection After Exoneration, in New Orleans, Louisiana, is one such organization. It is led by people who have themselves been exonerated. The agency assists individuals with a place to stay, job training, health care, mental health counseling, and guidance services. Some staff members of another group, Witness to Innocence, based in Philadelphia, Pennsylvania, were once on death row and have since been exonerated. The group works to educate the public and to abolish the death penalty in the United States. It also aids people convicted of capital crimes they didn't commit.

Exoneration groups are also working for change. David Moran, codirector of the Michigan Innocence Clinic (MIC), states, "Our plan is gradually to do more and more work to advocate for reform. Part of the idea of an innocence clinic is that we don't exonerate people quietly, and so a big part of our mission is to publicize these cases and explain what went wrong, and then use them as tools to try and convince policy makers and the public that these same mistakes shouldn't be made in the future." In Michigan, for example, the state bar association (a network representing attorneys practicing in the state) has created task forces to examine some of the issues that com-

> "A BIG PART OF OUR MISSION IS TO PUBLICIZE THESE CASES AND...CONVINCE POLICY MAKERS AND THE PUBLIC THAT THESE SAME MISTAKES SHOULDN'T BE MADE IN THE FUTURE."
> —David Moran, codirector of the Michigan Innocence Clinic, 2011

monly lead to wrongful convictions and to suggest remedies. One of the pilot research projects demonstrated that video recording of police interrogations helps avoid false convictions. In fact, the procedure actually improves the rate of proper convictions. Such findings will hopefully build support for other reforms and lead to new laws to help prevent future wrongful convictions.

The general public pays a big price for wrongful convictions. In Michigan, for example, the incarceration of each innocent person costs the state about $30,000 per year. People in prison are also not able to support their families financially. So, their families may have to seek welfare and other support payments from the government. After exoneration, financial compensation to the victims of unjust guilty verdicts costs taxpayers millions of dollars each year.

The greatest costs to society are not measured in dollars, however. When the actual perpetrators of serious and violent offenses get away with their crimes, they are free to commit additional unlawful acts. For example, evidence in four of the first five exonerations obtained by the MIC identified the real perpetrators. Those guilty individuals were alleged to have committed at least an additional six murders, a carjacking, and other offenses that could likely have been prevented. All those crimes took place after police mistakenly focused on innocent people as responsible for the real perpetrators' initial crimes. The general public also pays for false convictions by the damage they do to our trust in the legal system, which is fundamental to society.

SCIENCE AND JUSTICE: DOING THE RIGHT THING

The sciences of psychology, criminology, police science, and forensics work hand in hand with the legal system to prosecute and punish people whose actions break the laws that bind us into a community. One of the primary foundations of science is questioning. Good science, like justice, requires a willingness to keep an open mind and to consider all alternative possibilities when seeking truth. The mission of those involved in the science and service of justice is to never lose sight of the uncertainty that underlies all human endeavors, including their own. Criminal investigation and prosecution processes are complex and rely on people, who are all capable of mistakes. When errors are made, we must be open to correcting them.

The US Constitution establishes many rights. Along with these rights, Americans bear responsibilities to the government and to each other. As a society, each of us must strive to do our best and to attempt to be an ethical person of great character. All of us must aim to avoid situations where our integrity could be compromised. If we find ourselves in a moral dilemma, we must be strong in our convictions to do the right thing. We are called upon to respect authority. If we find ourselves as part of that authority—as a police officer, forensic scientist, judge, lawyer, or member of a jury—we must always aim to be worthy of that respect. Like the Innocence Project, the Center on Wrongful Convictions, and the Michigan Innocence Clinic, when we witness abuses of the legal system or people being treated unfairly, we too must work for change.

EXONERATED: DESHAWN AND MARVIN REED

In March 2000, twenty-two-year-old Shannon Gholston was driving in Ecorse, Michigan, just south of Detroit. He was turning left at an intersection when a bullet came through the window behind the driver's seat. The bullet hit him in the back of the neck and instantly paralyzed him. His car crashed into a fence, and when someone stopped to help and asked who had shot him, Gholston said

DeShawn Reed (left) and his uncle Marvin Reed (right) were imprisoned in 2001 for a drive-by shooting they did not commit. They were released in 2009 but struggled to get their lives back on track. In 2012 the city that investigated the men awarded the pair a $3.1 million settlement.

he didn't know. By the time he arrived at the hospital, he could barely whisper. A police officer shared with Gholston that people in the neighborhood were saying that either Gholston's former classmate, twenty-four-year-old DeShawn Reed, or his thirty-three-year-old uncle, Marvin Reed, was the shooter. The officer told Gholston to blink twice if DeShawn was the gunman. Gholston blinked twice. The officer asked the victim to blink twice if Marvin Reed was also involved in the shooting. Gholston again blinked two times.

Within the next few days, De-Shawn and Marvin Reed were arrested and charged with assault with intent to commit murder. Both insisted they were innocent. A few weeks later, Gholston whispered sworn testimony from his hospital bed. He reported that Marvin was driving, with DeShawn as his passenger, when they pulled up alongside Gholston's car. Gholston reported that DeShawn (who is left handed) fired the shot from a gun in his right hand. When that testimony was presented at a preliminary hearing in 2000, a judge ordered the Reeds to stand trial the next year. DeShawn

and Marvin believed the truth would win out in time, once they got their day in court.

No physical evidence linked the Reeds to the crime, and the men had six alibi witnesses. Several eyewitnesses claimed they saw a man fire a couple shots from an alleyway behind Gholston's car, contradicting the victim's story. In fact, at least one witness had earlier told police the shooter was Tyrone Allen, who lived in the neighborhood and was involved with Gholston in a stolen car parts ring. Much of that information, however, never made it to trial. Allen himself couldn't be questioned. Police had shot and killed him during an attempted carjacking in the months just after Gholston was wounded.

It was clear the Reeds had had poor defense attorneys at trial. The judge himself stated that the complete story had likely not come out in court. All the same, he convicted both men of the murder and sentenced each to a minimum of twenty years in prison. Eight days after the Reeds were sentenced, the results of forensic bullet testing were released. Analysis showed that the bullet taken from Gholston's body at surgery matched the striation pattern on a bullet test-fired from a gun found on Allen after he had been shot by police.

The post-conviction bullet testing was new evidence that could not be used in the standard appeals process. Appeals were denied all the way up to the Michigan Supreme Court in 2005. DeShawn's younger brother then hired a private investigator. The investigator ultimately got Shannon Gholston to admit on videotape that he had not actually seen the person who shot him. Gholston claimed that once he had accused the Reeds and been backed by his entire family, he couldn't bring himself to say he had lied all along.

In 2007 a Reed family friend took the story to Northwestern University's Center on Wrongful Convictions. From there the case was passed to lawyer Bridget McCormack, who was forming the Michigan Innocence Clinic for non-DNA cases. She and another attorney prepared a motion requesting that the appellate court consider additional evidence. They found that the original police account of Gholston's eye-blink testimony in the hospital had been wrong. The officer had actually told him to blink twice if he did not know who had shot him, not if he did know. The MIC team also scientifically demonstrated that a bullet from a shooter in the alley in which Allen was supposedly standing could have easily penetrated Gholston's rear window on the driver's side, hitting the back of his neck as the car turned left. The alleged scenario—in which the shooter's car pulled up alongside Gholston so that the victim would have seen the shooter— was actually impossible.

The appeals court also reviewed evidence that before the Reeds' 2001 trial, Allen's girlfriend had told her uncle (a deputy sheriff) that Allen confessed to her that he had shot Gholston. The deputy notified the Ecorse police, but they apparently did not follow up on that claim.

The appeals court judge considered that information and ruled for a new trial. Before the trial took place, the charges were dropped in July 2009.

Third-year law student Zoe Levine (under the supervision of faculty members) represented the Reeds during the appeals process. She said of the experience, "I think when you're in that courtroom it's impossible not to feel . . . the stakes. You try your best to . . . make sure you do everything that you need to do for these clients because their lives are in the balance. They're also sitting there at the table with you . . . and behind you is their family and everyone is highly invested in this case, and so the pressure is very strong. The way to overcome that is preparation."

THE GIFT OF HOPE

DeShawn Reed said the exoneration team brought him the gift of hope. As a prisoner, he had not seen his four children grow up. The career goals he had been working toward when arrested were a thing of the past. DeShawn felt particularly bad, believing he was to blame for the conviction of his uncle Marvin and for all the years both men had spent in prison.

During the first four years of confinement, each man had spent twenty-three hours a day in his cell. Every time they were transferred to a new prison, they were strip-searched. Their cellmates were murderers, rapists, and other violent men. Once, in a case of mistaken identity, another prisoner stabbed DeShawn in the arm with a homemade knife. Marvin was put in solitary confinement for two days after a prison fight. Each man wondered whether having to defend himself against a fellow inmate might forever destroy his chances for a new trial.

The Reeds were finally set free in 2009. But they walked into a world that had changed both personally and technologically. Not wanting to wait twenty years for his release, the mother of DeShawn's children had moved on. Marvin had been newly married before his conviction, but his wife had divorced him while he was incarcerated. The two men left prison without a dime during one of the worst recessions the US economy has ever seen. They quickly discovered that convicts who are paroled after rightfully serving their time receive more help starting over than those who are wrongfully convicted.

DeShawn and Marvin Reed were each scheduled to receive $500 from the Ken Wyniemko Foundation. Wyniemko had started the fund after his own 2003 exoneration following a false conviction. DeShawn looked into getting his GED. He found that it was difficult to find work. Potential employers "want to know why you haven't been working for the last nine years. I still end up explaining the whole thing," he said. Complicating the men's ability to find work, their names remained in Michigan's online offender-tracking system until 2012 as part of state policy. Marvin took on odd jobs for a family member, saying, "I'm just trying to do an honest day's work."

In 2010 the MIC helped the Reeds file a wrongful conviction suit against the Ecorse Police Department. The men were awarded $3.1 million in 2012. Their story is one in which a close-knit neighborhood and three families were torn apart by a series of senseless acts. Shannon Gholston is a quadriplegic, Tyrone Allen is dead, and DeShawn and Marvin Reed spent years in prison for crimes they did not commit. The Reeds try never to be bitter about the time they spent behind bars and have forgiven Gholston.

EXONERATION PROFILES

The exoneration stories in this book are only a handful of the thousands of wrongful conviction stories in the United States. Below are brief sketches of a sampling of additional cases. To learn more about other exoneration stories, visit the National Registry of Exonerations website at https://www.law.umich.edu/special/exoneration/Pages/about.aspx Most cases have multiple causes for wrongful conviction.

Julie Baumer. In a 2003 Michigan case, twenty-seven-year-old Baumer was caring for her six-week-old nephew when he became ill. Hospital doctors suspected head trauma, perhaps from shaken baby syndrome. Baumer was charged with child abuse. Medical testimony disagreed on the injury's timing and cause, but Baumer was convicted and sentenced to ten to fifteen years. The appeals process resulted in a new trial at which six medical experts testified the baby had suffered a childhood stroke following a difficult delivery. Baumer was acquitted and exonerated in 2010.

Levon Brooks and Kennedy Brewer. A three-year-old girl was abducted, raped, and murdered in Mississippi in 1990. A forensic dentist named Dr. Michael West matched Levon Brooks (an ex-boyfriend of the child's mother) to the crime through bite-mark analysis. Brooks was convicted. A similar crime against another three-year-old was committed in the same town. Kennedy Brewer (the boyfriend of that child's mother) was convicted of that crime using bite-mark testimony from the same dentist. DNA testing exonerated both men in 2008 and uncovered the true perpetrator, who confessed. He said he had never bitten either girl, further calling into question the reliability of the forensic dentist, who was later discredited in numerous cases.

Francisco Carrillo. In a California case, police picked up Carrillo when he was fifteen for killing a man in front of the man's son and five other boys during a drive-by shooting. One witness claimed to have seen the gunman and told the others it was Carrillo. All six witnesses testified against Carrillo at trial, which ended in a hung jury. At his second trial, in 1992, Carrillo was convicted and sentenced to life in prison. While reviewing his own conviction case files in 2003, Carrillo discovered that a defense investigator had uncovered the real shooter. The shooter had confessed, but the judge had not permitted that testimony. The eyewitnesses eventually recanted and Carrillo was finally exonerated in 2011.

Rubin "Hurricane" Carter and John Artis. While preparing for the world middleweight boxing title in 1966, Carter and a friend, John Artis, were arrested for killing three people and wounding another in a New Jersey barroom shooting. After the grand jury failed to indict the men, police produced two informants. (They received reduced prison sentences and payments for their testimony.) Carter and Artis were sentenced to three life terms each. The informants recanted in 1974 and the convictions were overturned. However, the prosecution retried the men and they were again found guilty in 1976. Carter and Artis's convictions were finally reversed in 1985. Carter, who died in 2014, became one of the pioneers of and champions for exoneration.

Rolando Cruz and Alejandro Hernandez. Trying to gain a $10,000 reward for information related to the 1983 kidnapping, rape, and murder of a ten-year-old girl in Illinois, Rolando Cruz concocted a fake story. The plan backfired, and twenty-year-old Cruz, along with fellow gang member Alejandro Hernandez, age nineteen, were instead charged with the crime. The lead detective resigned in protest. Prosecutors tried the men anyway. They were sentenced to death, partly based on informant testimony. A serial killer named Brian Dugan had already confessed to the girl's murder, but that information was not presented at trial. An appeals court reversed the convictions based on legal errors, and the men were retried--this time as Dugan's accomplices. Both were again convicted. An assistant attorney general resigned, refusing to fight against further appeals, which were granted. The men endured a third trial before police corruption was revealed and DNA testing proved that the serial killer alone had been responsible. Cruz and Hernandez were freed after twelve years in prison.

William Dillon. In a 1981 Florida case, when he was twenty-one, Dillon was arrested for murder days before he was to try out for major league baseball. Five days after the murder, police picked up Dillon on the beach where the killing had occurred. Dillon admitted he knew about the case; it had been heavily covered in the news. A scent-tracking dog allegedly linked Dillon to bloody evidence, and he was arrested and later convicted, partly based on perjured testimony from his ex-girlfriend, who became romantically involved with the lead detective during the investigation. After Dillon had served almost twenty-seven years in prison, DNA evidence helped clear him in 2008.

Gary Dotson. In 1977 a sixteen-year-old Illinois girl told police she had been raped. The police collected her torn clothing and found a semen stain. After the girl described her attacker, police directed her to a photo of Dotson, who resembled the girl's description. Dotson was convicted in 1979. In 1985 the "victim" admitted she had made up the story. She had torn her own clothing, fearful of becoming pregnant after consensual sex with her boyfriend. The woman's attorney contacted the prosecutor's office that had convicted Dotson, but the office refused to investigate. In 1987 an attorney took on Dotson's case after learning about the confirmation that new DNA testing could provide. Dotson was finally exonerated in 1989.

Dennis Fritz and Ronald Williamson. In an Oklahoma case, Fritz (age twenty-two) and Williamson (age twenty-nine) were both convicted in 1988 for raping and killing a young woman whose body had been found six years earlier. A day before charges against Fritz were to be dropped for insufficient evidence, Fritz's cellmate alleged that Fritz had confessed to him. Another witness perjured herself against Williamson, who later came within five days of execution. Both men were exonerated in 1999 after DNA testing showed that one of the prosecution's witnesses who had testified against Williamson was the actual rapist. The book *The Innocent Man: Murder and Injustice in a Small Town* by John Grisham covers this case.

Barry Gibbs. In New York, a witness claimed to have seen a man wearing red pants dump a woman's body from a gray car. Detective Louis Eppolito heard that Gibbs knew the victim and brought him in for a lineup. The witness identified Gibbs. A jailhouse informant testified Gibbs had confessed to him while awaiting trial. Evidence included a pair of red pants police allegedly discovered in Gibbs's apartment, although they didn't fit him. Gibbs also had a gray car, but it was inoperable and had flat tires. Gibbs was convicted of murder in 1988. The police file in Gibbs's case and DNA evidence went missing, complicating appeals. In 2005 police began investigating Eppolito, who had retired, and found Gibbs's missing file in his home. Later, he and another officer were convicted for eight murders and other crimes they had committed for the Mafia. The witness against Gibbs admitted that Eppolito had threatened him and his family if he did not help frame Gibbs. After spending more than seventeen years in prison, Gibbs was exonerated in 2005.

Calvin C. Johnson Jr. Two women, both raped in Georgia in 1983, ultimately identified twenty-five-year-old Johnson as their attacker. One woman picked him from among a group of photos. However, she could not identify him later in a police lineup. The second woman did not choose Johnson from a photo array but did select him during a lineup. Despite the conflicting eyewitness identifications, Johnson was convicted in one of the rape trials and was acquitted in the other. Johnson served sixteen years of a life sentence, and in 1997, DNA testing showed that he was not the rapist. In 1999 a judge ordered a new trial, but based on the DNA results, the district attorney dropped charges. Johnson's case is the subject of the 2005 book *Exit to Freedom*.

Koua Fong Lee. After ramming his Toyota into another car and killing three people in Minnesota, Lee was sentenced to eight years in prison for vehicular homicide in 2007. Lee claimed the car had accelerated on its own, and he had tried to stop. Lee's defense lawyer told the jury his client may have hit the gas pedal while intending to hit the brake, since there was no evidence of skid marks at the scene. Lee's appeal attorney indicated the antilock breaking system on his car would not have caused skid marks even if he had tried to stop. Based on the initial lawyer's negligence, Lee won a new trial. He was released in 2010, as evidence of problems with vehicle acceleration mounted.

Jerry Miller. In 1981 an Illinois woman who routinely used the same parking garage was shoved into her car, beaten, robbed, raped, and then forced into her trunk. When the perpetrator tried to drive out of the garage, the gate attendant recognized the victim's car and confronted the driver, who ran off. Two parking employees helped generate a police sketch. Police arrested twenty-three-year-old Miller. He resembled the sketch, and both garage attendants picked him out of a lineup. The victim was unable to identify Miller from photos. However, at trial she claimed he resembled her attacker. DNA testing finally exonerated Miller in 2007. He had already been released by this time, however.

SOURCE NOTES

4 William Blackstone, *Commentaries on the Laws of England,* 4 vols, (Oxford: Clarendon Press, 1765-1769), bk. 4, ch. 27. Available at http://library.law.harvard.edu/justicequotes/explore-the-room/south-4/.

7 Ken Burns, Sarah Burns, and David McMahon, *The Central Park Five,* directed by Ken Burns, Sarah Burns, and David McMahon (New York: IFC Films/Sundance Selects, 2012), DVD.

8 Alice Cantwell, "Sentencing in Central Park Attack," *New York Daily News,* January 10, 1991, accessed May 27, 2014, http://www.nydailynews.com/services/central-park-five/sentencing-central-park-attack-article-1.1304989.

8 Sarah Burns, *Central Park Five: A Chronicle of a City Wilding.* (New York: Knopf, 2011), 150.

8 Lizzette Alverez, "Central Park Attackers Sentenced to Max," *New York Daily News,* September 12, 1990, accessed May 27, 2014, http://www.nydailynews.com/services/central-park-five/central-park-attackers-sentenced-max-article-1.1304884.

9 Burns, Burns, and McMahon. *The Central Park Five* (DVD).

9 Ibid.

9 Ibid.

10 Benjamin Weiser, "5 Exonerated in Central Park Jogger Case Agree to Settle Suit for $40 Million," *New York Times,* June 19, 2014, accessed June 22, 2014, http://www.nytimes.com/2014/06/20/nyregion/5-exonerated-in-central-park-jogger-case-are-to-settle-suit-for-40-million.html?smid=fb-share&_r=2.

12 Calvin C. Johnson Jr., and Greg Hampikian (with an afterword by Barry Scheck), *Exit to Freedom: The Only Firsthand Account of a Wrongful Conviction Overturned by DNA Evidence.* (Athens, GA: University of Georgia Press, 2003), 271.

24 Innocence Project, "DNA Exoneree Case Profiles," accessed April 11, 2014, http://www.innocenceproject.org/know/.

36 John Grisham, *Innocence Project: John Grisham Discusses "The Innocent Man,"* clip from Innocence Project annual benefit video, 2008, http://www.innocenceproject.org/news/Video/?id=tpEQfagdfXk.

48 Decca Aitkenhead, "Betty Ann Waters: 'We Thought Kenny Was Coming

Home'," *Guardian,* December 10, 2010, accessed June 16, 2013, http://www. theguardian.com/film/2010/dec/11/betty-anne-waters-interview.

48   Ibid.

50   Jennifer Thompson-Cannino, Ronald Cotton, and Erin Torneo, *Picking Cotton: Our Memoir of Injustice and Redemption* (New York: St. Martin's Press, 2009), 68.

57   Ibid., 172.

57   Ibid., 271–272.

58   Christopher Ochoa, "My Life Is a Broken Puzzle" in *Surviving Justice: America's Wrongfully Convicted and Exonerated,* compiled and edited by Dave Eggers and Lola Vollen (San Francisco: McSweeney's Publishing, 2005), 19.

65   Lisa Chavarria, "Chicago Mom Freed after Serving Seven Years on Wrongful Conviction," *myFOXChicago.com,* June 24, 2013, accessed April 30, 2014, http://www.myfoxchicago.com/story/22614447/ chicago-mom-freed-from-prison-after-7-years-on-wrongful-conviction#ixzz2WaGPYcPz%3Cbr%20/%3E.

65   Ibid.

66   Innocence Project, "National Academy of Sciences Urges Comprehensive Reform of U.S. Forensic Sciences," February 18, 2009, accessed June 12, 2014, http://www.innocenceproject.org/Content/National_Academy_of_Sciences_Urges_Comprehensive_Reform_of_US_Forensic_Sciences.php.

73   Francis X. Clines, "Work by Expert Witness Is Now on Trial," *New York Times,* September 5, 2001, accessed June 16, 2013, http://www.nytimes.com/2001/09/05/us/work-by-expert-witness-is-now-on-trial.html.

74   Rob Warden, *The Snitch System: How Snitch Testimony Sent Randy Steidl and Other Innocent Americans to Death Row* (Chicago: Center on Wrongful Convictions, 2004), 2. Available at http://www.innocenceproject. org/docs/SnitchSystemBooklet.pdf.

77   Ibid., 15.

78   Alexis Wilcy, "New Evidence Could Lead to Convicted Detroit Man's Exoneration," clip from *myFOXDetroit.com,* November 20, 2012, accessed June 15, 2014, http://www.myfoxdetroit.com/story/20144768/new-evidence-could-lead-to-convicted-murderers-exoneration.

79 Alexis Wiley, "Local Man Wrongly Convicted of Murder to Be Set Free," clip from *myFOX9.com,* December 13, 2013, accessed June 15, 2014, http://www.myfoxtwincities.com/story/24219389/local-man-wrongly-convicted-of-murder-to-be-set-free.

80 Peter Rose, "People Don't Know How Lucky They Are to Have Their Liberty" in *Surviving Justice: America's Wrongfully Convicted and Exonerated,* compiled and edited by Dave Eggers and Lola Vollen (San Francisco: McSweeney's Publishing, 2005), 439.

87 Brooke A. Masters, "Missteps on the Road to Injustice: How Earl Washington, Jr. Was Sent to Death Row for a Crime He Did Not Commit," *Washington Post,* November 30, 2000, accessed May 27, 2014. Available at http://truthinjustice.org/missteps.htm.

90 National Registry of Exonerations, *Exonerations in 2013,* February 4, 2014, https://www.law.umich.edu/special/exoneration/Documents/Exonerations_in_2013_Report.pdf, 4.

96 Christina Schockley, Zoe Clark, and What's Working, "Michigan Innocence Clinic Works to Free Those Wrongfully Convicted," *Michigan Radio,* June 24, 2011, accessed June 22, 2014, http://michiganradio.org/post/michigan-innocence-clinic-works-free-those-wrongfully-convicted.

102 "Out of the Blue: The Michigan Difference: Innocence Clinic," *University of Michigan,* Michigan Television Production, n.d., accessed June 16, 2013, http://web.law.umich.edu/flashmedia/public/Default.aspx?mediaid=133.

103 James Dickson, "After Eight Years of Wrongful Imprisonment, the Reeds Are Free with the Help of University of Michigan's Innocence Clinic. But Now What?" *Ann Arbor News,* September 17, 2009. http://www.annarbor.com/news/exonerated-but-now-what/.

103 Ibid.

SELECTED BIBLIOGRAPHY

Acker, James R., and Allison D. Redlich. *Wrongful Conviction: Law, Science, and Policy.* Durham, NC: Carolina Academic Press, 2011.

Bohm, Robert M. *Capital Punishment's Collateral Damage.* Durham, NC: Carolina Academic Press, 2012.

Committee on Commerce, Science, and Transportation, United States Senate, Hearing before the One Hundred Twelfth Congress, First Session, December 7, 2011. *Turning the Investigation on the Science of Forensics.* Washington, DC: US Government Printing Office, 2013. Available at http://www.gpo.gov/fdsys/pkg/CHRG-112shrg77805/pdf/CHRG-112shrg77805.pdf.

Committee on Identifying the Needs of the Forensic Sciences Community, National Research Council. *Strengthening Forensic Science in the United States: A Path Forward.* Washington, DC: US Department of Justice, 2009. Available at https://www.ncjrs.gov/pdffiles1/nij/grants/228091.pdf.

Garrett, Brandon L. *Convicting the Innocent: Where Criminal Prosecutions Go Wrong.* Cambridge: Harvard University Press, 2012.

Harris, David A. *Failed Evidence: Why Law Enforcement Resists Science.* New York: New York University Press, 2012.

Lassiter, G. Daniel, and Christian A. Meissner. *Police Interrogations and False Confessions: Current Research, Practice, and Policy Recommendations.* Washington DC: American Psychological Association, 2010.

Medwed, Daniel S. *Prosecution Complex: America's Race to Convict and Its Impact on the Innocent.* New York: New York University Press, 2012.

Petro, Jim, and Nancy Petro. *False Justice: Eight Myths That Convict the Innocent.* New York: Kaplan Publishing, 2011.

Simon, Dan. *In Doubt: The Psychology of the Criminal Justice Process.* Cambridge: Harvard University Press, 2012.

Walker, Jeffrey R., and Craig Hemmens. *Legal Guide for Police: Constitutional Issues,* 9th ed. Cincinnati: Anderson Publishing, 2010.

Zalman, Marvin, and Julia Carrano. *Wrongful Conviction and Criminal Justice Reform: Making Justice* (Criminology and Justice Studies). London: Routledge, 2013.

FOR FURTHER INFORMATION

Borchard, Edwin M. *Convicting the Innocent: Sixty Five Actual Errors of Criminal Justice.* Scotts Valley, CA: CreateSpace, 2010 (republication of Garden City, NY: Yale University Press edition, 1932).
The 1932 edition is available in its entirety at https://archive.org/details/convictinginnoce00borchrich.

Burns, Ken, Sarah Burns, and David McMahon. *The Central Park Five.* Directed by Ken Burns, Sarah Burns, and David McMahon. New York: IFC Films/Sundance Selects, 2012. DVD.
This documentary covers the story of five teens, Antron McCray, Kevin Richardson, Yusef Salaam, Raymond Santana, and Korey Wise, who were wrongfully convicted in 1990 for rape and were exonerated in 2002.

Burns, Sarah. *The Central Park Five: A Chronicle of Wilding.* New York: Knopf, 2011.

Center on Wrongful Convictions, Bluhm Legal Clinic, Northwestern University School of Law. http://www.law.northwestern.edu/legalclinic/wrongfulconvictions/
This website provides information about wrongful convictions and related issues, includes a list of exonerated, and features videos, news segments, and a blog.

Connors, Edward, Thomas Lundregan, Neal Miller, and Tom McEwen. *Convicted by Juries, Exonerated by Science: Case Studies in the Use of DNA Evidence to Establish Innocence after Trial.* US Department of Justice, Office of Justice Programs, National Institute of Justice, 1996. PDF.
These studies are available by cutting and pasting the following URL into your browser: http://permanent.access.gpo.gov/lps53435/lps53435.pdf.

Edds, Margaret. *An Expendable Man: The Near Execution of Earl Washington Jr.* New York: New York University Press, 2003.

Eggers, David, and Lola Vollen, eds. *Surviving Justice: America's Wrongfully Convicted and Exonerated.* San Francisco: McSweeney's Publishing, 2005.

Fritz, Dennis. *Journey toward Justice.* Santa Ana, CA: Seven Locks Press, 2006.

Gray, Pamela. *Conviction*. Directed by Tony Goldwyn. Los Angeles: Fox Searchlight Pictures, 2010. DVD.
This film tells the true story of Kenny Waters, who was wrongfully convicted of murder in 1983. His sister Betty Anne Waters became an attorney and helped to exonerate him. He was freed in 2001.

Grisham, John. *The Innocent Man: Murder and Injustice in a Small Town*. New York: Doubleday, 2012.

Innocence Project. http://www.innocenceproject.org/
This is the official website of the Innocence Project, affiliated with the Benjamin N. Cardozo School of Law at Yeshiva University in New York. The site provides case profiles of its exonerees and information about the causes of wrongful convictions, including video segments to highlight facts and figures.

Johnson Jr., Calvin C., and Greg Hampikian (with an afterword by Barry Scheck). *Exit to Freedom*. Athens: University of Georgia Press, 2005.

Junkin, Tim. *Bloodsworth: The True Story of One Man's Triumph over Injustice*. Chapel Hill, NC: Algonquin Books, 2005.

Loftus, Elizabeth F. *Eyewitness Testimony*. Cambridge, MA: Harvard University Press, 1996.

Loftus, Elizabeth, and Katherine Ketcham. *Witness for the Defense: The Accused, the Eyewitness, and the Expert Who Puts Memory on Trial*. New York: St. Martin's Press, 1991.

Meili, Trisha. *I Am the Central Park Jogger: A Story of Hope and Possibility*. New York: Scribner, 2003.

Michigan Innocence Clinic at Michigan Law
https://www.law.umich.edu/clinical/innocenceclinic/Pages/default. aspx This is the website of the Michigan Innocence Clinic, where information about the causes of wrongful convictions and case summaries (for non-DNA exonerations) can be found, as well as a 2009 video (on the "In the News" page) about the exoneration of DeShawn and Marvin Reed, the clinic's first two clients.

Münsterberg, Hugo. *On the Witness Stand: Essays on Psychology and Crime,* (n.p., 1908, revised in 1925).

These essays are available at no cost from Classics in Psychology at
http://psychclassics.yorku.ca/Munster/Witness/index.htm

National Registry of Exonerations
http://www.law.umich.edu/special/exoneration/Pages/about.aspx
The registry lists all known exonerations since 1989 and includes
exoneree case information and other resources to help site visitors better
understand wrongful convictions.

Center on Wrongful Convictions, Bluhm Legal Clinic, Northwestern
University School of Law
http://www.law.northwestern.edu/legalclinic/wrongfulconvictions/
This website provides information about wrongful convictions and
related issues, includes a list of exonerated people, and features videos,
news segments, and a blog.

Scheck, Barry, Peter Neufeld, and Jim Dwyer. *Actual Innocence: When
Justice Goes Wrong and How to Make It Right.* New York: Signet,
2001.

Shelton, Donald E. *Forensic Science in Court: Challenges in the
Twenty-First Century* (Issues in Crime and Justice). Lanham, MD:
Rowman & Littlefield, 2011.

Thompson-Cannino, Jennifer, and Ronald Cotton, with Erin Torneo.
Picking Cotton: Our Memoir of Injustice and Redemption. New York:
St. Martin's Press, 2009.

Warden, Rob. *The Snitch System: How Snitch Testimony Sent
Randy Steidl and Other Innocent Americans to Death Row.* Chicago:
Center on Wrongful Convictions, 2004. Available at http://www.
innocenceproject.org/docs/SnitchSystemBooklet.pdf.

Warden, Rob, and Steven A. Drizin. *True Stories of False Confessions.*
Chicago: Northwestern University Press, 2009.

Wells, Tom, and Richard A. Leo. *The Wrong Guys: Murder, False
Confessions, and the Norfolk Four.* New York: New Press, 2008.

Westervelt, Saundra D., and Kimberly J. Cook. *Life after Death Row:
Exonerees' Search for Community and Identity* (Critical Issues in
Crime and Society). New Brunswick, NJ: Rutgers University Press,
2012.

INDEX

American Civil Liberties Union, 16

amicus brief, 26

appeals process, 22–23, 82, 83, 101, 102, 104

arresting and charging; process of, 14–15, 17–19

attorneys and lawyers; Castelle, George, 73; Drizin, Steve, 65; Kunstler, William, 8; Levine, Zoe, 102; Mason, C. Vernon, 8; McCormack, Bridget, 101; Moran, David, 96; Morgenthau, Robert, 9; Neufeld, Peter J., 26–27; Rosen, Richard, 57; Scheck, Barry C., 26–27

Bill of Rights, 16

blind lineup, 59

Buckhout, Robert, 51

Carter, Matenis, 78

Central Park Five, 6–11

constitutional rights, 16, 17, 20, 39, 40

courts; appellate (circuit) courts, 22, 26, 82, 83, 101; Michigan's Wayne County Circuit Court, 79; the Seventh Circuit Court of Appeals in Chicago, 65; trial (district) courts, 22; US Court of Appeals for the Tenth Circuit, 76

crimes; arson, 33, 72; assault, 5, 7, 33, 55, 100; attempted murder, 7, 11, 79, 100; kidnapping, 33, 104–105, 105; murder, 8, 28, 49, 64, 72–73, 78, 85–86, 88, 93, 97, 100, 102 104, 105, 106–107; rape, 5, 7–8, 11, 28, 56–57, 72, 86, 88, 93, 104, 105, 106, 107; robbery, 5, 15, 33, 47;

sexual abuse, 7

criminals; Allen, Tyrone, 100–101, 103; Dugan, Brian, 105; Eppolito, Louis, 106–107; Pitchfork, Colin, 28; Poole, Bobby, 56–57; Reyes, Matias (East Side Rapist), 8–9; Tinsley, Kenneth M., 88

cruel and unusual punishment, 87

Dancy, Diante, 63–65

Dancy, Jaquari, 63–64

Dancy, Sta-Von, 63

death penalty (capital punishment), 11, 17, 22, 23, 31, 87, 91, 94, 96

deoxyribonucleic acid (DNA); diagram, 30; in exonerations, 26–28, 49, 57, 67, 73, 88, 91, 93, 104–107; lack of, 69–70, 106; technology, 28–31

evidence; circumstantial evidence, 42, 43–45, 48, 68, 77; class evidence, 43; direct evidence, 42; DNA evidence, 28–31; individuating evidence, 43, 44–45, 69, 72; physical evidence, 7, 20, 26, 27, 39, 79, 100; scientific evidence, 41–42; trace evidence, 37, 42–43, 69; video recorded evidence, 62

exoneration agencies and innocence advocacy, 25–28, 31–35

exoneration laws; inadequacies, 94–95

exoneration organizations; Center on Wrongful Convictions, 31–33, 64–65; Innocence Network, 34–35; Innocence Project, 24, 26–28, 32, 33, 34, 35, 36, 48–49, 51, 54, 68, 71, 84, 88, 98; Michigan Innocence Clinic (MIC),

32–33, 96–97, 101, 103

exonerees: Artis, John, 105; Baumer, Julie, 104; Borchard, Edwin, 46; Brewer, Kennedy, 104; Brooks, Levon, 104; Buckland, Richard, 28; Carrillo, Francisco, 104–105; Carter, Rubin "Hurricane," 105; Central Park Five, 6–11; Cotton, Ronald, 55–57; Cruz, Rolando, 105; Dillon, William, 105–106; Dotson, Gary, 106; Fritz, Dennis, 106; Gibbs, Barry, 106–107; Harris, Nicole, 63–65; Hernandez, Alejandro, 105; Johnson, Calvin C., Jr., 12, 107; Jones, Elroy "Lucky," 78–79; Lee, Koua Fong, 107; McCray, Antron, 8–10; Miller, Jerry, 107; Reed, DeShawn, 99–103; Reed, Marvin, 99-103; Richardson, James E., Jr., 72–73; Richardson, Kevin, 6,8,10; Salaam, Yusef, 6–11; Santana, Raymond, 6, 9–10; Smith, Donald, 44; Washington, Earl, Jr., 85–88; Waters, Kenny, 47–49; Williamson, Ronald, 106; Wise, Korey (also Khorey or Kharey), 6–10; Wyniemko, Ken, 103

eyewitness misidentification; and psychological defense mechanisms, 53; and weapon-focus effect, 53; cross-race identification bias, 52; environmental factors, 52; memory and recall, 53–54

false statements and incentivized testimony, 75–76

Federal Bureau of Investigation (FBI), 33–34, 68–70

Fifth Amendment, 16

forensic analysis, 69–71

forensic misconduct; falsifying evidence, 67–69, 72–73, 87

forensic tests, 9, 29, 71

Gilchrist, Joyce, 67–69

hearings; arraignments, 17; court hearings, 15, 17; grand jury hearings, 18; preliminary (evidentiary) hearings, 18, 22, 42; pre-sentencing hearings, 17; sentencing hearings, 21–22

informants, 75–77, 79, 105–106

interrogations and false confessions, 6–7, 60–62, 64–65, 86

investigations and investigative reports, 33–34, 68–69, 72–73, 106

jurors, 8, 18–21, 40, 44, 64, 71, 76, 77

jury selection, 19

jury trial, 17, 19, 21

Justice for All Act, 94

Ken Wyniemko Foundation, 103

law schools; Benjamin N. Cardozo School of Law, 26–27; Northwestern University, 31; University of Michigan Law School, 32–33

lie detector (polygraph) tests, 62

Locard's Exchange Principle, 37

Loftus, Elizabeth, 46

McCormack, Bridget, 101

Miranda warning, 16

Münsterberg, Hugo, 45–46

National Academy of Sciences (NAS) forensic sciences report, 70–71

National Registry of Exonerations (NRE), 33–34, 76, 89, 90, 91, 92, 104

Neufeld, Peter J., 26–27

peer and assistance organizations, 95–96

plea bargains, 17–18, 21, 75, 91, 95

police lineups, 54, 56, 57, 59, 62, 78, 79, 106, 107

police misconduct; hostile interrogations, 7, 60; physical and verbal abuse, 64

poor lawyering and prosecutorial misconduct, 81–84, 87

probable cause, 14–15, 31, 39

pro bono public work, 28

psychological evaluations and intellectual disabilities, 85–87

reasonable doubt, 8, 14, 21

reliable science, 69–70

search warrants, 39

Scheck, Barry C., 26–27

serological testing, 28–29

supreme courts; Michigan Supreme Court, 101; New York State Supreme Court, 9; US Supreme Court, 16, 23, 65, 87

testimony; expert testimony, 18, 20, 41; eyewitness testimony, 20, 26, 32–33, 42, 45–46, 51, 57, 59, 78–80

US Congress, 70, 94

US Constitution, 14, 16, 39, 41, 87, 98

US legal system, 13–14

victims; Brow, Katharina Reitz, 47–49; Coleman, Genai, 44; Dancy, Jaquari, 63–64; Gholston, Shannon, 99–101, 103; Gilfilin, Kelli, 72–73; McDougal, Cleo, 78; Meili, Trisha, 5–10; Thompson, Jennifer, 55–57; Weeks, Helen, 85–86, 88; Williams, Rebecca Lynn, 86, 88

Waters, Betty Anne, 48–49

wrongful convictions; and appeals, 48, 57, 65, 79, 87, 101–102, 104–107; and concealed evidence, 49, 73, 100; and costs to the public, 97; and financial compensation, 10, 73, 88, 94–95, 97, 103; and lawsuits, 10, 87–88, 103; and lost years, 9, 93–94; and prison sentences, 49, 57, 65, 73, 79, 88, 102–103; and racial prejudice, 6, 34; and settlements, 73, 95, 99; and trials, 7, 56, 64–65, 73, 78–79, 86–87, 100, 104–105, 107; books and memoirs, 45–46, 57, 106, 107; films, 9–10, 47

Zain, Fred, 72–73

PHOTO ACKNOWLEDGMENTS

The images in this book are used with the permission of: © iStockphoto.com/fpm (prison bars); © iStockphoto.com/VallarieE (rusty barbed wire); © iStockphoto.com/Trevor Hunt (newspaper tear); © fhogue/Thinkstock, p. 4; © Michael Nagle/The New York Times/Redux, p. 10; © iStockphoto.com/WSS, p. 12; AP Photo, p. 16; © iStockphoto.com/Terraxplorer, p. 24; Courtesy of The Innocence Project, p. 27; © Laura Westlund/Independent Picture Service, pp. 30, 92; © iStockphoto.com/dvan, p. 36; AP Photo/Steven Senne, p. 47; © iStockphoto.com/redhumv, p. 50; AP Photo/The News & Observer/Takaaki Iwabu, p. 55; © Ivan Bliznetsov/Getty Images, p. 58; © Zbigniew Bzdak/Chicago Tribune/MCT/LANDOV , p. 63; © iStockphoto.com/dra_schwartz, p. 66; AP Photo/The Daily Oklahoman, Roger Klock, p. 68; © David Schalliol/Moment/Getty Images, p. 74; © Bryce Duffy/The Image Bank/Getty Images, p. 80; AP Photo/Steve Helber, p. 85; © motorenmano/E+/Getty Images, p. 90; © Lon Horwedel, p. 99.

Front cover: © iStockphoto.com/GlobalP (crow); © iStockphoto.com/fpm (prison bars); © iStockphoto.com/VallarieE, (barbed wire).

LERNER

SOURCE

Expand learning beyond the printed book. Download free, complementary educational resources for this book from our website, www.lerneresource.com.

ABOUT THE AUTHOR

Dr. Elizabeth A. Murray has been an educator and a forensic scientist for more than twenty-five years. Her primary teaching focus is human anatomy and physiology and forensic science. She is one of only about seventy anthropologists certified as an expert by the American Board of Forensic Anthropology. Dr. Murray was scientific consultant and on-camera personality for the miniseries *Skeleton Crew* for the National Geographic Channel and a regular cast member on the Discovery Health Channel series *Skeleton Stories*. She has written and delivered two lecture series, *Trails of Evidence: How Forensic Science Works and Forensic History: Crimes, Frauds, and Scandals,* produced on DVD by The Teaching Company's The Great Courses. Dr. Murray is also the author of *Forensic Identification: Putting a Name and Face on Death* and *of Death: Corpses, Cadavers, and Other Grave Matters* for teen readers.

ACKNOWLEDGMENTS

Many thanks are due to my longstanding friends Chief Magistrate Michael L. Bachman and court reporter Linda Mallory, both from the Hamilton County, Ohio, Court of Common Pleas, for reviewing legal aspects of this work. Chief Deputy Mark Whittaker of Darke County, Ohio, once again assisted me with a deeper understanding of best police practices. My sister Kathy Isaacs and my dear friend Elizabeth Villing provided thoughtful comments on the first draft. Thanks to Domenica Di Piazza of Lerner Publishing Group for her patience and wise responses to my many questions. I want to express gratitude to my family for understanding all the times I was busy. Finally, I wish to recognize the exonerees whose public stories of battles won have allowed me to include them in this book. May your cases, and the too many others like yours, inspire all of us to consistently strive to prevent injustices, whenever and wherever we see them.

Coq au Vin

Also by Charlotte Carter

Rhode Island Red

CHARLOTTE CARTER

Coq au Vin

THE MYSTERIOUS PRESS

Published by Warner Books

A Time Warner Company

Mysterious Press books are published by Warner Books, Inc., 1271 Avenue of the Americas, New York, NY 10020.

A Time Warner Company

The Mysterious Press name and logo are registered trademarks of Warner Books, Inc.

Printed in the United States of America

First printing: February 1999

10 9 8 7 6 5 4 3 2 1

Library of Congress Cataloging-in-Publication Data

Carter, Charlotte (Charlotte C.)
    Coq au vin / Charlotte Carter.
        p.   cm.
    ISBN 0-89296-678-5
    I. Title.
    PS3553.A7736C6   1999
    813'.54—dc21   98-22565
                                                                CIP

For Drew Gangolf

Acknowledgments

For friendship and support offered, for the examples they set and for the luck they have brought me, I wish to thank Lisa Carlson, Larry Eidelberg, Susanna Einstein, Estelle Gerard, Margo Jefferson, Martha Jones, Patricia Spears Jones, Frank King, Bill Kushner, Bernadette Mayer, Suzanne McConnell, Mark McCormick, Jackie McQueen, Shirley Sarris, Laurie Stone, Serpent's Tail, Lynne Tillman, Gary Woodard.

CHAPTER 1

Travelin' Light

Damn, I was tired. My saxophone seemed to weigh more than I did.

I had awakened early that morning and immediately commenced to fill the day with activity—some of it necessary but most of it far from pressing.

I played for a time midtown, a little north of the theater district; made some nice money. That wasn't my usual stomping ground. I had picked the corner almost at random. I don't know why I did so well. Maybe the people had spring fever, hormones working, calling out for love songs. In fact the first song I played was "Spring Fever." When you play on the street, you never know why you're a hit or a bust. Is it the mood of the crowd? Is it you? Is it the time of day or the time of year? Anyway, you do the gig and put your money in your belt and move on.

Next, I power-walked up to Riverside Park and played

there for a while; did my two hours volunteer work at the soup kitchen on Amsterdam; bought coffee beans at Zabar's; took the IRT downtown; bought a new reed for the sax on Bleecker Street; picked up some paint samples at the hardware store; then played again on lower Park Avenue, closer to my own neighborhood.

Makes me sound like a real flamer, doesn't it? A go-getter, a busy bee. Not true. I'm lazy as hell.

What I was doing was trying to outrun my thoughts. That's what all that busy work was about.

Over dinner the previous night, the b.f. (the shithead's name is Griffin) had announced, number one, he wouldn't be spending the night at my place because he had other plans, and number two, he had other plans . . . period.

I should have known something was up when he said to meet him at the little Belgian café I like in the Village—the other side of town from my place. He hated the food there, but it was convenient for his subway ride home.

This kind of thing has happened to me before. The relationship is at some critical point—or maybe not; maybe it's simply that a certain amount of time has passed and I'm re-evaluating it. I meet his family. Mom wants to know if this is "the real thing." I'm asking myself constantly, Is the sex really that good? Should I stay in or should I get out?

And then, a couple of weeks later, before I come to a final decision, he splits.

What's with that?

I always seem to end up asking myself that question. What is with that?

I didn't spend the night crying or anything. I merely came in and stripped out of my clothes and snapped on the radio and finished whatever brown liquor I had in the cabinet. Temper tantrum aside, breaking the porcelain planter in the living-room window had been more of an accident than anything else.

Sleep was a long time coming. Yes, I had decided about two A.M., the sex *had* been *that* good. And when I awoke in the morning, I just started moving like this—manic.

Now I was exhausted. I packed up my sax and started the short walk to my apartment near Gramercy Park.

Our homeless guy was back. It had been so long since anybody had seen him on the block, we all figured he was dead. But here he was again, in a neck brace, evil as ever, begging for dollars and cussing at anybody with the nerve to give him coins. "Why don't you comb your hair?" he called after me when I stuffed a single into his cup.

I made a quick run to the supermarket and then into the benighted little corner liquor store where a white wine from Chile is the high-end stuff.

I had poured myself a glass, turned on the radio, and read through the mail before I remembered to check the answering machine.

"Nanette, it's me. About tonight. You're still coming over to eat, aren't you? Because I've got something to tell you. It's . . . I'm . . . Well, I'll tell you when you get here. I'm going out now to pick us up some food at Penzler's. You still eat pork, don't you, baby?"

Mom!

Oh shit.

I had forgotten. Two weeks ago I had said maybe we'd have dinner—I walked over to the kitchen calendar—tonight.

I was in no mood to see anybody tonight, let alone Mom, for whom I'd have to put on an act—make out that things were fine between me and Griffin, and that my fabulous—and utterly fictitious—part-time job teaching French at NYU was going great. I'd have to be careful never to mention the sax or my street friends or anything remotely connected to my career as an itinerant musician on the streets of Manhattan. She might have been able to handle it if she ever found out that the teaching job was a lie (I was getting steady translation work, at least). But she would have gone absolutely crazy if she knew I blew sax on the street corners with an old fedora turned up to catch the cash. *And* I'd have to haul my ass on the F train out to Queens.

Well, I just wasn't going to make it. Not with all these papers to grade. Not with this pneumonia, cough cough. Not tonight. Tomorrow maybe, but not tonight.

I've got something to tell you.

I turned that gossipy, girlish phrase over in my mind. What was there about that locution that troubled me so? It didn't sound like Mrs. Hayes, that's what. It just did not sound right. And, come to think of it, there was a bit of a quaver in her voice, too.

Oh, God. She's sick. Heart. Cancer.

I rushed to the wall phone and dialed her number. No answer.

I threw my jacket on and locked up.

Halfway to the subway, I realized I was probably being crazy. There were only about three million other reasons my mother might have had to sound worried. Maybe it really was something about her health, but that didn't have to mean that death was knocking on the door.

So why hadn't she answered the phone? She was probably still at Penzler's—Elmhurst's answer to Dean and Deluca—inspecting the barbecued chickens and braised pork chops and waiting on line for a pound of potato salad. Or out in the backyard. Or over at the Bedlows' house, picking up one of Harriet's cobblers for our dessert.

By then I was at Sixth Avenue. I turned downtown instead of north to the Twenty-third Street station. It was a spur-of-the-moment thing. I had suddenly decided I needed a drink before heading out there, and I needed a little reassuring from the one person whose level head and unfailing equilibrium I could always depend on: my one and only homegirl, Aubrey Davis. Who works as a topless dancer.

We knew early on, at about age nine, that I was the whiz at sight-reading music, inventing lies more believable than the truth, and forging my mother's signature. "Very bright, but a bit unfocused," one of my teachers had told Daddy on parents' night.

Aubrey, however, was the one to call when you wanted to see some dancing. She struggled mightily to teach me one or two moves. But it was no good. I could work the shoulders, and I could usually work the hips too—just not at the same time. To this day, when I hit the dance floor I look like a holdup man who realizes too late that his victim is carrying a taser. By the time we were fourteen we'd both thrown in the towel on my dancing career.

It was about that time, on a summer day, that Aubrey's mother abandoned her. She went off to play cards with some people and just never came back. In school, I was the brightest star in the heavens, but Aubrey, when she deigned to join us, was the butt of the kids' pitiless taunting—about her clothes, about her poverty, about her mother, and in time, about her morals. The oddsmakers wouldn't have laid ten cents on Aubrey's chances of getting through life in one piece. They'd have lost. She is a genius at taking care of herself. And my girl never wastes a second looking backward.

Anyway, Aubrey is now one of the bigger draws at Caesar's Go Go Emporium, which is exactly the kind of place it sounds like, tied however circuitously to the mob and located in that one dirty corner of Tribeca where Robert De Niro has not yet bankrolled any emigre restaurateurs.

She performs topless, like I said, and what she wears over the nasty bits is barely worthy of the term "panties." Between weekly pay and tips she makes a pretty impressive salary, only a fraction of which gets declared to the tax folks. I don't know all the details, but I believe Aubrey has an enviable little portfolio going, thanks to one of her Wall Street admirers. I can always hit her up for money, but I made a vow long ago never to do so unless I was starving. See, if you ask her for a couple of hundred, the next thing you know, she's putting down a deposit on a new co-op for you. She is that generous. She is also a great beauty, and I love her madly. So does my mother, who took turns with the other grown-ups in the neighborhood in trying to raise her.

I heard the pounding bass line from halfway up the block. Caesar's. I hate that fucking place. I hate the white men in their middle-management ties who come in for their fix of watery scotch and flaccid titties. I hate the rainbow coalition of construction worker types in their Knicks T-shirts drinking Coors and spending their paychecks on blow jobs. And I've got zero patience with all of them. Not Aubrey, though. She understands men—all kinds of men. And boy, do they love her and her Kraft caramel thighs and her cascades of straightened hair and her voice like warm apple butter.

It is little wonder that Aubrey became a superstar, if you will, at Caesar's. A lot of the other dancers are distracted college girls who'd rather shake their ass in a dive than work behind a cosmetics counter somewhere, or they're skanks strung out on crack and pills. But Aubrey, who isn't even much of a drinker, is focused, engaged, thoroughly there when she's dancing. She has a fierce kind of dedication to her work, and the guys seem to pick up on that immediately. It is the damnedest thing, but they appear to respect her.

There was no one on stage when I walked into the darkened room. The girls were taking a break. I walked double time through the crowd of horny men, and had almost made it back to the dressing rooms when I heard a male voice call my name. My whole body stiffened for a few seconds. I kept walking, but the voice rang out again: "Hey, Nan!"

I stopped and turned then. I couldn't believe that any man

who actually knew me would not only be hanging in a place like this but would actually want me to *see* him in here.

To my relief, it was only Justin, the club manager. He was standing at the end of the bar, his signature drink, dark rum and tonic, in one hand and one of those preposterously long thin cigarettes in the other. Justin, self-described as "white trash out of Elko, Indiana," is Aubrey's most ardent fan. Of course, his admiration for her has no sexual dimension; he is as funny as the day is long.

Justin has a benign contempt for me that actually manifests itself as a kind of affection. I'm just not a femme—his word for a certain kind of lady that he idolizes. (Femmes, you see, are a subgenre of women in general, all of whom he refers to as "smash-ups.") In any case, he is absolutely right—I am no femme: I don't sleep all day, as Aubrey does, and then emerge after sundown like a vampire; I never paint my nails; I don't own a garter belt or wear spike heels before nine P.M.; my hair is Joan of Arc short; I don't consider the cadging of drinks one of the lively arts; I don't share his and Aubrey's worship of Luther Vandross; and, probably my worst sin, I cannot shake my boody. The truth is, he thinks I'm overeducated and a secret dyke. Justin does not understand going to college and does *not* approve of lesbians. But he likes me in spite of himself and, giving the devil his due, he says my breasts are "amazing." We've been out drinking together a couple of times, once just the two of us and once with an old lover of mine, an Irishman who is still turning heads at age forty-two. Yeah, Tom Farrell garnered me quite a few Brownie points with Justin. On the other hand, Griffin, my ex, met Justin once, and the two of them scared each other half to death.

I saluted Justin, raising a phantom glass to his health, and continued walking backstage.

Aubrey gave out with one of those Patti LaBelle–register shrieks when she saw me swing through the door. She was busy applying some kind of sparkly shit all over that flawless body and she didn't have stitch one on.

"Christ, Aubrey. Put some clothes on," I said. She made me feel like I had the body of a Sumo wrestler and the skin of Godzilla.

"This just makes my night! What are you doing here, sweetheart?" She slipped into a peach-colored robe as she spoke.

"I just thought I'd drop in for a minute on my way out to see Moms. Is there anything to drink back here?"

"Yeah, just a minute." She walked to the door and called out into the ether: "Larry, get me a Jack Daniels, baby. Tell him don't put no ice in it."

The glass was in my hand almost before I could blink. I took a healthy drink from it.

"You look kind of funny, Nan," she said. "Wait a minute . . . don't tell me that nigger is trifling with you again?"

"No, it's not Griff. It's my mother."

"How is Moms?" she asked me, back at her dressing table.

It was taking me a long time to answer. "What's the matter with her, Nan?"

"Probably nothing," I finally said.

"What does that mean?"

"I know you're going to say I'm crazy, but . . ." I repeated, a bit abashed, the phone message that had set me spinning.

"Nanette, you *are* crazy, girl. How you know it ain't something good instead of something terrible? She could be getting married again for all you know."

"Aubrey, I know you're a relentless optimist. But give me a break, huh. Moms is getting married? To who?"

"How do I know that?"

"Or me, for that matter."

"That's what I'm saying, Nan. You don't know all her business."

I took another deep drink of the bourbon. "Trust me, it's not wedding news."

"Okay, fool. She's not getting married. But that still don't mean she got cancer, do it?"

"No, you're right, it doesn't. But I'm still a little freaked. Which brings me to the reason—another reason—I came here. I thought if you could get a couple of hours off tonight, maybe you'd go out there with me."

"Oh shit. I can't, baby. I *am* taking some time off tonight—but I gotta meet somebody for a couple of hours."

"Oh." It flitted through my mind to ask who she was meeting, but then I remembered myself, and who I was talking to, and who she worked for. I didn't want to know any of the particulars. Of course, it might have been something perfectly innocent, but I thought I'd better let it go.

I stayed a few minutes longer, until it was almost time for her to go on again. She insisted on having one of the guys run

me out to Queens in his car. I ran through my head the possibility of staring at the thick neck of some club gofer while
I sat in the backseat all the way across town and then over the
Long Island Expressway to Elmhurst. Or maybe, I thought
with a shudder, he might try to chat me up. We'd talk about—
what?—Heavy D's latest, or some new designer drug? My
heart sank.

Then I mentally put myself on the subway, stop after stop
after stop. I didn't even have a newspaper to distract me.

I went for the car.

I left with the promise that I would call her the next day to
give her a full report on Mom's news, whatever it turned out
to be.

On the way out I ran into Justin.

"What's happening, Smash-up?"

"Same old, same old, Justin. You know."

"Have a quick one with me, girlfriend."

"I can't."

"Got a date?"

"Yep. Dinner. With my mother."

"Ooooh. Bring me back some cornbread."

I guffawed. He didn't know how funny that was.

The kitchen was spotless, as always. But then, why shouldn't
it be? Mom never cooked. Everything was take-out or pre-
mixed or delivered in stay-warm aluminum foil.

"Mom, I'm here! Where are you?"

My mother's cotton dress was as surreal as the kitchen
counters in its neatness. Decorous pageboy wig bobby-pinned

in place. Makeup specially blended by one of the black salesladies at the Macy's in the mall.

It must be eight, nine years now since Daddy left her. But if I no longer remembered the exact date that had happened, Mom sure did. I bet she could tell you what she'd eaten for breakfast that day, what shoes Daddy was wearing when he broke the news to her. On those rare occasions when Mom talks about him, she never uses his name, referring to my father only as "him."

My father soon remarried: a young white teacher on his staff at the private school where he was now the principal. Outside of the occasional birthday lunch, Christmastime, and so on, I saw very little of him. He was happy enough, I suppose, in his new life. And he never missed an alimony payment.

"Nanette, what have you got on your feet?"

"They're called boots, Mother."

"Those things are something you wear down in the basement when you're looking to kill a rat. Don't tell me you dress like that for—"

"Holy mackerel, Mother, what is it you have to tell me!"

"It's about Vivian," she said grimly.

I fell into a chair, suddenly exhausted. No melanoma. Thank God. No wedding.

Vivian, my father's sister, had been my idol when I was a kid. Breezing into town and swooping me up, Aunt Vivian meant trips into Manhattan and eating exotic food and hanging with her hip friends and my first sip of beer and every other cool thing you can imagine when you're ten years old and your father's baby sister is a sophisticated sometime-fashion-model who drinks at piano bars and parties with people who actually make the rock 'n' roll records you hear on the radio.

My father felt about his little sister Vivian the way Justin feels about dykes. He disapproved of her friends and her nomadic ways and her prodigious consumption of vodka and her way-out hairdos and everything else about her lifestyle, which he didn't understand at all.

My mother didn't understand it any better than he did, but she loved Vivian just the same. Maybe that was due to the same kind of sympathy with strays that had moved her to take Aubrey to her heart. Mom looked on with pity while Auntie Viv blew all her money and drank too much and got her heart broken by trifling pretty men and then recovered to start the cycle all over again.

In time Vivian married and divorced—two or three times, if I remember right—and moved out of New York and then back again, half a dozen times—to L.A. and Mexico and France and Portugal—wherever the job or the party or the boyfriend might take her. Daddy and she finally had one final royal blowup during the cocaine-laced eighties and stopped speaking to each other altogether. We didn't even know where she had been living for the past eight or ten years.

And now, apparently, some disaster had befallen her.

"Is she dead?" I asked. "How did it happen?"

"No, no. She isn't dead."

"She isn't? Then what happened to her? What about Vivian?"

"She's in trouble. Wait here a minute."

Mom vanished into the dining room.

I sat looking around the kitchen in puzzlement, at last fixing on the covered Styrofoam plates that held our dinner, waiting to be popped into the microwave. And I thought the day had been long and weird *before* I crossed the bridge into Queens. What the hell was going on here? Well, at least my mother hadn't tried to reach me at NYU. That sure would have resulted in an interesting phone message. But I had always discouraged her from calling me at work, telling her that as a part-timer I didn't really have an office of my own.

"Look at these."

She handed me two pieces, one a standard tourist postcard with a corny photo of the Eiffel Tower, the other a telegram.

I turned the postcard over and read:

"Long time No see. Hate to ask you but I'm strapped. Can you spare anything? Just send what you can—if you can. Love, Viv."

The postmark on the card was about three weeks old.

There was an address beneath her signature. A place on the rue du Cardinal Lemoine—my Lord, Viv was in Paris.

I looked up at Mom and began to ask a question, but she ordered me to read the telegram first, which was dated a week or so after the postcard.

JEAN
DID YOU GET MY CARD?
WORSE. I CAN'T GET OUT.
VIV.

"What's this about?" I asked, the fear rising in my voice.

"I don't know, honey. I don't know." Her spine stiffened then and her eyes took on a glassy look. "I finally called . . . him. I mean, he is her brother."

"You're kidding! You called Daddy?"

She nodded.

I tried to imagine White Mrs. Daddy picking up the phone in their apartment near Lincoln Center. Handing the receiver over. Jesus, the look on his face when she told him who it was.

"What did he say?" I asked. "Did Viv write to him too?"

"Yes. But he doesn't want to know anything about Vivian. Says he tore the card up without reading it. It's a sin. I told him I hoped one day he would be hurting in the same way and when he reached out for help—well, never mind. I told him I think it's a sin, that's all."

I shook my head. "Wow. This is so weird. What are you going to do? You don't have any money to send her, and if Pop won't do it—"

"He wouldn't give it to her, but I managed to shame him into giving me something for you."

"*Me?* What do you mean?"

She pulled out a chair for herself then and sat down in it before answering. "Listen, Nan."

"What?"

"*I* don't have any money to spare. But—well, I do have it, but it's not mine. As a matter of fact it's Vivian's money."

"What are you talking about, Mother?"

"I mean I actually do have some money for Vivian—especially for her. When your grandfather died he left most of what he had to your daddy, naturally. And you got enough to take that beautiful trip. But you know how he was. He feuded with Viv just like your father did, but at the end he wanted to come to some kind of peace with her. Nobody even knew where Vivian was at the time. So he left her some money, and gave it to me to keep for her. It's in a special account. Waiting. There must be close to ten thousand in it by now."

"Ten thousand dollars! That sure sounds like enough to bail her out of trouble. And you mean you've had this money all along?"

"Yes. I knew sooner or later we'd hear from her again."

"But not like this," I said.

"No. Not like this. And so . . ." She glanced away from me then.

"What is it?"

"I know it's a lot to ask, Nan. You haven't seen Viv since you were a kid. I just know she's over there drinking, broke, stranded somewhere. Maybe even sick. I wouldn't know where to begin to help her. I don't know how I'd even get out of the airport over there. But I thought—since you've been there so many times—I thought maybe you could go over there and help her—take this money to her and help her get home. Like I said, I managed to shame your father into giving me enough for your expenses."

Expenses?

"What are you saying, Mother? You want me to go to Paris!"

"Yes. Would you do it? If—I mean, only if you could take

the time from work. You're going to be on spring vacation soon, aren't you?"

"It started yesterday, Mom. No problem."

A lot to ask! *Holy*—

I felt a kick right then. Right on the shin. I knew who that was: my conscience, Ernestine. I just kicked the bitch right back. Yes, I'm a liar, I told her; a deceiver, a coldhearted Air France slut. I was thinking not of my Aunt Viv in a French drunk tank but of the braised rabbit in that bistro on the rue Monsieur le Prince.

A lot to ask? Coq au vin, here I come!

CHAPTER 2

Can't We Be Friends?

I know I'm a fool. A sentimentalist. A sucker for a sad song. The same old hokey things undo me every time.

I was crying so hard I could barely see out the window of the taxi, one of those workhorse Renaults with a driver who smoked Gitanes, a beautifully dappled Dalmatian asleep beside him on the front seat. It was April and the trees were budding and we had just passed the Arc de Triomphe and it was tearing my heart out.

It helped a lot that I had sucked down about fifty glasses of Veuve Clicquot on the flight over and been hit on big time by both an African diplomat in a vintage Armani and a sublimely big-nosed Frenchman.

Drying my eyes, I recalled that first time I saw Paris, from the window of a train. I was still a student and traveling on the cheap. I took a charter flight into Amsterdam, where I met up with a couple of classmates and their European boyfriends. After a couple of days of museum going and smoking pot till I was pixillated, I took the train into Paris. That first sight of the roof of the Gare de Nord, alive with pigeons, had produced the same kind of waterworks.

By the time the cab deposited me at the picturesque little square in the 5th arrondissement, I was working on one hell of a hangover. The address on Vivian's postcard turned out to be a clean but decidedly unglamorous little hotel at the top of a rise in the pavement. Their one-star rating was not mere modesty—nothing fancy about the place. I set my valise down and walked over to the *reception*.

There was no such American madame as Vivian Hayes registered at the hotel, the well-fed gentleman behind the desk reported. Perhaps my friend was at the small hotel at the other end of the square? No, I said, checking the postcard again, this was the address given. It occurred to me then that Aunt Viv might be using either of two—or was it three?—married names. So I began to describe her, thinking even as I did so that she had probably changed so much since our last meeting that the description might be worthless. I was just about to dig into my bag for a twenty-year-old snapshot of Vivian, when the monsieur suddenly realized who I was seeking.

A sneer pulled at his lips. "Oh yes. I recall your friend now." I waited for him to go on. "This Madame Hayes," he said contemptuously, had checked out more than ten days ago.

"Checked out" was not exactly the phrase he used to describe her departure. Apparently Vivian had left without paying the last week's rent, abandoning her suitcase and clothing and personal items. She had simply gone out one afternoon and never returned.

Not good.

I had counted on some kind of trouble. Still, I didn't have to hit the panic button yet. I might have to mount a search for her. On the other hand, she might be able to raise a few dollars from somewhere, in which case she would show up again to pay her bill and collect her things.

But I couldn't think about that at the moment. My head was pounding and I needed some sleep—real sleep, not airplane nodding. This hotel was not exactly what I'd had in mind as a base of operations, but it would do for now. Hell, dowdy French hotels short on amenities but rich in character had been the sites of some of my most delightful adventures.

I asked for a room and, to forestall any problems, paid for a few days in advance. I pulled the envelope with the Thomas Cook money orders earmarked for Aunt Vivian out of my carry-on bag and committed it to the hotel safe. Mom had asked if it wouldn't be better to buy traveler's checks in my own name, but I wanted to guarantee I wouldn't be tempted to start dipping into those funds for my own use. In Vivian's place, I don't think I would've appreciated any messenger messing about with my inheritance, even if it was a totally unexpected gift from heaven.

I splurged on the best room in the house. Even so, the toilet was down the hall. The bidet had been cracked and repaired half a dozen times. The bureau smelled faintly of mildew. But the room was a good size, and the view wasn't bad. Not bad at all: my room, on the sixth floor, looked out over the busy square with its ancient copper fountain. I put in five minutes at the open window just looking at the people, pulling the air into my chest—and thinking about Aunt Vivian, somewhere out there. I didn't know yet what kind of shape I'd find her in. But I did know she wouldn't be high stepping in her designer jeans and smart black pumps. She wouldn't be laughing her tantalizing laugh that put lights in her clear brown eyes. She wouldn't be young anymore.

I thought, too, of my first trip to Paris and all the subsequent ones; of the friends I'd once had here, all dispersed to other places, other lives, now; of my summer in Provence; the meals, the men; the just plain fun. I'd been happy, ecstatic, in Paris—drunk on it—and yet I'd also known that peculiar *tristesse* that could fasten around your heart like a vise, for no particular reason, and suddenly make you feel so very alone.

Tiredness overtook me then. I closed the shutters tight. I turned back the covers on the creaky iron bed and slipped between the ironed white sheets. And then—darkness.

The trick is not to let yourself sleep too long lest you fall victim to jet lag. It was the only travel tip I could ever remember. You've got to crash and allow the old ankles to lose the swelling that results from sitting constricted in one place for so long. Nap, yes. But you mustn't sleep too long, or you'll be on the way back home before your body clock is running right again.

I was groggy when I pulled myself out of dreamland—and ravenous. I opened the metal shutters. *Pam!* Night had fallen. Those inimitable lights were all around me, and, down below, the canopies of a thousand cafes. I went and cleaned up quickly in the communal shower room and then jumped into some black trousers and a leotard. I threw my long raincoat over that and I was ready to roll.

I did a quick turn around the Pantheon, where I had often gone in the dark of night to sit and think and sometimes consume a couple of *boules* of rich ice cream purchased at one of the carts dotting the landscape. Then I headed back across the square and the boulevard St. Michel, pulsating with young people.

I hit boulevard St. Germain, or rather it hit me. It was Friday night and the street was hopping. Traffic was the predictable nightmare. I took a deep breath and ran, snaked, bullied my way across the street, heedless of the color of the traffic lights. I headed north then, away from the worst of the crowds. I had decided to eat at the Café Cloche, which was on the pricey side, but my mouth was watering for a couple of their beautiful spring lamb chops. I remembered that they didn't take reservations—the only reason I had for believing I'd get a table on a Friday night. The cross streets were beginning to look familiar now. Yes, this was the block. The café was near.

Except it wasn't. It was not there. The Café Cloche, where I'd once been seduced by a chain-smoking academic from Toulouse over a fine *daube* of beef, was no more. I stared stupidly, dejected, at the darkened window of the boutique that had replaced the restaurant.

Well, what was the big deal? Things change. So I'd find someplace else to eat dinner. A restaurant closing was a small thing, yet, inexplicably, it unsettled me. I walked back slowly into the heart of the crowd and found a friendly looking if undistinguished place where I ordered foie gras and then went on to langoustines and a half bottle of white wine. Afterward, I browsed somnolently through a few of the late-night book-stores on St. Michel, buying nothing, and found my way back to the hotel.

I got into my nightgown almost immediately. It was cool in the room but I opened the window wide and let the low night sky fall in on me. Another one of those singular Paris mo-ments. The lights on the Pantheon were silver blue and I watched them for a long time, wondering how many others were doing the same thing, their hearts moving in their chest. But, curiously enough, I had stopped crying.

I made a bet with myself as I called downstairs to order breakfast. At every hotel I'd ever lived in on this side of the Seine, the maid's name was Josette. I figured that would never change.

I lost. Marise bid me good morning in her musical colo-nial accent—was she from Antigua? maybe St. Croix?—and set the wooden tray bearing my soupy black coffee and crois-sants down at the foot of the bed.

I spent the late morning and all afternoon checking out the really low-rent hotels on streets like Gay Lussac, thinking that Vivian might have got her hands on a few bucks to live on, but not enough to go back to the hotel in the Square. The next day, I figured, I'd go another rung down on the ladder and try Pigalle and the parts of Bastille that had not yet been gentrified. Then, if I didn't turn up any leads, I'd head out to the edge of the city, Buttes Chaumont or someplace, where I'd probably be mugged and left for dead somewhere.

I put in a full day. Nothing. At six o'clock I returned to the hotel and put in a call to my mother, reporting on my progress, or rather lack of progress.

I took a long soak in the pay-per-bath room down the hall and changed into something slightly slinky. There was a fabulous wine bar on the rue du Cherche Midi that I loved. It had been the scene of two or three major flirting triumphs.

They sold lighting fixtures there now. I stood on the pavement watching the clerk clear the register and begin to close up for the evening. I could have cried.

I wandered down into the métro and took the train to Pont Marie, on the right bank. Surely the much more staid wine bar that a friend's father had once taken us to would still be there. And it was. But it was obvious there would be no lighthearted seductions taking place that evening. Oh no. No sharing a steak frites with a cute translator and then a nightcap at some avant garde jazz loft. No and no. Average age of the patrons at this stately establishment: 55 by my calculations. Successful businessmen and their co-workers, or their Chanel-clad ladies. I put away two lovely glasses of Medoc and was on my way.

I walked along the Seine in the twilight, feet hurting in my strappy heels. The magazine/postcards/junk stands on the quai were all closed now. Here and there I could hear voices down below, along the water. I had to smile. One thing you never forget, your first kiss on the banks of the Seine. I just

know it's one of those pictures that go flying across your vi-
sion as you lay dying.

I had had nothing to eat except the breakfast croissant and
a yogurt taken on the run midday. I was starving but I hated
the thought of eating alone again.

What choice did I have, though? I went to Au Pactole, a
perfectly nice place on St. Germain, just the tiniest bit stuffy,
up the block from a hotel I'd once lived in—the Hotel de
Lima. It was almost pleasurable to behave so formally with
the maître d', like playing a role, or wearing a disguise.
*Hmmm—she is black and French speaking. Must be an immigrant.
Spinster on vacation from the provinces,* I could almost hear the
young waiter thinking. *Trying to dress Parisian. Not bad looking.
Needs to get laid, though.* I was the only solo table in the good-
sized room, which was awash in fresh white flowers and
skyscraper-tall candles. After an already too heavy meal, I
pigged on goat cheese and a big-time dessert.

The thing is, I mused during my meandering walk home
along the quai, the main thing is: the police have to be
avoided.

If nothing happened with my search for Vivian in the next
day or so, I might have to contact the American embassy. But
not the French police. It was half instinctual cop-o-phobia
and half worry that maybe Vivian had wandered into something not on the up and up; then there was the plain gut-
clenching terror based on the Gallic mind-set. Guilty until
proven innocent was not a metaphor over here, it was the law.
You just did not fuck with cops in this country—not even
traffic cops.

What does a foreigner do when he or she is broke, in trouble—no friends, no resources? I didn't know. True, I had bummed around Europe before, hitchhiked with companions, smoked dope with kids I met at discos, and so on. But I had never been anything like stranded or in trouble with the law. I always had a return ticket in my pocket, and help was a collect call away. I thought about the asshole white boys who thought they were slick enough to get away with smuggling hashish out of Turkey. I found myself shuddering.

The *Herald Tribune?* What about placing an ad there— "Aunt Viv: You're richer than you think. Call home. All is forgiven." Something to that effect.

Not a likely venue. Vivian had lived in Paris before. She had enough French that if she read the newspapers at all, she'd read a French one.

I was at the Pont Neuf. Shit, I had been so lost in my thoughts that I'd overshot the hotel. I was beat, my toes crying out for release.

Give me your tired, your poor . . . your Manolo Blahniks . . . your tart tatin.

Not just tired now. I was slappy. Maybe I hadn't escaped the jet lag after all. I stood on the quai for a few minutes more. Well, good night, old Notre Dame. And if it's not too much trouble, help me find Aunt Viv before I have to go to the 19th. Amen.

I visited at least fifteen fleabag hotels and hostels the next day. I was seeing the side of Paris they don't print up on the picture postcards. The homeless, the druggies, the bag ladies, the nut jobs were nowhere near as numerous, as filthy, or as desperate as their New York cousins, but they did nothing for tourism either.

Just to make myself feel less like a mendicant, I went and had lunch in an overpriced, overdecorated restaurant in Montmartre and then took the funicular up to Sacré Coeur. I looked out over the city while the shutterbugs swarmed all around me. Maybe there is a heaven, I thought, and it's nothing more than these rooftops.

As long as I was doing the American in Paris bit, I figured I'd go to American Express, on the very remote chance that Vivian had left a message there. Of course, she'd have to know I was in Paris. But what did I have to lose? Perhaps she had spoken to my mother by now.

No such luck. And now I was stuck in the busy 9th, clogged with crazed shoppers and sightseers, the traffic like a million killer bees. I had to admit, the Opéra was looking a great deal spiffier than the last time I'd been in Paris. Choking on exhaust and too weary to do any window shopping of my own, I zigzagged across the boulevard des Capucines and went down into the métro station.

Home at last, thank the baby Jesus. The alert, generous-bosomed madame who seemed to rule at the hotel was having her afternoon *tisane* when I stopped at the desk for my key. I must have looked about as frazzled as I felt, because she offered me a cup.

French businesswomen are about the least homey human beings imaginable. Anybody would be scared of them. I know I am. This one, however, told me she had noticed my saxophone, and wondered if I was in Paris to play an engagement somewhere. She had always admired *le jazz*, she said, and at the time of their wedding anniversary each year, she and her husband enjoyed making an evening of it at the music club just off St. Germain des Pré. You know—the one with the likeness of Satchmo in black plaster in the entryway.

I told the madame, in as little detail as possible, about my search for Aunt Viv. She was sympathetic—genuinely so, I believed—and when she offered further assistance, I jumped on it.

The madame's husband relieved her at the desk while the two of us climbed into the taxi she had ordered. We were going to La Pitié Salpêtrière, a giant medical complex in the 13th arrondissement that also housed the city morgue. It made sense, didn't it, to check there first? Oh yes, it was quite sensible, my companion agreed. After all, if, heaven forbid, Vivian was at La Pitié, then there was little point in canvassing the hospitals and the emergency rooms and hospices and so on—our search would be over.

The office where we waited had a beautiful view of the Jardin des Plantes. As the lady from the administrative office led us along the corridors the worst kinds of morbid one-liners were running through my brain. I couldn't help it. It was like whistling in the graveyard.

Back in the fresh air, I went weak with relief, happy to know that Viv was not one of the bodies in those human filing cabinets. The madame and I rested for a few moments on a bench in the Jardin des Plantes and then caught another cab home.

Back at the hotel we worked out a fair way of computing the phone charges I was racking up calling the appropriate municipal offices to determine if anyone fitting my aunt's general description had been admitted to a Paris hospital. It seemed only right, I told her gratefully, that I also pay the week's rent that my aunt had skipped on. That was most responsible of me, she said. Would I like to pay that now, or should she add that sum to my own bill at the end of my stay?

None of the hospitals had any mysterious amnesiacs in residence who might be my poor aunt. So, as far as we knew, Aunt Vivian was still alive, somewhere out there. She had to be. If she was broke, how was she going to get out of Paris? I was going to have to bite the bullet and go to the embassy soon, it seemed.

It was time for me to clear out of Madame's way and let her get her dinner started. I thanked her for all her efforts— the tea and sympathy not the least of them—and went upstairs.

About seven o'clock I put on a fresh shirt and jeans and left the hotel, with no particular destination.

I wound up at one of the revival cinemas near the place everybody referred to as the Beat Hotel, a dump with character over on the rue Gît le Coeur, which I had checked out the previous day. Its reputation had been made by William Burroughs and his crowd in the fifties, and I guess its legend was still going strong. Not a single vacancy.

The street was clogged with kids of all nations, hanging out, playing guitars, smoking reefer, dry humping in doorways, eating *frites* and souvlaki, and just glorying in being alive and young and stupid. A few paces away was perhaps the world's narrowest, shortest street, which I had searched for years ago, on my first visit to the city, because its name was so intriguing: rue de Chat-Qui-Peche. The Cat Who Fishes? What the hell was the point of that? Right after finding it, I had had an even bigger disappointment. I had wandered over to the rue Mouffetard, where, I had been told, a lot of cute third world students ate cheap Middle Eastern meals. I was promptly groped and nearly kidnaped by a tobacconist with hideous b.o., and had never again set foot on that street.

At least the movie was no disappointment. How many times had I seen *Children of Paradise* since my college roommate and I first caught it on campus? Too many to count. I cried again anyway.

Lord, what a beautiful night. There was no way I was going to dinner alone again. Maybe I should turn into the first bar I saw and make a fool of myself by begging some stranger to come eat with me—or perhaps I should just pick up a sandwich someplace and call it a night.

I went for the sandwich. I would not have been good company for anybody.

After coffee the next morning an idea came to me. No, I hadn't yet thought of my next move for locating Vivian. It was something a lot goofier than that.

In fact, it was probably about the goofiest idea that had ever come my way: I decided to take my sax down into the métro and play for change. Reckless. Silly. Ill-considered. Preposterous.

Formidable, I'd do it.

It was the stuff of fantasy. Maybe I didn't have the chops a lot of my fellow street musicians back in Manhattan had, but at least I'd be able to say I played in Paris. I got cleaned up and dressed in a hurry. I wanted to get out of the room and down into the métro before I had a chance to wimp out.

I got a polite *bonjour* along with an indulgent smile from the old monsieur behind the reception desk as I tripped past him, my instrument case festooned with an old India print scarf I often use as a strap for the sax.

I bought a booklet of métro tickets and passed through the turnstile. It was an act of supreme hubris to set up shop at Odéon, one of the busier stops in the city. What with the number of hip Parisians who lived in or passed through the neighborhood every day—students, intellectuals, musicians, jazzaholics of all stripes—I was betting half of them had heard better horns than mine before they'd finished their morning coffee.

But what the hell. I wasn't playing to pay the rent; I was living out a fantasy. I settled myself at the mouth of the passageway connecting the Clignancourt line to the Austerlitz, took a deep breath, and started to blow. I began with "How Deep Is the Ocean." Hardly anyone took notice of me. That was okay, because my playing was a lot rustier than my French. I didn't sound so great.

Still, I pressed on. I chose "With a Song in My Heart" next. Not bad, if I do say so myself. And indeed, a cool-looking man in an expensive trench coat stood there attentively until I'd finished, and then began to dig into his pocket for change. The sound of the francs hitting the bottom of the case made my heart soar. I gave the guy a big shit-eating grin and immediately launched into "Lover Man." I felt so good, anything seemed possible. Maybe even a certifiable miracle. Maybe I'd see Viv bustling along the tunnel, running to catch a train.

The late morning crowd was replaced by the noontime one, people bustling along to lunch appointments, or going to do their shopping, or heading home for a leisurely meal and maybe some quick nooky—or vice versa—before returning to work.

I had to chuckle at the idea I'd had earlier in the morning—that if I kept at it all day, maybe I could make enough in tips to buy Moms and Aubrey some nice perfume. Ha. I barely made enough to buy a Big Mac. It really didn't bother me, though. I was having a good time.

I went above ground about two o'clock and found a cart that had nice-looking crêpes. I strolled along the Seine as I ate, and then turned into a beautiful old tabac on the Quai Voltaire, where I had a *grand café* and bummed a cigarette from a waiter who was tall enough for the NBA and weighed about ten pounds.

I couldn't wait to get back to my post in the subway. And when I did, I hit the ground running. I had never managed to make "It Never Entered My Mind" sound like that before in my life. And my "Green Dolphin Street" ran a close second. I even got a nice round of applause from a group of older women with folding umbrellas.

Don't *ever* get too comfortable. It's just one of a thousand lessons that I have never truly taken in. My mother has been cautioning me about it since I was old enough to crawl. And Ernestine, my conscience, never tires of saying it. But I always forget.

It was about five-thirty. I got through a couple of bars of "You Took Advantage of Me" before I realized something strange was up. I was hearing the same licks being played— note for note—not twenty feet away. On a violin, of all things. It startled the shit out of me. In fact, for a moment I thought I was hallucinating. I looked into the passageway and saw a long-legged, light-skinned black man with demure dreadlocks and wire-rim spectacles gazing directly, defiantly into my eyes while he bowed absentmindedly.

I stood where I was, seething, until he finished, and then strode over to the gangly Caribbean-looking prick. "What the fuck do you think you're doing? I was here first," I told him in rapid-fire French.

His eyes bugged behind the glass of his spectacles.

"*Idiot!*" I shouted at him. And then went on to ask him if he was deaf, and then if he was under the mistaken impression that he was funny. I finished with "Who the hell do you think you are—Marcel Marceau?"

There was plenty of anger in his eyes, but he said nothing. Which only increased my fury.

"*Eh bien, salaud? Pourquoi tu me reponds pas?*"

"I'm not answering you," he said, acidly, and in English, "because I don't know any gutter French yet."

"Oh my God. You're . . . an American."

At this point he chose to answer me in French, adding a

Gallic smirk to his little repertory of expressions: "No need
to be so snotty about it. So are you—obviously."

"Obviously?" I began to splutter. "Oh, so I don't know
how to speak French? Is that what your lame-ass little riposte
is supposed to mean?"

More smirk.

I got right up in his face then. "Don't even think about
criticizing my accent, mister. You speak French like a pig."

"That's because I am an autodidact. I hope to polish my
accent while—"

"An au-to-di-dact," I repeated, and then began to roar with
scornful laughter. I was being the schoolyard bully picking on
the kid with the bulging book bag. It was cheap and unwor-
thy of me, but I couldn't put the brakes on it. "Jesus, this is
unbelievable. I have to come all the way to Paris to deal with
an evil, pretentious, bourgeois asshole from the hood—"

"I was thinking the same thing about you."

"Hey, you see here! I may be pretentious, but I am not bourgeois—and I sure as hell am not from your hood."

"Bitch, you can be from Jupiter for all I care," he said,
abruptly ending our absurd argument. "Just as long as you
move your ass along. This is my spot."

"What do you mean, your spot? You own it or something?"

"I mean I got a right to play here at this time four days a
week. I have a piece of paper that says so."

"I don't believe you."

"I have no interest in what you believe. I'm a legal resident
of the city of Paris and I have an artist permit to play here."

I was going to slice into him about his prissy-sissy attitude, but suddenly all the wind was gone from my sails. Suddenly I knew who I reminded myself of: a monster-gold-earring-wearing gangsta girl on the IRT; hunching her shoulders, threatening, gesticulating wildly, using her high-polished fingernails like a garden trowel as she read out some enemy in subliterate slang.

"You know what?" I said, calm now. "You can die on this fucking spot, mister legal resident. Forget you."

I turned on my heel and walked back to my case.

As I climbed the stair at the other end of the tunnel, I could hear him playing "How About You?"

His playing was effortless, swinging, like something humming inside your own head.

I'd like to show you some New York in June, I thought bitterly.

Oh, but shit, he was good.

Well, that was nice and ugly.

"Ugly" didn't really capture the essence of it, though. It was, to use some prissy language of my own, mortifying. Jesus—why did I do that!

I hated myself.

Above ground again, my face burned with shame. Two black Americans, strangers, meeting in Paris under those singularly strange circumstances—it should have been an occasion for rejoicing. But what do we do? Rather, what do I do? Ridicule. Curse. Clown. Fight over a little patch of pee-soaked concrete. Goddamn, it was horrible. And the more I thought about it, the more thoroughly depressed I became.

I walked for a while, trying to get myself in hand, shake off the bad feelings. I sat in the Jardins du Luxembourg for a little while, smelling the sweetness of the grass, despising it. I watched the parents as they sauntered home with their kids; the lovers as they kissed in parting. Everybody seemed to be carrying a baguette for that night's dinner. Man, it would be so nice to be invited to somebody's house for dinner. I was yearning for somebody just to call me by my name—for something familiar like that. A plain meal in an apartment I'd visited many times, and a couple of hours of aimless, civilized conversation. I am still civilized, I told myself. Despite that appalling interlude in the métro. I'm not the asshole who behaved that way. I'm better than that—really.

I went and had a drink at the Café Flore. In fact, I had a few of them.

Like every musician, probably, I had often wondered what it was like to play high on drugs. All the cornball stuff crosses your mind: does the heroin unlock some door in your soul? Does it make you better? I don't just mean, does it make you play better. I mean, are *you* better, however briefly.

For all my musical forefathers, it had to do more than just make the pain go away. God. Negroes and their pain. What the fuck were we going to do if suddenly it all did go away? Would we even know who we were anymore?

The waiter was looking at me, the bottle in his left hand, the smile on his lips like a question mark.

I shook my head. No more, *merci.*

I wasn't exactly merry, but I'd had enough wine to make me lighten up somewhat. Enough with the clichés, Nan, I cautioned myself. No more being blue in Paris. Gotta lose that "Azure-tay," as Nat Cole sang.

So, back to work. I walked for a few blocks and then descended into the station called St. Sulpice. The crowds had disappeared. I set up and began to play again. Not many passersby, but what did it matter? The sounds of my horn ricocheted hauntingly off the tiled walls. I felt almost as though I was in my own private city, the occasional visitor dropping a few francs into my case like a toll to enter the gates.

I played "Something to Live For" and another Ellington, "Come Sunday."

I think what happened was, I pushed it too far. One minute I was playing the break on "Ill Wind," my eyes closed, and the next moment I was seeing stars. I had thought I heard a kind of scuffling noise farther down the tunnel, but I was so wrapped up in playing I paid no attention.

All I know is that suddenly they were on me: two white guys in denim and swastika-ed leather, short haircuts, bad teeth. And one of them was banging my head against the tiles.

I began to flail around, hit out blindly, but my fists never connected with anything. I became dimly aware of shouting—somewhere far off—and then I heard a ripping sound. They were tearing the pockets off my jeans, going after my money, I guess. The instrument case must have gotten overturned, because the few coins that had been inside it, I heard rolling up the tunnel floor. Someone was pulling at the strap of the sax now, but it was all twisted around my head. I heard the unmistakable epithet, negre, spoken through clenched teeth as I took a blow to the face. I once saw a film clip of Thelonious Monk playing at the Five Spot in New York. When the spirit moved him, he got up from the piano and spun himself around madly, like a holy drunk. That's how I felt right then, as if someone had set me spinning, like Monk, and I was never going to stop.

My head and heart were drumming hard. I raised my hands to cover my ears. Something on my face. Something on my hands. Wet. That was blood. Blood! Was I cut up?

So this is how it ends, I thought fleetingly. Me beaten to death by skinheads. Aunt Viv starves to death in a back alley or rots in prison. Mother, grief stricken, carted off screaming to the insane asylum. Daddy, riddled with guilt, commits suicide. Negro angst turned Wagnerian.

"Ends" is the right word. One of them is coming back to finish me off now. His face comes into focus. Wish I had the strength to kick him in the balls.

But wait—it's not a white face. And this guy's got a mop of curly hair and wears glasses.

And, somehow, all the noise has stopped.

CHAPTER 3

I Didn't Know About You

W hite sheets. Creaky bedsprings. My old suitcase open on top of the bureau. Unless heaven was a budget hotel room with no TV, I was still alive.

Oh yes. There was something else in my room that tipped me off I wasn't dead: a fine-looking, long-legged, high yellow black man, snoring softly, sitting on a hard chair, his big bare feet propped up at the foot of my bed. He wasn't wearing any pants. Gray T-shirt over matching briefs.

Lord-a-muzzy, I am still alive.

"How's it going, sleeping beauty?"

Shit. He caught me staring at his shorts. How gross.

"I'm okay, I think. My nose hurts a little. Is it broken?"

"Nothing broken," he said, a little patronizing.

There followed a long and awkward silence.

"Last night's still fuzzy to you, I guess," he said, yawning and getting to his feet. He reached for his trousers and turned his back while he zipped up. "I asked if you wanted to go to the hospital, but you wouldn't do it."

"Yeah, one member of the family in trouble is enough," I mumbled.

"What?"

"Doesn't matter. I remember now. You rescued me and got me back here."

He didn't respond. Instead, he went over to the basin and began to splash water on his face.

"Damn nice of you," I said, laughing a bit, too embarrassed to do much else. "After that scene I pulled—going out on you like that in the métro—you should have let them kill me."

He shook his head. "Forget it."

"God, I haven't even asked, how are you? What are you— Hercules or something? There were two of those freaks. Did they hurt you?"

"Not really. I'm not much of a hero. I was screaming like a white lady and three or four other folks came running to help us out. The Aryan League didn't even manage to get your wallet."

I suddenly buried my face in my hands and moaned.

"What is it?" he said, alarmed. "Headache?"

"No, no, no. I'm just cursing my fucking karma. I don't know why I'm so surprised when stuff like this happens to me. You know what I mean?"

"Uh—"

"What's the story downstairs, by the way? Did you bring me in here all bloody and stuff? And what did they say—'Be out by tomorrow morning'?"

"I told them I witnessed two thugs trying to rob you. The madame is the one who supplied the sleeping pill for you."

"Oh."

"Why did you ask that?" I distinctly heard lofty censure in his voice. "You think they figure anything that happens to a black person, it's gotta be his own fault? Some flour-faced Nazis just tried to kill you. Why are you worried about how it looks to some white people? Think you're letting the race down?"

Oooh. Touched a nerve there. Big time.

She's a little middle-class hypocrite playing the bohemian. Was that what he was thinking? What did we have here? A truly enlightened brother? Or was he mixing me up with himself? Was he talking about his own fears? Or had he really zeroed in on mine?

I decided discretion was the better part of etcetera and—for once—held my tongue.

"All right," I said. "You nailed me trying to be exemplary. I've been chastened, and you paid me back for what I said about you being bourgeois, okay? But it's a little more complicated than that. The management here is just not having the best luck with the coloreds from Elmhurst, Queens lately."

He looked at me questioningly but didn't press for any explanations.

The silence fell again. "How about handing me that mirror?" I finally asked.

He plucked my makeup mirror from the bureau top and gave it to me. He stood at the foot of the bed quietly examining me while I examined my face. He was right: nothing broken. The bridge of my nose was a bit tender and there was a little lump on the back of my head. That was all. I didn't look half as bad as I imagined. In fact, the tonic effect of a good night's sleep seemed to be right there on my face. Satisfied, I nodded and handed the mirror back.

"Think you're going to be okay now?" he asked.

"Fine."

"Good. I just didn't want to leave you until I was sure."

"Listen," I called out to him as he prepared to leave, "you *do* have a place to stay, right? I mean, you really are living—uh—somewhere?"

I saw that little smirk on his lips.

"Yes. I don't need any help."

"Right, right," I said quickly. "I kind of forgot for a minute there. I'm the one who needs all the help." *You're Mr. Perfect, aren't you, you prick?* Damn, was there nothing I could do right with this guy? He just kept outclassing me. He was a living reminder of my incompetence. Bet if he was looking for his aunt Vivian she'd be cleaned up and firmly in hand by now, her ass in a seat on TWA.

"What's your name?" he asked mildly.

I began to laugh then. That's right. We hadn't been introduced, had we?

"Nan."

"My name's Andre."

"Okay. Thanks again, Andre. I owe you one."

"You really do speak French very well," he said.

"I've got an idea, Andre. Why don't you start polishing your accent, like you said yesterday. Why don't you pick up the phone there and order two breakfast trays with extra coffee."

I got one thing right, at last. Cheerful little Marise, the maid, was sick that day. Her replacement was indeed called Josette. She had never served me before, so she didn't even raise an eyebrow at finding two of us in the room.

I carefully moved his violin case aside and opened the shutters wide to let in the morning air.

"Keep polishing, Andre. Speak to me in French," I said, pouring more coffee.

"I don't know if I can hold up my end all in French," he said.

"That's okay. Do the best you can." I then began to speak in my senior-year seminar French accent, enunciating clearly but keeping my vocabulary colloquial, everyday: "First off, tell me what you're doing over here, if it's any of my business. Are you in school?"

"No. I got a little bit of money after my mother died—insurance—and I just headed straight over here. I'm planning to be . . ."

"Be what?" I asked when he hesitated.

"Famous maybe."

I cracked up.

"Well, you sure can play that violin. Is that what's going to make you famous?"

"Yeah. Well, yes and no. I want to do something with the music, sure. But I'm also taking notes for this book I'm thinking about writing."

"No kidding? What kind of book?"

"About black people in Paris. Musicians mostly, but others too—dancers, soldiers, poets, whoever I come across. And not just the big ones like Josephine Baker and Wright and them. I mean people who worked to get over here and would do anything to stay. They were excited—proud to be here. Not like tourists, you know? Like there was something really at stake for them. People like me." He paused there. "And you."

I couldn't help it. I was fucking happy he had included me.

"I want to walk around in their footsteps," he continued, "look up their friends and families, if they had any, visit the places where they lived. Give them their due. It's hard to do something like that—start over in a strange place. Hard. Lonely. Scary. There's more than one way to be a black hero—to me, anyway. I want to tell people how admirable some of those folks were."

"*Formidable*," I said. "So there is a little of the race man in you after all."

His face went scarlet around the edges. But, thankfully, he laughed rather than bristled.

"Where'd you study music?" I asked.

"I went to Curtis."

"You're from Philadelphia?"

"No. Detroit, originally." There was a sourish expression on his face.

"Sounds like you didn't like it much."

He shrugged. "Wasn't just Detroit. I didn't like anything that much in the States."

"I can hear that," I said.

I wanted to say something more than that, but I couldn't quite form the words yet. The permutations of our relationship to the whole of America were endless. You could hate white people but not hate America. You could come to terms with the racism but never accept the insipid culture. You could view our disenfranchisement as a kind of massive swindle—all that blood, sorrow, loyalty, hope, and patience deposited over the centuries, and the check keeps bouncing. You could simply self-destruct. Like I said, endless. I figured I'd hear the particulars of his take on the thing soon enough.

"Like Baldwin said, 'I had to get out before I killed somebody.' Is that how you felt?"

"Something like that," he answered, not looking at me. "More than likely, if anybody was gonna end up dead, it would have been me. Like I told you before, I'm hardly anybody's idea of fierce. Keep in mind that when I was little I used to have to walk home carrying a violin. *And* these thick glasses. It was like wearing a sign that said KICK THE SHIT OUT OF ME."

"Kids are real nice to each other, aren't they?" I said, chuckling, but angry too. I was thinking about my friend Aubrey's treatment at the hands of some of our peers. "Who was it that saw your musical stuff and put you in school?"

"My mother. She could talk you out of your teeth. Got me scholarships to everything. We didn't have much. My father died when I was seven."

"What was she like, your mother?"

"White. Which made things even more interesting than they might have been."

Yeah, I thought as much. Aggressive as our DNA is, there were still little hints of the other in his face. "Tell me more," I said.

I divided the last of the coffee between our two cups. Boy! did I want a cigarette.

"Well, like they say, nothing lasts forever," he said. "You get over yourself, one way or another. I stopped running from fights. And the fellas stopped wanting to fight me around the time we all discovered sex. See, the girls liked me."

I grinned. "Yaaay, Andre! So you went from being the four-eyed sissy to the neighborhood pussy magnet."

"You got it. For however brief a time, I was a hero."

"Fierce at last!" I raised the fist to him.

"No, I told you, I'm not. But I'll tell you who was. My mom. I don't know how she did it, exactly, but she's the one who—" He stopped there and didn't talk again until he had drained his cup.

When he spoke again, his voice had become thick. "A lot of things make me want to kill. And a lot of things I just don't give a fuck about anymore. All I care about now is becoming excellent at my work and being legit over here. Getting my papers, steady gigs, an apartment, whatever. 'Cause I am *not* going back. By the way, that was a load of crap I gave you about being a legal resident and having a permit, just in case you didn't already know.

"About the only thing that makes me want to fight now is

other people telling me who I am and what I ought to be doing and who I ought to be doing it with."

"You mean you don't like having your blackness challenged?"

"My blackness is not open to challenge. My father was black, so that means I'm black. Period. I guess what I mean is, my people deserve to be honored by me, and I'm serious about doing that—but I deserve some honor too, right? Who doesn't?"

"Yeah," I said. "Who doesn't? Are you all on your own now? No family?"

"No."

"How long have you been in Paris?"

"Five months."

"Made any friends yet?"

He shook his head. "Not really. Just some guys I met playing around town. The place I'm staying at belongs to one of my profs, but he isn't there now. I'm subletting from him."

"What are you—"

He cut me off. "Just a minute! Hold up! Question after question after question. We're only talking about me. I want to know something about you and your stuff."

"You will, you will," I said. "Tell you what. Wait for me in the café downstairs while I get ready."

"Ready for what?"

"We're going to get seriously drunk."

"Are you joking?"

"Seriously, intentionally drunk."

"It's only ten-thirty," he said giddily. "In the morning."

"I know. But I'm about to tell you my life story, right? That's not something you do sober, my brother. And you've got to show me your Paris before I show you mine."

He picked up his violin and practically danced over to the door.

"It's good to be an international nigger, don't you find, Nan?"

"Yes, *mon frère*. It is kind of da bomb."

Instead of waiting downstairs, he had run home to drop off his violin.

By late afternoon, we'd been walking and talking and drinking for hours.

I didn't figure on another excursion to the Right Bank so soon. But that was okay. Andre and I were wending our way all over the 8th while his nonstop Negro-in-Paris history rap unreeled like a guided tour cassette. The kid was amazing.

He had just given me the complete history of the concert hall called the Salle Pleyel, on the rue du Faubourg St. Honoré, where every famous brown person who had ever set foot in Paris—from the players in the old la revue Negre to W.E.B. Du Bois to Herbie Hancock to Howlin Wolf—had drawn an audience.

We stopped briefly for another drink, exchanged more life story tidbits, and pressed on.

It was Andre who pointed out the American Embassy building to me, near the place de la Concorde. But more important to him was the spot a couple of buildings away where once had stood the deluxe club Les Ambassadeurs. I heard all about Florence Mills's success there in 1926 and how Richard Wright had brought Katherine Dunham's dance troupe there to perform in the forties.

As we swept up the Champs Elysées, he listed what Chester Himes and his wife had had for lunch at Fouquet's in 1959. All right, all right—slight exaggeration.

Sidney Bechet this, Henry Tanner that, Kenny Clarke this, Cyrus Colter that . . . Was I aware that *Art Blakey aux Champs-Elysées* was the only live jazz record that . . . Did I want to visit the site of Chez Josephine, la Baker's nightclub, before or after we saw the cabaret where Satie, Milhaud, *and* Ravel used to hang with her . . . In 1961, you know, both Bud and Dexter backed up Carmen McRae at the Paris Blue Note, but it wasn't called that anymore . . .

Who had told this child he wasn't black enough? Not to play amateur Freudian, but his encyclopedic knowledge of our people in Paris was way past the maybe-I'll-write-a-book stage. It was obviously at the level of obsession. Who was he trying to vindicate?

It was late and I was starving. "I'm buying," I told Andre. "What do you suggest?"

"You shouldn't treat," he said. "You've been buying all day."

"It's okay. I'll write it off on my taxes under Educational Expenses."

"You know, there is a place I want to try."

"Name it."

"Bricktop's. It's in the ninth."

He was putting me on. "Oh sure," I said, laughing. "Maybe we'll run into Mabel Mercer and her friend Cole Porter. Scott and Zelda, too." Bricktop, the oh-so-sophisticated cabaret singer, and the club bearing her name were roaring twenties legends, I knew. He had to be putting me on.

"No, no. It's there. Really."

I looked at him then, truly worried. "Jesus. You're really over the edge. I mean, you think we've been transported back to 1928, don't you? I understood that Bricktop's closed about sixty years ago."

He grinned mischievously at me. "Yes, you're right. It did. But there's a place with the same name now. I'd like to see what it's like."

"That's better," I said. "I guess we won't have to get the net for you after all. Are we dressed for it?"

"I think we're cool. It's just a place with down-home food and a piano player."

Back to funky Pigalle. I had crisscrossed most of these streets before, in my scattershot search for Vivian. Well, this time I wasn't sitting around in the lobbies of grunge hotels, searching for down-and-out bars or the Parisian equivalent to a soup kitchen. I was being escorted around the hallowed grounds of our ancestors, so to speak. The hotel where Bud Powell lived. The cabaret (at least the address where once there had been a cabaret) where one celebrated musician reportedly shot another to death. And, of course, the site of the original Bricktop's on the rue Fontaine.

I felt a flash of guilt about having taken the day off like this. That would be old Ernestine trying to shame me: Vivian's suffering! she was reminding me. Vivian's lost—broke—

Vivian's dying! And here you are, drinking the day away *with some man*, chasing after some phantom of the glamorous black past.

Yes, ma'am, I answered meekly. I *am* having too much fun and he *is* too good-looking. Tomorrow I widen the search for Aunt Viv. I swear.

Cole Porter and Mabel Mercer were definitely not in residence. No ladies in bare-back evening gowns and diamonds. Not a tuxedo in sight. The new Bricktop's was African-American kitsch. Autographed photos of the namesake lady herself, of Louis Armstrong and Lady Day, Alberta Hunter and you name them. Stuffed piccaninny dolls. Posters for Oscar Micheaux movies. Laminated Bessie Smith records. Items on the menu named after this or that famous personage. The food wasn't half bad, though. We devoured hot cornbread and smothered chicken and collards while we goofed on the place. The generic old black gentleman at the baby grand played terrific stride.

They were doing a fairly brisk business in the place, too. Mostly older black people occupied the tables, but quite a few younger couples—black, white, black and white—were chowing down as well. Some musician types were drinking and bullshitting with the bartender up front.

A loquacious elderly gentleman we took to be the owner, because of the deference being paid him by what appeared to be the regulars, was holding court at a large round table near the back. The drinks were flowing back there and spirits were high. One woman at his table we recognized as an up-and-coming diva from the States—you know, in one meteoric arc she goes from the church choir in Stomach Ache, Mississippi, to rave reviews at the Met. When Andre kept glancing over there, I assumed it was Miss Thing that he was staring at.

But no, he said, he was looking at the old man. There was something about him—something vaguely familiar—that he couldn't quite put his finger on.

"He was probably Eubie Blake's butler or something—somebody only you would know," I said mockingly.

He blushed. At least he had enough perspective to be embarrassed.

I called for the check.

What a day it had been. We began the long walk back to the 5th, still talking, confiding in each other the way you do in the early stages of a friendship. Occasionally I'd point out a café or a restaurant or a street corner where I'd dined with friends, met a lover, made a discovery of one sort or another.

Back at last at the hotel, we were reluctant to say good night. I invited Andre up for a glass of the brandy I'd been smart enough to purchase and lay away in the armoire.

We set our chairs in front of the open window and went on talking. It wasn't long before a weird kind of chill went up my back. I knew it wasn't from the night air. It was a bizarre sensation and I managed to push it away quickly enough, but I had become somewhat distracted.

"I think I got it!" Andre exclaimed, seemingly out of the blue.

It was as if his voice were coming at me from the bottom of a well. "What? What did you say?"

I had been staring, transfixed, over at the top of the bureau.

"You know that old man—the one who owns Bricktop's?"

"Yeah. What about him?"

"Didn't someone call him Mr. Melson—or Melons?"

"I may have heard somebody call him something like that. Why?"

"I think I know who he is."

"Who?"

"Morris Melon. That's it. He was a teacher. Anthropology, wasn't it? Or sociology. Yes, right. He wrote a book—one of those pioneering studies about the black community in Chicago. Or am I thinking of *Black Metropolis?* It was something like that, anyway. Damn, what was the name of that book? Or was it the study of the Gullah Islands? I should interview him sometime. Find out his story."

He went on chattering. I was only half listening. I got up and began to walk around the room slowly, a sense of fear rising steadily inside me.

Andre had pulled himself out of his compulsive trip down memory lane. "What's the matter, Nan? What are you doing?"

I began to open the bureau drawers then, checking, I'm not sure what for. I looked inside my sax case and all seemed well there. I could find nothing missing. But I knew that someone had been looking through my things. I just knew it: earrings placed at the right-hand corner of the bureau instead of the left; a tube of hand lotion set on its side rather than on end; pantyhose rolled up with the toes outside rather than in. But things disturbed so minutely that it was possible I was imagining the changes. I told Andre what I was thinking. More-

over, I said, I think it might have something to do with my
aunt.

"What do you mean? It was probably just the maid."

I shook my head. "No. No, something's . . ."

"What? What were you going to say?"

"Something's happening."

"Like what? What's happening?"

I had to shrug my shoulders. I had no idea what I meant.

He smiled at me and got me settled down again, almost
convinced me that it was my imagination. I sat back at the
window with him and finished my drink, but that weird feeling never went completely away.

"I'd better go," Andre said a while later, his voice low. "You
need to get to bed."

I nodded. "So do you, friend."

He nodded, too.

A darkness moved across his face then. I didn't understand
it. We stood for a minute in the doorway, saying a final good
night, and then he left.

Seconds later, there was a knock at the door. He had come
back.

"Forget something?" I asked.

"No. Look—uh . . ."

I waited in silence. The darkening in his face was full-
blown midnight by now. Something was very wrong.

He dropped the bomb then:

"You think I'm a fag, don't you?"

"Of course not." Oh yes, I did.

I hadn't known it before, but of course I did. What else

could it mean for a handsome young man to be staying *chez* "one of my profs."

"I'm not," he said, threatening. He reached for my wrist but at the last moment pulled back. "I'm not gay."

I caught my breath. I didn't speak. He was looking at me so intently that I lowered my gaze from his.

"I'll come over to have breakfast with you tomorrow—if that's okay," he said finally. "We have to do something about your aunt."

We have to do something?

I nodded. "See you in the morning."

Okay, so maybe he wasn't a closet case. But surely there was more to his life story than brilliantly gifted mixed-race kid fights his way out of the ghetto and becomes the toast of Gay Paree. It wasn't that I suspected what he had told me was untrue; there simply had to be some juicy bits that he'd left out.

We.

When he was gone I locked the door and placed my grip in front of it.

CHAPTER 4

It Could Happen to You

I was showered and in street clothes when he arrived.

He was carrying a white box tied with string.

"Coffee's on the way up," I said. "What's that?"

"Decent croissants," he answered, "and sliced ham and some fresh fruit. I stopped at the market near my place." He lifted the sack in his other hand. "And the morning paper."

He laid out all the items on the bureau. "This is the kind of stuff even I can afford," he said.

"Don't worry, boyfriend," I said. "You're going to be rich and famous soon enough."

Thank God, last night's heaviness seemed to have gone from his face, and from the air between us. The tray was delivered a minute later. He sat next to me on the bed and we breakfasted royally.

I felt good, happy, so much less alone.

Unfortunately, when I looked down at the headline under

the fold of the morning paper, that warm and fuzzy feeling instantly went away.

AMERICAN WOMAN BRUTALLY MURDERED

My heart stopped beating for a moment.

Andre noticed the headline a second after I did. We began to read frantically, looking for the name of the victim.

Polk. Mary Polk. A white woman.

I could breathe again.

For about two horrible minutes, I had been absolutely convinced that it was Vivian who had been murdered. But now it was just another story in the news. We read on.

The woman had been bludgeoned to death in the alleyway out back of Le Domino, a seedy bar in Pigalle. She was apparently in France on business, working for a wine wholesaler. She had been registered at a perfectly respectable hotel in the 1st, and was probably indulging some wish to see the wicked side of Paris after dark.

The article went on to say that another patron of the club, one Guillaume Lacroix, had been detained for questioning but already released. The police said Lacroix (street name Gigi) was a petty thief and one-time pimp with a long record, but there was no evidence linking him to the dead woman. The continuation page of the story showed a mug shot of Lacroix looking like a freeze-dried trout.

Another possible suspect, unnamed, was being sought. Authorities believed for now that robbery was the motive for the murder: all Mary Polk's cash, jewelry, and credit cards were taken.

In the gruesome crime scene photo Mary Polk lay dead, a

bloody tarpaulin over her upper body, exposed from the knees down. There was something lurid, and at the same time touching, about her shapely ankles in the high heels. Also pictured was the murder weapon—a paperweight wrapped in a "blood-soaked kerchief, olive green in color and with a red insignia sewn on the upper left corner," the news account said.

Sipping at my coffee, I put the paper aside for a minute. Andre picked it up and continued to read, narrating the rest of the story to me as he did so.

I was still thinking about my aunt Vivian. Vivian in her disco-going, coke-snorting, party-animal heyday. I had always admired the way she put herself together—stark black, tight-fitting dresses or bell-bottomed jumpsuits in startling colors. She would scour the flea markets for antique hats and jewelry and shoes. And she almost always wore a scarf. Not a flowing chiffon number, but something more like a cowboy ban-danna—a kerchief. She said it added just the right element of fun to her outfits, kind of a throwaway. There was one sort she was especially fond of. A Girl Scout kerchief. Her waist was so tiny she could wear one of those as a sash. In fact, she collected them. She must have had a half dozen of those ban-dannas.

I grabbed the newspaper from Andre's hands and stared hard at the bloody scarf wrapped around the lethal paper-weight. Of course, it was impossible to make out any details in a photo like that, but—No. No, it was crazy. What I was thinking was crazy. It couldn't be. It couldn't.

I jumped off the bed, startling Andre.

"Where are you going?"

"I must be the stupidest cow who ever lived," I said, jamming my feet into my boots.

"What are you talking about? Nan, where are you going?"

"Reception!" I shouted, fumbling with the door. "I'm going to get her suitcase! I should have looked in her suitcase!"

Her valise was humongous. I dragged it onto the birdcage elevator, off again, and into my room.

The case, an old one, was not locked. We hefted it onto the bed and unsnapped the fasteners. It had been packed tight as a drum. All manner of stuff sprang out and onto the coverlet—sweaters, trousers, pantyhose, shampoo—even a photo album.

"I wonder how long she intended to stay," said Andre. "There's a lot of crap in here."

"Yeah," I said, "you're right. And look at the kind of crap it is—I mean, the variety of crap."

There was an impressive panoply of stuff: hair curlers, an old matchbook from the Brasserie Lipp, a portable radio, light clothes, heavy clothes, a couple of mateless earrings, photographs, an empty perfume bottle. A lot of the things seemed more like mementos than travel necessities.

"You know what?" I said. "It's like she grabbed the minimum stuff a person would need to set up housekeeping. Almost like she was going to start a new life."

"She wasn't planning to go home, you mean."

"Maybe. The strangest thing of all is why she would leave it all behind."

"But you said she skipped on the bill."

"Yeah, I know. But if you're deliberately going to skip on the bill, wouldn't you find a way to take a few things out, you know, one at a time in a shopping bag on your way out one morning and nobody would think anything of it. If you were really planning to escape without paying the weekly rent, you'd smuggle your clothes out somehow and just leave the empty suitcase—or something.

"This makes it seem like she left here on the run. Like she hadn't planned to skip at all."

"Could be," he said, picking up the hefty photo album. "Do you remember this?"

"No. I hadn't seen her for a long time. I don't know what kind of things she would have kept at home—wherever that was."

We opened the cover of the album to the first page of photographs.

"That's my grandmother!"

In truth, I had never met my father's mother. She died young. But I recall this photograph of her; my father had a copy of it that used to adorn the chest of drawers in my parents' bedroom.

"God, how strange," I said. "It's so weird seeing that picture again after all these years."

Andre leafed slowly through the book. "He looks like you. Is that your father?" He was pointing to a tall, serious-looking young man in cap and gown.

"Yeah. He looks like he'd rather be someplace else, doesn't he? Like always."

"You don't get along with him?"

"I don't know if I'd put it that way. I don't see him often enough to get along or not get along with him. I was never really sure how Pop felt about me. I was grown up when he left, but it was almost as if when he stopped loving my mother he stopped loving me, too."

"I don't believe it works like that," he said, lingering another minute before he turned the page. "Wow—is that *you?*"

"Where?"

The little girl in pigtails was wearing a polka-dot playsuit, grinning at the camera.

Lord, what a geek I was. I took control of the album and turned hurriedly past the next page or two lest we encounter any shots of me accepting spelling bee or good citizenship prizes.

"There's Vivian!" I cried.

She was wearing a white suit and matching pumps, and a bridal veil. A black man I did not recognize was the groom.

"She's beautiful," Andre said. "Who's the man?"

"Uncle number one, I suppose. She's awful young there. I don't remember him."

"Look here," said Andre. "Looks like another wedding."

Yes, it did. I instantly recognized City Hall in Lower Manhattan. Viv, in a scalloped-neck sheath, her hair teased to giddy heights, and a devilishly handsome man—with an Afro as big as the Ritz—holding up a copy of their marriage license on the steps of the courthouse. Him, I had a vague memory of.

We continued to turn the pages.

Hubby #3 looked familiar, too. Jerry, that's what he was called. "The Cracker," I believe, was my father's pet name for him. Jerry was a musician from L.A. By the look of things, he and Viv had gone to Venice on their honeymoon. And here they were in swim clothes, on a hotel balcony, the Adriatic like a chip of sapphire behind them.

We saw Viv in one of those jumpsuits at a table in some bar. A second-level Motown crooner from the sixties was pawing her. Andre put a name to the guy's face: Chuck Wilson.

There she was again, in a colorful African hat, receiving an autograph from a nice-looking black man, the chairs and tables of a cabaret visible in the background. "That's Oscar Brown Jr.," Andre pronounced.

"You know, I think you're right," I said. "Who's this?" I pointed to the gentleman in another photo, seated at a Steinway, who was shaking hands with Vivian.

"I believe it's Wynton Kelly."

"You're kidding."

"No."

"And what about her?" I said, turning to a snap of Viv in her black evening finery, wineglass raised in salute to a sleepy-eyed lady, also at the piano of some boîte. I slipped the photo out of its cellophane jacket and turned it over, cupping it with my hand so that he could not see what was written there: "Shirley Horn at the Blue Note, 1971."

"Shirley Horn," said Andre.

"Boy, you are fucking amazing. Who's this handsome guy—playing the bass?"

"Ray Brown."

Again, I took the snapshot out and looked at the back of it. He was right again. "Damn, you're good," I said.

He shrugged, trying to hide his swelling chest.

I took out another one and looked at it front and back. "I'm going to stump you on this one, I bet."

"Why?" asked Andre. "Let's see it."

This time I handed the photograph to him. Vivian was pictured with a sweet-faced black man no taller than she was, but beautifully built. They stood with their arms around each other's waist under a sign that read in French EXOTIC GARDEN—THIS WAY.

He studied the man's face for a long time. "Well, I guess you got me," he admitted. "I can't identify him. Let's see who it is." He turned the photo over.

"Picnic With Ez, near Èze! (Ha ha)" was written on the back.

"What does it mean?" Andre asked. "Where is Èze?"

"On the Riviera. We'll have dinner and make a night of it in this incredible hotel someday. When we've got two thousand dollars to blow."

"You mean you've been there?"

"Uh-huh. Once."

"Who took you?"

I gave him a little world-weary sigh. "Oh, you know. Jekyll and Hyde shit. A mistake wearing pants."

"He hit you or something?"

" 'Something.' Yeah, it was more like 'something.' That's the trouble with guys who know a lot more than you: they know *a lot* more than you. Anyhow, I guess I come by my occasional bad taste in men honestly. God knows, Viv had her lapses, too."

He looked down at the snapshot again. "So maybe this guy Ez turned out to be one of Vivian's mistakes. But you say you don't know him?"

I shook my head. "Never heard of him."

We played the game for a few minutes more and then I dived back into the suitcase. More crap, as Andre had called it. But nothing to lead us any closer to Viv. No address books, no airline tickets, no names or phone numbers jotted down on paper napkins. And no Girl Scout bandannas. I guess Viv's waistline wasn't what it used to be.

Finally I came across a fraying denim jacket. I stood up and tried it on. A couple of sizes too small for me and my friends up top. I stuck my hand in one of the chest pockets and pulled out a filthy piece of paper, rolled up tightly like a reefer. I unrolled it. It was, to my astonishment, a hundred dollar bill, U.S. currency.

Andre and I began a thorough search, turning pockets inside out, feeling along seams, opening jars, and so on, but we could find no more cash.

"This was her emergency money, I guess," I said.

"Yeah," he said. "And from what you told me—her telegram to your mother and everything—she had a real emergency. Why didn't she spend it?"

It was a good question.

I put the money back and closed the case, sitting on the lid to get it refastened.

"Know what I think?" I said. "I think Viv left her room one day, just like always, and something happened to her on the outside. I don't know—she saw something or somebody who scared the shit out of her or grabbed her or . . . whatever.

"Either that, or she came back here to the hotel once and found somebody or something waiting for her, and she was too spooked to even come up and get her stuff."

I waited a few seconds, and when he didn't reply, I asked, "Doesn't that sound logical to you?"

This time it was Andre who made a sudden move. All at once he was clearing up the debris from our breakfast and opening the armoire where I kept my things and flinging open the drawers.

"What are you doing that for?"

"Get your stuff," he said. "We're getting out of here. You're leaving this hotel."

"And going where?"

"To my place."

"Why?"

He didn't answer.

"Why?" I asked again. "You think something's going to happen to me here. Is that what you're saying?"

"I don't know. But I think you should leave. You could save the money, in any case."

"You believe somebody was here last night now—is that it?"

"No—I mean, I don't know—it's possible. But aside from all that, I want you to come. I want you to stay with me."

I called downstairs and told them I would be checking out

and that I'd need to retrieve the envelope I'd stashed in the safe.

"You know, Andre," I said when I had finished packing, "I bonded like this—with a strange man—once before. Only once."

"What happened?"

"Not good. Not good. It ended up terrible."

CHAPTER 5

Straight Street

I sprang from the cab.

"Holy shit. You live on the rue Christine?!"

"Yeah," he said. "Didn't I mention it?"

"You most certainly did not, Andre."

"You're tripping because you know Baldwin once lived on this street. Is that it?"

"No, fool. I'm 'tripping' because I love this goddamn street like a schoolboy loves his cherry pie. When you said you got the ham in the market, you meant the market at rue de Buci, didn't you?"

He answered, but I wasn't even listening.

I was running up the stairs ahead of him.

"What floor?" I called down to him while he struggled with Viv's suitcase.

"Top."

Holy shit!

The tea shop across the street, with the madeleines to die for. The blind man in the fountain pen shop. The fifty-seat cinema at the end of the block. There was a time when I'd have become a common prostitute to live on this block, sold my grandmother, given away my soul. I had been walking on the street perpendicular to this one, rue de Seine, one summer afternoon—I was nineteen years old—and I'd turned down this street and opened my arms to it. I couldn't even have told you why; there were far more beautiful places to live right in this neighborhood. But I had returned to this street again and again, walked it at all times of the day and night, observing the life that went on, pretending I lived in the apartment over the lingerie store. I used to see this street in my dreams after I'd returned to school that fall.

And now Andre was turning the key in the lock and letting me into—holy shit! A skylight. The apartment was tiny, but so beautiful. Was this really happening? I was flying around that room, touching everything—the lamp, the kitchen sink, the stereo.

I turned to face Andre, who was regarding me as if I were insane. I suddenly began to laugh helplessly. No wonder he thought I was nuts. I was acting like—like a schoolgirl version of Andre, when he had some Negro arcana in his teeth.

By the time my fit of laughter was over, his expression had changed. I knew that face: desire. Wrong word. Desire was the least of it. His face read, as clearly as the headline in the morning paper, You are going to be fucked. No preliminaries. No talk. For better or worse. Fucked.

I didn't contradict it, I didn't examine it. I was too busy tearing out of my dress.

I ran—ran—to my valise and tried to claw it open, looking for a condom. But he overpowered me, pinned me where I stood. I stopped struggling, fearing he would snap my windpipe with the strong hand at my neck. Fearing, period. I was afraid of him, but even more afraid of the brute strength of my own desire, which had me grunting like a half-wit as we fell to the rug with him tearing at my underpants.

He was on me. Everywhere. Prying me open. Sucking. Thrusting inside me like a wild boar. Crying out. With my nail, I had accidentally opened a small gash over his left eyebrow. We were either going to come together or kill each other.

There was unbearable grief in his throat when he finished. I dug my fingers into his hair, pulled his head up off my breast momentarily and looked into his eyes. His face was pasty and wet and he was sobbing. I covered his mouth with mine and we rolled over and lamely began to fuck again.

Through his tears he spoke for the first time since we had entered the room. What he said was, "Belong to me."

"I do," I said, not missing a beat.

He made coffee with his back to me. Nothing on except his shorts. That wonderful barely there butt of his seemed to wink at me like a pornographic sign. A warming breath blew across my desire, heating me up again. Inside my head, I went to the next time I would lie gasping under him, barely able to lift myself to him; the next time I'd lick at the sweat in the hollow of his neck in syncopation with the stroking of his finger inside me. Greedy Nan, greedy girl. I pushed the image aside, busied myself with unpacking.

He got the windows open, then poured coffee and brought mine over to me in a small yellow cup.

"Nan?"

I looked up at him.

"I have never done anything like that before," he said. "Not even close."

"Neither have I," I said, "and I'm a slut. By some standards, I mean."

The next forty-eight hours went by in a blur. I know I phoned Mom to tell her I'd—ahem—changed residences and to give her a no-progress progress report. I know Andre and I had two or three quick meals in the café across the street from the apartment. I know we made a couple of scouting excursions to low-down hotels and hostels to inquire about Vivian, and in desperation we did place an ad in the *Trib*. But mostly those two days, those hours, went by in a haze of the headiest, funkiest, sexiest sex I had ever taken part in.

The caveman-type coupling gradually faded into long looks and longer kisses and driving each other wild with touches and tongues, and doing it in the bathtub, and feeding each other cheese with our fingers, and generally going through each other like two kids with a box of cookies.

It was damn hard to keep my mind on Aunt Viv and her troubles. But on the third day the fog began to lift and I was able to focus a little better.

Andre and I went back to the hotel on Cardinal Lemoine that afternoon, just on the chance that Vivian had come back to pay her bill and collect her things. No such luck on that score. But the madame, to whom we presented a staggering bouquet of flowers, was good enough to conduct another phone search for us: this time to determine whether Vivian was in jail under any of her various names.

Andre and I were still unable to keep our hands off each other, but we had at least come back to earth sufficiently to be hungry for a homemade meal. On the way back to the apartment we stopped to acquire groceries and wine in the open-air market. I put the chicken in the small oven and set about peeling some potatoes. While I worked, he supplied a beautiful serenade—a medley of standards that sounded utterly fresh and even downright foreign on the violin.

After dinner the concert resumed. I was eating his "Don't Worry 'Bout Me" with a spoon, when he stopped mid-note, the queerest look on his face.

"What?" I said, pulling myself out of the reverie.

"I just got the greatest idea."

Wasn't it wonderful, my beloved had an idea.

"What idea?"

"You know 'Sentimental Mood,' don't you?"

"Sure," I said.

"Okay. And—let's see—what else? Do you know 'Blue Room'?"

"Of course."

"Go get your sax."

Duets!

Why the hell not? Talk about your peas in a pod. Two jazz-drunk African-American neo-francophiles.

I'd never given much thought to jazz violinists before I met Andre. Now I kicked myself for not making an effort to see artists like Regina Carter or Maxine Roach and the all-female group she was involved in back in New York: the Uptown String Quartet.

I was now of the opinion that violinists made the perfect musical colleagues. Stuff Smith had collaborated most successfully with Dizzy, and with Nat Cole and Ella. Who else? Joe Venuti, of course. Then there was the old gentleman they called "Fiddler"—Claude Williams, who, if he only had four arms, could accompany himself on the guitar. And, almost too obvious to mention: the Grappelli-Reinhardt combination.

The world thought I was just little old me from Queens. Ha! Little did they know, I was Django's illegitimate gypsy granddaughter.

CHAPTER 6

Lush Life

It was time for a bold move.

Time was flying away from me. Before Vivian became nothing more than a memory, I had to do something forceful, something concrete. And I had to do it now.

That is why I made the decision to dip into the murky end of the pool, going once again to Pigalle.

As far as we knew, Vivian wasn't dead or dying. But that didn't mean she wasn't still in trouble. The way I saw it, if she was indigent, hungry, unable to go back to the hotel for her money, and surely unable to get any kind of job over here, she might well have turned to something not so legit, if not outright felonious. And so I decided to seek help from the only French criminal I knew—make that *knew of.*

The first bold step I took was to tell a whopping big lie to Andre. I said that I'd run into an old classmate in the drugstore. She was living in Paris and she and I were going to get together for a night of drinking, roasting men, and catching up. It was to be girls-only, I told him; next time we got together, I'd ask him to join us.

See, I knew he would go nuts if I told him what I was really planning to do. So he spent the evening playing with a couple of other musicians way out in Passy, while I joined my mythical girlfriend for dinner.

The newspaper accounts of the murder of Mary Polk, the American businesswoman, had made Le Domino, the club where she was killed, sound like sin central. But in fact it was sort of like the French version of the dive where my friend Aubrey danced in New York. A lot of drunks. A few ambulatory junkies. Watery booze and skinny whores and a bunch of randy men who ought to know better.

I chatted up the bartender and tipped outrageously and hung around long enough drinking donkey-piss beer to get my reward: Gigi Lacroix, the ex-pimp who had been questioned and released in the Mary Polk investigation, put in an appearance about one A.M.

Yeah, he was a bit oily. But I had been prepared for that. I didn't expect a guy in a beret carrying a marked-up copy of *Nausea* or humming Jacques Brel's greatest hits. I predicted a certain sleaze factor and I got it. Gigi was a thin fellow with a thin mustache, a bad haircut, and a line of bullshit as long as a summer day in Stockholm.

The thing was, with his big Charles Aznavour eyes and Popeye swagger, he was kind of adorable along with it.

Gigi said he had not run a stable of hookers in more than ten years; "that nonsense" was all in the past. To hear him tell it, he was an old coot now—enjoying his retirement, and for all he knew, "looking up the ass of death." Guillaume Lacroix claimed he was now just a regular *mec* who liked his dinner hot and on time, and of course a glass of wine now and then. *But* . . . if a nice man was in dire need of female companionship, or if one person with something to sell needed an introduction to another person with the wish to buy? He broke off with that emblematic Gallic shrug. *"Entendu?"*

Understand? Sure I did, I said, managing to slide my hand out of his grip and signal the bartender for another round.

Unlike a lot of his stuffy countrymen, Gigi adored Americans, he assured me. Especially Al Pacino. Did I love the movies as much as he did?

Oh, absolutely.

Was I, or this fellow I was traveling with, involved in any way with the film industry?

Sadly, no, I had to admit, but we were both musicians— did that count for anything?

"Not really," said Gigi. "Paris is lousy with musicians—no offense." In any case, he said, he wasn't the one to talk music with. His lady friend Martine was the music expert. She'd probably be dropping in around two-thirty.

I saw no reason to fence with Gigi Lacroix. He was no more a cop lover than I was. I laid out the Aunt Viv story for him. Let's say it was the edited version of the Viv story. Leaving out any mention of the ten grand I was going to give her, I stressed how worried the family was about her; I was on a mission, out to rescue my adventurous aunt, who drank a little and who'd always had more nerve than brains.

While Gigi listened he casually downed another in the army of Pernods I was paying for.

"Hmph," he uttered at the end of the tale. "I don't know the lady. She sounds like an exciting woman, though."

"Do you think you could help me? Do some asking around?"

There went another defining gesture: the puffed-out lips accompanied by raised eyebrows and a slant of the head. Maurice Chevalier in polyester. The guy cracked me up.

I figured we could come to terms.

"*Écoute*, Gigi," I said, "you're not going to be able to retire to the mountains on what I can pay you, but I think we can work something out. There's just one thing I've got to get straight."

"Of course," he said expansively.

"Did you have anything to do with Mary Polk's death?"

The false bonhomie fell away from his face then and he shook his head once. "The unfortunate victim," he said, "was another lady I never had the pleasure of meeting. We simply happened to be in the wrong place at the wrong time—both of us."

I had a sudden image of that Girl Scout bandanna. It just flew in and out of my thoughts. "Did you get a look at the death scene? Out back I mean, where the police found her?"

"Me? No, my friend. I'm no ghoul. I have no curiosity about the dead. Especially when the police are involved."

I took that in without comment.

It was a bit like the time I found my dream chair on sale at a furniture outlet store back in New York. The price was unbelievably low. I couldn't find a thing wrong with it, and I knew that if it turned out to have been put together with spit, I'd never get my money back. I knew, furthermore, the salesman was the last person I should look to for reassurance. Yet I did. I also told him that at the first sign of a hidden defect, I'd come back there and get postal on his ass. I had absolutely no means of backing up that threat. But he took me at my word, and I left the store with his personal unconditional guarantee in hand. One of those rare occasions when racism works for you rather than against you.

So it was that I threw in with Gigi the aging pomaded pimp—with the promise that if he tried to fuck me over he'd have to call in Al Pacino to get me off his case. I'd make his retirement uncomfortable as hell, even report to the police that he'd told me he knew who killed Mary Polk as well as my aunt.

Did he take my threats seriously? Not very, I wagered. But I decided to go with him anyway.

It was while he was comparing *Godfather III* to the other installments in the saga that Martine walked in. Gigi Lacroix was like a thousand other trifling guys I'd seen in the world: unregenerate larceny in his heart, living off the weaknesses of others, quick-witted, shrewd, and lazy. When all was said and done, a colorful underworld character, no more. His lady friend Martine, on the other hand, scared the bejesus out of me.

For starters, my girl had a *scar*—jawbone to neck. No taller or more powerfully built than he, but there was menace in her very walk. She locked glances with Gigi, ignoring me utterly until he introduced us, at which time she swept her burning eyes across my face and torso. I looked down at her stiletto-heeled shoes, which consisted entirely of straps and laces that crawled up her ankles like garter snakes.

Martine seemed to take up all the space at the bar. She and Gigi went into a wanton lovers' clutch for a couple of minutes and then he ran down my story for her. She took it in without comment, helping herself to a belt of Gigi's Pernod.

It was after 4 A.M. when I got back to the rue Christine apartment. Andre was sleeping peacefully, waking only long enough to ask if I'd had a good time with my fictitious chum—and he wasn't one of the guys we roasted, was he?

No way, I said, and pressed his head back onto the pillow. Then I went in to shower the stale tobacco and barroom funk out of my pores.

When we got up the next morning, I'd have to tell him the truth about the evening and prepare him for Gigi.

As predicted, he was not amused. I saw the worst of his play-it-safe side as he turned into my father for fifteen minutes. He blasted me for my foolishness in going into that din of iniquity; preached at me for jeopardizing our status as nice colored foreigners; ridiculed my private-eye fantasies, and so on.

I sat there and took it, goddammit. But, under my patient, reasoned, point-by-point defense, he had to agree in the end that playing it safe was getting us nowhere with the Vivian quest.

Once we had a late breakfast and hit the streets, he contin-

ued to punish me for a couple of hours with all the quick-
step melodies he could think of. I was hung over, but I'd be
damned if I wouldn't keep up with him.

The folks at the outdoor tables loved our ass. They were
giving us an overwhelming round of applause. Andre's violin
case was stuffed with francs. We had played duets all over
Paris, and this was one of our favorite spots. We made just as
much or more here as at Au Père Tranquille or the gargantuan
café on rue St. Denis, where the hookers sometimes helped us
with our pitch, or playing for hours in the métro.

"Could you *play* any faster than that?" I said through my
teeth.

"Stop being sarcastic and concentrate," he said. There was
that smirk again. I wanted to slap him.

Not really true. Number one: whenever I looked at that
mouth of his, smirking, smiling, whatever, all I wanted to do
was die in his arms. Number two: he had done the impossible—flogged me, metaphorically that is, until I learned to
play Bird's "Segment" at the proper breakneck speed. How
could I be mad at him? Andre believed I was a better musician
than I did, and whether he was right or wrong, I had, beyond
question, improved immensely. I could feel it happening,
evolving, every day I spent with him. It was as if I were top-
ping myself in a cutting contest with me.

"We're knocking off now—right?" I threatened, already
packing up. Little or no sleep last night, I was exhausted.

"Yeah, right," he said. "Let's go home."

He put an arm around me and together we tripped across
the avenue de la Grande Armée in the kind spring air.

Through the traffic, across the noisy boulevards and the narrow streets we went, not talking at all. We were heading back to the apartment to clean ourselves up, and inevitably to make love, before going to meet Gigi for dinner. Life was so good it almost scared me.

Almost. There was no need yet to feel the gods were about to lower the boom on my perfect life. Because of course life wasn't perfect. I had not found Vivian. Indeed, I had not come within a mile of finding her—not a single lead—and it was starting to eat me up inside. I'd be happy if Gigi turned up even the slightest little piece of information.

Back in the safety of the little love nest on rue Christine, I took a nice nap in the afterglow of afternoon sex. Odd how afternoon dreams are the worst, but afternoon fucking is usually the best.

Around seven that evening Andre and I pulled into virtually matching outfits: black jeans and white shirts. Each checking the other out and gaining assurance that we looked really cool, we left the apartment and caught the métro at St. Michel, heading for the bistro in the Bastille where Gigi liked to eat.

The place sure had the right smell. Onion and rosemary, rabbit and scallops, sweetbreads and hundred-year-old cheese and rich red wine danced around my senses. I searched the noisy, plain room for Gigi, but he had not yet arrived. We took a table, the burner under my appetite suddenly cranked up to red alert. Andre and I were devouring olives when I caught sight of Monsieur Lacroix, the lovely Mamselle Martine in tow.

We had a sensational meal. And I bet there wasn't another foursome like us in the place: Gigi and I doing most of the talking as he reported on the people he'd asked about Aunt Vivian; Andre looking a little uncomfortable but gamely trying out his newly mastered French idioms on Gigi; and Martine, who clearly thought Gigi's mission was preposterous, barely speaking at all but commanding and drinking wine as though—well, as though she was paying for it.

"We are fairly sure your aunt is not in the life," Gigi pronounced.

Well, that was nice to hear. Aunt Viv, as far as Gigi could determine, was not currently a streetwalker. I stole a quick glance at Martine, who was guffawing.

Martine seemed as eager to show off her rather good English as Andre was to master colloquial French. "So what is this story?" she said expansively, helping herself to more wine, "the two of you are playing what? That . . . *jazz?*" She formed the word as if it were something gross she had come upon in the refrigerator.

"That's right," I said. "What's the matter? Don't you like jazz?"

She shrugged. "It is useless. Anyone can play popular music."

"Oh really?" I said mildly. *Oh really? Is that so, you charmless whore?* "What sort of music do you admire, Martine?"

"Ze blues," she answered immediately.

Andre and I exchanged looks. I had to admit, his was more amused than mine.

"People are always speaking about these jazz men," Mar-

tine said dismissively. "How brilliant they are, how sophisticated. I say 'shit' to sophistication. The only real American
music is the blues. Can you and your man with his silly little
girl's pigtails do what John Lee Hooker does? (*Jean Lee Ook-
heir*, she pronounced it actually.) Do you have his pain? Do
you have his *cri de coeur*? Or Lightning Hopkins (*Op-keens*)?
No! You can play your childish ballads all you want, but you
will never make anyone feel the way Muddy Waters did. No.
You *have* no feeling compared to them. No soul. I do not care
how black you are."

What could I do? If I got up and bitch slapped her, which
was what she deserved, it was going to cause no end of trouble. Somebody might panic and call for help. Gigi might pull
out of the deal and leave me right back where I started. Or,
just as likely, Martine, despite the thirty pounds I had on her,
might end up kicking the shit out of me. I kept my seat. It
had to be the high road for now.

"Well, thank you, Martine," I said crisply. "That was most
informative. Tell me, is Muddy Waters your very favorite
noble savage?"

"Do not patronize me."

"Patronize *you*?" Andre repeated, not so amused anymore.

She shirked off his remark. "If you are really interested in
who I like—for me, there is no one like Haskins. He was the
best blues man of them all."

Haskins? Who the hell was that?

I looked to Andre, Mr. Negro Music, for help. But apparently he, too, was drawing a blank on the name.

"It does not surprise me that you have not heard of him,"

Martine said sniffily. "See, Mr. Pigtails? I told you, you know nothing about the soul."

The three of us—Gigi, the slow-boiling Andre, and I—all sat back as Martine launched into her lecture.

"Little Rube Haskins," she said, "was a giant. A hero. He was unfairly locked up in your racist Mississippi prisons. But he escaped, first to Canada and then to Marseilles. Finally he came to Paris. He was the last in a line of giants like Leadbelly and 'Owling Wolf."

Andre listened intently as she rattled on. "Listen, Martine," he said when at last she stopped for a breather, "are you telling me this Haskins was living and singing in Paris in the 1970s?"

"Yes, that is right."

"And he wrote all these songs himself, you say?"

"That is right."

"But . . . but how come I don't know anything about this genius? I mean, why doesn't his name turn up in anybody's book? Why don't we see him listed as the composer on any folk music? How come I never once even heard the guy's name?"

Martine used Gigi's disposable lighter to fire up her cigarette. She took a luxurious puff from it and then told Andre, "You expect me to explain your ignorance to you? This I cannot do."

Sharp intake of breath. Like he was counting to ten. "I don't suppose you have any of his records?"

"Records!" Martine scoffed. "Records? He had no records. The music industry is interested only in money, not in the truth. Haskins was appreciated only by the aficionados. Besides, just as he was about to go into the studio to make an album—he died."

"So how did you hear him? You went to these places where the aficionados hung out? Or to some kind of underground concerts?"

"What are you talking about, you ignorant man? I never saw him in my life. How old do you think I am? I was only a girl then. I've heard the tape recordings made of him at the clubs. They're collector's items today."

Andre gave her a lingering look of appraisal, full of skepticism.

Gigi, draining his glass, placed a proprietary arm around Martine's shoulder. "My Martine is like an encyclopedia, you know. Full of information—and opinions—no?"

"Yeah," said Andre, in English. "Full of it."

I gave him a sharp look.

"Hey, Martine," he challenged, "what's your favorite song by this giant—what's-his-name—Rube Haskins?"

" 'The Field Hand's Prayer,' " she snapped right back at him.

"The what?!" He reared back in his chair, openly laughing at her.

This time, the look I threw him had broken glass in it.

"You find it funny?" Martine said, going red at the ears. "You think Haskins could not write a song better than the weak, pitiful white immigrants you jazz musicians worship? You would rather hear something by Cole Porter than the words coming from the heart of the descendant of a slave? What sort of idiot does this make you?"

Oh shit.

To quote my friend Aubrey, *What you have to say that for?*

Andre's eyeballs were orbiting their sockets. Spittle at the corner of his mouth. Fists clenched. All the signs of a man about to go ballistic.

He leaned toward her threateningly. "Listen, you skank, what you know about the blues—" was all I let him get out before I smashed into his ankle with my low-cut boot.

"Andre!" I called into his face like a drill sergeant. "We'll have Martine over to the apartment for a night of shop talk some other time! We've got plenty of other stuff to talk about right now, don't we, Andre?"

He was fuming, but he shut up and, except for the stray wisecrack, remained that way while I passed a few more hundred francs to Gigi and listened to his rundown of where he was going to go later that night to ask about Vivian's whereabouts. I wrote down the phone number at the rue Christine apartment and he tucked it into his pocket.

Before the party broke up, Martine had an Armagnac and ordered espressos for all. Generous of the cow, wasn't it? I didn't want any goddamn coffee, but she had moved too quickly. I paid the check, glowering at her and at Andre.

We parted from them on the street, Gigi bursting with good manners and good will.

"Stop worrying," he said reassuringly. "I will find your wayward aunt."

"Y'all can stop worrying, too," Andre muttered under his breath. "Why don't you take a fucking cab to the Delta on our money? Check out some authentic blues."

I waited until our dinner companions turned the corner before loosing my rage on my lover.

"Andre, what the fuck do you mean, starting a fight over some lame ass singer with that dumb whore?"

"What the fuck do you mean, *starting*? I didn't start it! That 'dumb whore' had the nerve to talk to me about slaves!"

"Shut up, fool! You let that silly woman bait you. You let your know-it-all musical ego run away with you—like it was your balls on the line instead of finding Vivian. Finding Vivian! That's the real point here, remember? I wouldn't give a rat's ass for Martine's musical opinions either, but I can't afford to let this guy Gigi go yet. It'd be like flushing my money down the toilet, and we still wouldn't know anything. It's . . . It's . . . God damn, what is the matter with you, Andre!"

Our second public brawl. Screaming at each other—that's how this relationship had started. We went at it full throttle there in front of the restaurant, a few curious onlookers, non-English-speakers, I guessed, treating it as though we were the evening's entertainment: like we were street theater.

We used the walk home to cool down.

By the time we shut the door of the apartment behind us, I was exhausted all over again. I put on water for herbal tea and grudgingly made enough for Andre as well.

I plopped his cup down in front of him at the table.

"I'm sorry," he mumbled.

I grunted.

"I'm *really* sorry."

That sent me into his lap, tearing up and snuffling. He rocked me for a while.

"I'm trying to do what's right, Andre," I said. "I'm just trying to do right by Auntie Viv. I don't know, maybe I'm just feeling guilty because I used to wish Viv was my mother instead of—instead of my perfectly serviceable lovely mom. Pop treated Viv so bad, you know? Just because she decided she wasn't going to be a housewife in Queens—just because she wasn't all buttoned up and appropriate like him. Because she wanted to be free. I loved her for showing me that. I fucking *owe* her for that. Viv made a lot of stupid moves, but she lived her life—you know? I have to find her, Andre. Not just because of the money—I want to know she's okay."

"I understand," he said, trying to quiet me, wiping at my tears.

"I was awful to you, wasn't I?" I said. "Cussing and carrying on like that."

"Yeah, you're an awful bitch. A real *margère*—a shrew."

"*Mégère*," I corrected him.

"Thank you, teacher. Let's go to bed, let's go to bed, let's go to bed."

I laughed. "So a crying woman gets you hard, huh?"

"A paper clip gets me hard, Nan. I want inside you."

No time to undress. Push the hot tea aside. Straddling him on the little wooden chair. He unbuttons my jeans. Shirt over my face. My arms immobile. Can't see him, what he's doing. Just feel him, working his way in. Poking blindly at his eyes. Fight free of the shirt, buttons popping. Tugging on his braids. He's picking me up. I'm gummy with lust. Irradi-

ated.—"I'm sorry."—"I know."—"I love you."—"I know."—
"Don't leave me."—"I won't. Promise to play the Ravel for
me, after," I say through a giggle.—"Yes. All right. Oh yes,"
he says.

Pressed tightly up against my back, he soaped my hair.

"I've got a surprise in store for you," said Andre, straining
to be heard over the knocking of the old pipes in the shower
stall.

"Ha! That ain't no surprise, Geechee. You get one of those
just about every half hour."

"No, not that," he said. "This is something we have to go
outside for."

"What? Where?"

"It's on the street."

"What street?"

"I don't know the name of it. We just have to walk till we
find it."

"It" turned out to be a dusty, narrow shop near the
Comédie Française. It specialized in music scores and art re-
lating to music. The two older women who ran the place nodded warmly—maybe even conspiratorially—to Andre and let
us wander undisturbed all over the shop. I was in hog heaven,
oohing and aahing over a photo of Billy Strayhorn arm in
arm with Lena Horne, when Andre disappeared up the aisle.
I could hear him exchanging hushed words with one of the
ladies. In a minute the two of them approached me carrying
a framed pen-and-ink sketch.

Andre turned it so that I could see it full view.

"Monk!" I screamed.

"*C'est beau, oui?*" the owner said, smiling.

"It's beautiful," I agreed.

"And it's yours," said Andre.

"Mine?" I grabbed it out of his hands. "Really *mines?*"

"Yeah, I bought it—in three installments."

I gave him a dozen kisses.

We were having a great time in there. While the sketch was being wrapped, I continued to browse. I went up and down the rows, flipping through all kinds of memorabilia and photos. It was in the bargain rack marked "Miscellaneous" that I came across the most startling piece of all.

"Andre!" I shouted out.

They must have thought I'd been bitten by a fat sewer rat or something, because all hands rushed over to where I stood.

"What is it?" he asked in alarm.

"Look at this photograph!" I pointed to a shiny head shot of a pomaded black man trying to look pensive and irresistible. "Look at the caption and tell me if I'm dreaming."

"Jesus Christ," Andre said. Just that.

"Little Rube Haskins," I quoted the caption. "It says this is Martine's hero, Rube Haskins—right?"

"Yeah. It does."

"Man, do you know who this *is?*" I said, my eyes popping. "Take a good look."

"I don't have to," he replied. "That's your aunt Vivian's friend. Ez—from Èze."

CHAPTER 7

Pop!Pop!Pop!Pop!

Not that we had anything much to celebrate, but Andre and I went clubbing that night. Bricktop's.

The joint was jumping.

I had bought that amateur photo of Rube Haskins and we had run home from the music shop to compare it with the one in Vivian's scrapbook. No question about it; my aunt's Riviera companion and the obscure blues genius called Rube Haskins were one and the same man.

Sitting in the apartment, looking in bewilderment from one picture to the other, I got one of those shit! why didn't I think of it before? flashes. The original Bricktop had been a social lion. Everybody who was anybody in jazz-age Paris had passed through her door. Perhaps it was the same kind of thing with the present owner of Bricktop's. He might actually have known Haskins.

"Let's get over there," I urged Andre. We could talk to the owner before we hit the streets to play tonight.

It was one move that Andre had no trouble endorsing. It seemed safe enough to go and talk to Morris Melon. He was no ex-pimp with a razor-scarred girlfriend, and it seemed unlikely he'd make us pay by the hour for a little conversation.

I wriggled into my long, tight brown skirt with a matching sweater cropped so short that its bottom hem fell just below my nipples. I tucked the Rube Haskins head shot into my purse and Andre and I grabbed our respective axes and headed out into the night.

Like I said, the joint was jumping. In fact, the whole town was bustling. After all, it was springtime in Paris. Folks at Bricktop's were finger popping and flirting, eating and drinking with abandon, and gathering around the pianist to request their favorite song.

The elderly proprietor was just as much in the spirit as his customers. Morris Melon was drunk as a lord.

Leaning on his spiffy cane, he was up near the entrance greeting people as they walked in.

Small man, big voice. "Children!" his basso rang out when we stepped across the threshold. "*Bienvenu!*"

"*Merci*, Monsieur Melon," I said as he waved us to the crowded bar. "Will you allow us to buy you a drink?"

"Lord yes," he agreed, and joined us there.

Andre started out slowly enough, but was soon in high gear with his music and tell-me-about-being-black-in-Paris quiz. We listened attentively while the old man pontificated and reminisced and testified, though I suspect that Andre already knew the answers to most of the questions he posed.

After he had related yet another fascinating anecdote about his life in Paris—and to be fair, his stories *were* fascinating— we zeroed in on the real target.

"Mr. Melon," I said, "we have a French friend who's wild about a blues singer who used to live in Paris. I'd like to get her some of his records, but I can't find any of them for love nor money. Do you know anything about him? Little Rube Haskins was his name."

He burst into high-pitched, derisive laughter. " 'Rube' is right, *ma chère*. He was right off the boat. What the children in Chicago used to call a country nigger. To paraphrase that Ozark woman's song—a little bit country, a little bit rhythm and blues."

"You mean you actually met him?"

"Once or twice. You know what they say—if you stay in Paris long enough, you meet everyone in the world."

"Did you ever hear him perform?" asked Andre.

Melon rolled his eyes. "Yes, child."

"No good?"

"Good and bad didn't come into it. He was ridiculous. He could play that guitar well enough, I'll give him that, but his songs about his mule jumping over the moon or some such were so derivative and falsely primitive as to be preposterous. None of the sweetness, none of the heart, the grace of the rural Negro—no blessedness. And I should know, child. I'm a proud country nigger myself. I just found the man vulgar, to be candid. But then again . . . oh, I don't know why I'm fussing so much. I suppose he was just trying to enjoy the party, like the rest of us. To be fair, he did have a following here for a hot minute. But he was a footnote to a footnote, at best. I can't imagine that anyone let him make any recordings."

"When did you know him?" I asked. "How long ago?"

"Ah. Well, that's not so easy to say. Fifteen—eighteen— twenty years? Time doesn't mean a great deal to someone like me, you know. Not anymore." He laughed that marvelous deep laugh again and took the fresh martini the barman handed him.

"Might I just show you something?" I said.

"Of course. Show me everything, dear girl."

I retrieved the glossy photograph from my bag and held it close to his hand resting on the bar.

"Is that what he looked like?"

"Have mercy!" he said in wonderment. "Yes, that was him. Don't tell me your friend carries his picture around?"

"Well," I said, "she does adore him. All she's ever heard are a couple of badly recorded tapes of him. She found this in one of the stalls on the Seine."

He turned the photo over in his hands a couple of times. "The French are peculiar, *n'est-ce pas?*" he said philosophically. "Wonderful—but peculiar. And would we have it any other way?"

After a moment's appreciative laughter, Andre asked, "What happened to Haskins, Mr. Melon? We heard he died young."

"Umm. I think that's true. Died young and died tawdry, if I'm remembering it right. Let me see—must have been a drunken brawl somewhere—no—it was a jealous husband—or a woman scorned—something like that. He was shot to death in a car perhaps. Something absurd like that. He didn't have the decency to just choke on a pig's foot."

I couldn't help it: I let out a shriek of laughter.

"Oh, I'm mean, child," Mr. Melon said. "I'm just terrible, ain't I?"

Melon slid smoothly from his barstool, cane and all, when a party of five came barreling in, shouting their greetings at him.

I had to get in just two more quick questions before he took his leave of us.

"By the way," I said, "did you happen to know any of Rube's lady friends? One in particular called Vivian?"

"Oh dear, I don't think so." He pursed his lips then. "The only Vivian I recall from those days was a young man, not a young lady. A British chap, and the less said about him the better."

"Last question," I said. "Any idea if Rube Haskins was his real name? I mean, did you ever hear people call him by any other name?"

He shook his head "Just 'fool.' You two children should have some of that St. Emilion before you leave tonight. It's delicious. Ask Edgar to pour you some."

"He's something, isn't he?" Andre said when Melon was out of earshot.

"He's a stitch. But I wouldn't want him to read me. He's got one sharp tongue."

"What now?"

"Yeah. You got that right. What now? We know for sure now this is Haskins. But where does that leave us? How did he go from Ez to Rube—or vice versa? And which one was he when Vivian went picnicking with him?"

Andre began to speak, but he stopped short when Morris Melon reappeared at the bar.

"Is it true what I hear, children?" he asked us excitedly.

We looked at him blankly.

"That's right, play it coy, babies," he laughed expansively. "Don't be so modest! Some friends tell me you two are the talk of the town. They say *le tout Paris* is buzzing about the duets you've been performing. You must favor us with something."

His slow, steady clapping caught fire and before we knew it the whole restaurant was filled with coaxing applause.

After a brief consult with the pianist, we started with the old Nat Cole arrangement of "Just You, Just Me." A real up number. Everybody seemed to enjoy it. Then the old musician removed himself to a table and left us on our own.

Andre's beauty obligato for me on "Something to Live For" seemed to come out of nowhere. Gorgeous. I was inspired, and tried to return the favor for his solo work on "I Didn't Know About You." Someday you've *got* to hear that on the violin. We closed with "I Didn't Know What Time It Was."

I guess we killed. Applause like thunder. The waiters began to anoint us with complimentary drinks.

Andre and I recaptured our places at the bar and Morris Melon hurried over to clink his glass with mine. "You children are too beautiful to live," he cried in delight. "I want you to promise you'll come and play for us at least once a week."

Andre began to stutter.

"I won't take no for an answer," Melon pressed. "We'll feed you right, offer you our finest wines, and you can put your own tips bowl out on the piano."

Andre and I looked at each other and shrugged. We nodded okay at the old man.

"Babies," he said, grinning, "I couldn't be happier."

If you don't know what boulevard St. Germain looks like at four in the morning as you sit outdoors at the Deux Magots . . . I won't spoil it for you by talking about it.

We had received all those strokes from the fabulous Morris Melon; the street crowds had been supergenerous; we'd stopped at one of my old haunts, an all-night place, for a perfect little meal; I was actually living on rue Christine, my street of dreams; the low sky was showing Paris pink around the edges; and, not least, this beautiful man I was in love with, was in love with me, apparently to the point of stupidity.

Again, heaven seemed almost within my grasp. But I couldn't be happy. I couldn't rest. We were no closer to finding Vivian. She was, if anything, slipping further away.

"You gotta do something for me tomorrow," I said, turning to Andre.

He polished off his almond croissant. "You mean today, don't you, sweetheart?"

"Right. Here's the thing: Vivian knew this guy Rube Haskins."

"Check."

"Only he had a different name."

"Check."

"And he was murdered—maybe over a woman, maybe *by* a woman."

"Check—Wait a minute. You don't think your aunt was the woman—or the woman scorned?"

"The pig's foot, so to speak. Of course I don't know that she had anything to do with it. But at any rate, it had to be in the papers, right? There has to be some kind of investigation when anybody gets murdered. And Haskins was a public figure, even if he was a really minor celebrity—Mister Footnote. We have to find out if the police ever got the whole story. If they arrested anybody. Maybe somebody from his family came over here to claim the body. Maybe Vivian's name turns up as just someone the cops contacted for information."

"Maybe," he said. "So what is it you want me to do?"

"The murder happened, what, almost twenty-five years ago. I'm going to make a run to the library tomorrow, and make a phone call or two to some of the newspapers. I'll comb through the back issues. Not *Le Figaro*, it's too proper and conservative. But the tabloid types. That stuff's got to be on microfiche now, just like in the States. I'll try to find one of those books in English—you know, those music encyclopedias—*Who's Who in American Music*, or something like that—and see if Haskins's bio is there, and maybe his real name: Ezra Something, or Something Ezekiel—or whatever.

"What I need you to do is try to find back issues of the most obscure kind of music magazines you can think of. Canvass all your street player buddies and ask them if they own such things, or where to start looking. Maybe one of those music journals did a memorial piece on Haskins. Hell, maybe something a little more mainstream—like an early issue of *Rolling Stone*. Those shouldn't be too hard to find. Anything you can think of, no matter how nutty it seems. It's worth a try."

Try we did. None of the arcane, or nutty, sources panned out. But, as I had speculated, there was mention of Little Rube Haskins's death in the police blotter sections of the conventional press. The only report of any length turned up as an ordinary news item in a Paris paper that had long ago ceased publishing. Minimal information emerged on Haskins's career and background—not even where he was born. He was referred to as a black American folk singer who lived at a modest hotel in the 11th arrondissement. In the last report on file (the story had run for two days) Inspector Pascal Simard declared that police were still looking for the vicious killer who had left Monsieur Haskins's mangled body in the one-way street where he resided.

I kind of enjoyed playing the puppet master, dispatching Andre to do this or that spadework. While he was following up one potential lead, I gigged on the street all by myself, which was kind of scary but thrilling. But then the rest of my afternoon was shot, as I had to go hunting for pantyhose long enough for my endless legs. I finally found my size at a little lingerie store where only nuns shopped.

Controlling my other operative, Gigi Lacroix, was a tad

trickier. It was tough getting an appointment with him before sundown. He kept hours similar to my friend Aubrey's—the vampire schedule. Daylight must have been rough on his sensitive skin. He finally agreed to meet me at what he daintily referred to as tea time.

Gigi was waiting for me at a sedate "lady food" sort of café near the Louvre. The place was one of those unfortunate pissy hybrids of French and British culture where the waitress sneers at you if your shoes weren't made in Belgium. No trouble spotting Gigi among all the newly coifed girlfriends in that joint. But at least, thank the baby Jesus, the lovely Martine was not in attendance.

"I have a little news for you," he said, using his napkin to wipe a spray of powdered sugar from his mustache. "Don't get your hopes up too high though."

"What is it?"

"A friend who works the Eiffel Tower says he thinks he knows Tante Vivian."

"What!"

"Yes."

"What do you mean he works the Eiffel Tower? What kind of work?"

"He's a pickpocket. I'm going to see him tomorrow. Chances are he's full of shit and just looking to make a few francs for nothing. But I'll give you a report."

"You won't have to. I'm coming with you."

"No, no, my friend."

"Yes, yes, my friend."

"I said no!" he snarled, without a trace of his usual rueful

charm. "It's no fucking place for you, where I'm meeting him.
You'll only be in the way. Besides, you'll attract attention to
yourself—and me. The last thing I need."

"Well, what about what I need, buster? What the hell kind
of place is this where you're meeting?"

"No more questions. You're better off just letting me do
what you asked me to do. Anything could happen—*entendu?*
You're a Yank, remember. No matter how fancy your French
accent is. How would you like to end up deported? Who'll
rescue your sweet old aunt then?"

"Why do you put it like that—my 'sweet old aunt'? What
are you trying to say, Gigi?"

His laugh was almost as nasty as one of Martine's. "I'm
not so sure. But my friend says if this aunt of yours is the
same woman he's thinking of, she's up to her old tricks again."

"What the hell does that mean?"

"Hey! Don't break my balls, *'pute.* Those are not my words.
They're his. Like I said, he may just be giving me the
runaround, anyway. I'll call you. Here . . . try one of these."
He proffered his plate, which was crowded with cream-filled
delicacies. "A girl with an ass like yours doesn't have to watch
her weight. Am I right, *petite?*"

"Gigi," I said in exasperation, "get the fuck back into your
coffin."

CHAPTER 8

Mountain Greenery

There it was. Etched in stone: LE PALAIS DU JUSTICE. The palace of justice, eh? I'd be the judge of that.

Actually, police headquarters, which is where I was headed, is next door to the *palais du justice*. The lettering on the police building didn't say a damn thing about justice.

If I'm not mistaken, a number of famous French people—real and fictional—have been associated with the Quai des Orfèvres. The quai was where Inspector Maigret was based, of course. At the urging of my high school French teacher I had read all those George Simenon novels about the eccentric detective. And quite near police headquarters, someone had told me, Simone Signoret and Yves Montand had for years maintained an apartment, in the place Dauphine.

Gigi's news had set me off; although he'd told me to keep cool, that his friend's information might turn out to be bullshit, I couldn't just sit and wait. The more I thought about it the more agitated I became.

Yes, I was standing on the sidewalk looking up at the rather forbidding grandeur of the huge building, the uniformed *flics* buzzing and circling in their evil-looking capes like so many gossiping wasps. But no, I had not decided to throw in the towel and seek police help in finding Vivian. Not yet—not exactly.

I presented my valid passport and an old NYU identification, and I told the liaison officer my story: how I was an American law student doing a paper on police procedure in New York as compared to Paris. I would not presume to take up the time of any of the hardworking detectives on the force today, but I was wondering if he could put me in touch with an Inspector Pascal Simard, whose name I had come across in some old newspaper reportage. Surely the inspector was getting on in years now? and mightn't he have a little time on his hands these days?

Just enough of the truth, mixed with a few Nanette-type whoppers, to be believable. Or so I hoped. My reluctance to involve the authorities stemmed in part from the fear they'd discover Vivian was doing something not on the up-and-up, and the last thing I wanted to do was bring any heat down on her. On the other hand, if they embarked on some kind of investigation of *me*—so what? I had my passport, airline ticket, ˌd ample spending money. I was staying with a nice young ˌn in a borrowed apartment in a nice part of town and we done nothing wrong.

ˌe French had invented bureaucracy. Were they proud of

it, or embarrassed? I didn't know. But at least their red tape
appeared to work, sometimes with remarkable efficiency.
After the requisite number of phone calls and hours spent
waiting in this queue or that anteroom—and the inevitable
break for lunch—I was told that Inspector Simard, who had
retired to his home in the Loire Valley, had agreed to speak to
me. I was given his address and phone number in a town near
Amboise, some two hundred kilometers southwest of Paris.

Andre had never actually been outside the city limits and I
was letting him know how unParisian I thought that was.
After all, you have to spend time in the provinces before you
decide you hate them, right? So, wary as he was of my latest
plan, he agreed to make the trip with me. First of all, Andre
put no faith in anything Gigi or Martine said. He didn't believe I'd ever get that "report" on the Eiffel Tower pickpocket's
tip. And second, he probably would have insisted on going
with me to Simard's place anyway, to prevent me from doing
anything *too* dumb. We had not been together very long, but
already he had taken on the role of fool catcher: grabbing me
by the shirttails and pulling me back to safety whenever my
enthusiasm had me stepping off into the abyss.

We caught an early morning train at the Gare d'Austerlitz
and in about two hours we were in Amboise. A local bus took
us to the edge of Inspector Simard's village. We made a call to
him from the *tabac*, and from there, following the good inspector's directions to the letter, we walked the velvet-plush
paths until we arrived at his home.

Monsieur Simard had a full head of silky white hair under
the panama hat he tipped to us when we found him in his gar-

den. He must have been in his early seventies but there was no suggestion of a stoop in his bearing. He was as tall and up-right as Andre.

Before inviting us inside he turned to me with a question-ing look on his face. "I wonder if you know any gardening se-crets, mademoiselle."

"Me? Less than nothing."

"Pity," he said. "I have the feeling these flowers need more water. But then again one doesn't want to risk drowning them, you know. I've always liked the garden so much, but it was really my wife who tended to it. I've been slowly killing off one of her prized bushes after another ever since she died ten years ago."

As he invited us inside I thought I saw a mischievous little smile at the corner of Inspector Simard's mouth, but I couldn't be sure. So I just nodded my head in sympathetic under-standing.

In less than twenty minutes I had come clean with the in-spector. Simard, retired or not, had not lost his touch for eliciting confessions. I told him first about our interest in the Rube Haskins case, and this led inevitably to the saga of Aunt Vivian and my reluctance to involve the authorities. The only thing I left out was the Gigi Lacroix angle. It might be okay for me to make a clean breast of things, but I knew I had no usiness implicating anybody who'd been in trouble with the .

fter listening attentively to my tale, in a confession of his he admitted, "The Haskins case is one that still occupies nd. Even to this day."

"Because you never caught the murderer, you mean," said Andre.

"Yes, of course," answered Simard. "Of course because of that. But I also thought every other element of the case was, well, strange, for lack of a better word. The newspapers—and many of my colleagues, alas—either ignored this poor man's tragic death or dismissed it as a seamy sort of thing—as though Monsieur Haskins had probably lived the violent, dissipated life as a barroom performer and could expect no more than to die terribly."

"Just how terribly did he die?" I asked. "I remember one article referring to a 'mangled' body."

"Oh, believe me, it was a vicious murder. The hatred behind it—the passion, if you will—was quite apparent. But as for your acquaintance—the old gentleman who told you that Monsieur Haskins was involved in a drunken brawl—I'm afraid he has the story all wrong.

"Monsieur Haskins, who probably *was* a bit drunk at the time of his death, was cornered late at night in a little cul-de-sac and struck with a car. But that was not enough for the killer. He or she ran over the body repeatedly, deliberately. It made for a revolting sight."

The inspector sniffed at the air a bit and then lit a cigarette.

My God, I found myself thinking, are you French! I was captivated by the old man. Andre was, too, apparently. He couldn't seem to take his eyes off the inspector. I wondered fleetingly whether Andre would grow into a version of this kind of elderly gentleman—part De Gaulle, part Jackson (Milt, that is, the one from the MJQ).

"No," Inspector Simard continued, "there was no evidence that Monsieur Haskins had seduced anyone's wife or been involved in anything the least bit scandalous. He had no enemies as far as I could determine. He seemed to have been a decent man who was serious about his music and happy to be able to make a living out of it. Happy to have found a home in Paris, where he had a decidedly small but loyal following. The whole thing was not only a mystery but a pity. I've always liked and respected artists, you know."

"Don't tell me," Andre said, incredulous, "that you were a fan of Little Rube's."

"No," the inspector said, "I never heard of the man until he showed up as a file on my desk. I don't know a great deal about the American blues genre. Though I quite enjoyed the jazz I heard in New York years ago, when I was posted for a year with an anti-terrorist mission to the United Nations. I particularly enjoyed hearing Monsieur Getz at the Café Au Go Go. Tell me, is it still there?"

Andre and I exchanged amused glances. The pileup of musical coincidences was getting surreal: just last night we had discovered a cache of old vinyl in the apartment and we'd listened to Getz recorded live at the Au Go Go in 1964.

I related the story to the old gentleman, adding "Sometimes, the world seems a little too small for comfort, Inspector Simard. If you know what I mean."

French shrug. "But of course."

"Let me ask you this," I said to the inspector. "As I told

you, we're sure that Haskins was the man whose picture we found in my aunt's book. Only she called him Ez."

"Yes."

"All right. Number two: Haskins was born in America. This thing about his being an escapee from a chain gang in the South may be true or may be mythological. But suppose—whatever he did or was back in the States—suppose the person who killed him was somebody from his past in America. Could be that he tracked him here. Could have been someone who had no idea Haskins was here, but he finds himself in Paris on business or vacation. And then he discovers that his old enemy Rube is living in Paris and singing at a local club. Whatever wrong Haskins did to this person is still fresh in his mind. So he rents a car—or steals a car—or hires someone—whatever—and kills Rube Haskins and then goes sight-seeing and washes his hands of it. You never find the car that was used to commit the murder. The guy gets away scot free."

Simard smiled upon me. "All true, mademoiselle. Sound thinking."

Andre gave my hand a quick, strong squeeze.

"At the time, my thoughts turned in pretty much the same direction," Simard went on. "But there was a limit to how much could be done about all that. Monsieur Haskins held a Canadian passport, and the authorities there said he had no criminal record and no living relatives. Perhaps he obtained the passport with false documents—who knows? My inquiries to the United States never turned up any record of a Rube or Rubin Haskins as an escaped prisoner. But then, I never knew about this possible alias of his—Ez. And of course it was impossible to check on the whereabouts and background of every American tourist in town at the time of Monsieur Haskins's death. It was highly frustrating, you see. All those dead ends."

"And you have no memory of a woman's name coming up in your inquiries—Vivian Whatever?"

"I don't think so, no."

"Seems like this decent, humble little sharecropping poet covered his tracks very well," I commented sourly.

"I agree," said Simard. "And perhaps that helped to guarantee that we would never find his killer. A mystery and a pity, *n'est-ce pas?*"

"Hmm. Listen, speaking of small worlds," I said, "I don't suppose you have an attractive older black woman working in the bakery up the road who might be my aunt Vivian, do you?"

I got my laugh out of him. Then he insisted that we stay and share the lunchtime meal he was preparing.

The inspector asked me to pick a few flowers for the table. While I was doing so, I watched Andre as he played with Monsieur Simard's two old dogs. Yep, I could see my nearsighted love—who wanted so badly to be a Frenchman—in his gray dreadlocks, a retired professor, walking slowly through the village, lost in his thoughts, a few of the town children greeting him as he passed. Sitting by the fire and flipping through the books and recordings that had made him famous. Playing his violin for relaxation before he turned in. *But where am I?* Where am I in that silly daydream? Am I ten years dead, like Madame Simard? Did I die tragically in an automobile accident? Or did I simply leave him—or he me—in Paris, while we were still young?

Lunch turned out to be a near-inedible salad made with greens from his vegetable garden. The bread, however, was very good.

Parisian Thoroughfare

O h, what a head I have today, children!"

Morris Melon was drinking a fizzy concoction from the stainless steel tumbler of the bar blender.

The old wag-scholar-expatriate was looking ragged, his big bean-shaped head lolling around on his neck.

We all took our places at the long table where the Bricktop staff ate their supper before the doors opened for the dinner crowd.

The potatoes were superb and the steak with onions was fork tender. The collards had an indefinable Parisian spin—piquant but not too spicy. And oh those hot rolls! Taking second or possibly third helpings from the circulating platters, Andre was boarding, as my grandmother used to say of anyone going at his food with gusto.

I got up and refilled the ice pack that Morris Melon had been pressing to the back of his neck.

"Thank you, young girlfriend." He moaned and buried his face momentarily in the cold. "Oh . . . Oh, Father, that's better."

The meal proceeded—waiters gossiping and grousing, pitchers of lemonade and tea and wine crisscrossing and changing hands. It was the idealized image of restaurant worker camaraderie. A family *you* choose, rather than the other way around. The kind of thing you see as a lonely teenage nerd and fasten on. It takes actually getting a job as a waitress and standing on your foots seven or eight hours at a time—not to mention the asshole customer factor—to disabuse you of your romantic notions about restaurant work. I lasted about six minutes one summer, trying to make some bucks for the next semester at school.

Old Melon, about halfway back to the land of the living, retired to his office to nap, sipping from a glass of tomato juice as he shuffled off.

Gigi Lacroix showed good timing. Andre and I had just finished our set and repaired to the bar when I was called to the telephone. The pickpocket was not just pulling his chain, after all, he said. Gigi was in Les Halles now, and we should come to meet him in the square across from the Centre Pompidou. Martine would join us for a drink.

Oh goody. The four of us back together again. I knew Andre would be overjoyed to hear it.

I snatched my man's wineglass out of his hand and began tugging at him. "Let's go."

He grumbled and fussed the whole ride on the métro. Not only were we going to be rooked out of more money by the fatuous Gigi, he pointed out; we were heading into the night-time carnival that is Les Halles, which was always pumping with ugly tourists and junkies and panhandlers and runaways and the dreaded wandering mimes in their cheap French sailor shirts and ghostly white makeup.

"Just where I feel like going at the end of a long day," he spat at me.

I rolled my eyes and endured it. I could endure just about anything. We were closing in on Viv!

It took ten or fifteen minutes to locate Gigi. Lady Martine was the first pointer. I saw her moving toward us, more swiftly than I ever thought possible, considering the height of her heels. I damn near mistook her for one of those mimes; that's how white her face was. And her red mouth was hanging open in dumb amazement. In fact, even the wetness at the corner of her eye seemed to be frozen there, as if painted on—a comic teardrop.

I put out a hand to stop her, but she brushed right past me, moving even faster. When we began to follow, calling out her name, she became a human rocket. The night swallowed her up.

Andre and I walked back in the direction we'd started out. Gigi sat waiting for us not ten yards away.

A hapless young girl with an ice cream cone, who was about to sit down and rest on the same bench Gigi was occu-pying, must have seen what we saw at about the same mo-ment. Propped up against the armrest, Gigi was leaking blood from the gaping wound in his side. And those flirty, lying eyes of his: dead, dead, dead.

I caught the glint of a big thick blade on the ground.

I dug my nails into Andre's flesh so deep he nearly buckled. But we kept silent and kept right on walking.

Plop! went that ice cream. Lord, could that girl scream.

CHAPTER 10

What Is There to Say?

No, *no, no!* No you're *not!* You're *not* going! That's only your panic talking!"

It seemed to me that he was the one who was panicking. His voice was up in the ether and his body was shaking.

"Damn right, it's panic talking," I said. "Wouldn't you say it's about time to panic? Somebody just offed Gigi."

Andre swallowed, hard, and rushed over to the refrigerator. He upended the bottle of Vittel water and didn't stop drinking until it was empty.

"I'll tell you what you oughta be doing, my brother," I said tartly. "You ought to be packing your own stuff and leaving with me."

"That is not an option, Nanette." His voice had suddenly taken on that kind of deepness you might hear in an opera, when the baritone is letting somebody know he means business. "End of discussion."

"Well, okay, fuck you, end of discussion."

"Okay, okay, let's try to look at things a little more calmly here, Nanette. Let's make some tea or something and talk about this."

"I don't want any fucking tea!" I screamed.

He slammed the kettle into the wall and bellowed, "Then let's not fucking have any!"

That settled me down.

He began speaking very slowly, focused, oddly menacing. "What I'm trying to get at here, Nan, is this: something very bad has happened, yes. Gigi is dead, yes. But you didn't do it, and you didn't cause it. You're guilty of nothing—understand? Therefore, you have no reason to run. You have no reason to leave me."

"I'm leaving Paris, Andre, I'm not leaving *you*."

"Would you like to explain to me how you can do one without doing the other?"

"Okay, the way I put that was dumb. But you know what I meant. Look, I took on this insane project, to find my aunt, under totally false pretenses. I was bullshitting my mother and bullshitting myself—I admit that now. I thought I could use my Paris smarts to find her. That we'd have a fabulous reunion and I'd give her her money and I'd eat like a king and party like mad and go home happy. Slick little Nan, living by her so-called wits, puts another one over on the grown-ups and lives to tell the tale. I was supposed to rescue her, get it? I never dreamed things were going to turn out like this—so weird—so horrible.

"I'm in over my head now, sweetheart. Don't you understand? The old Nanette karma has kicked in again. Even when I set out with the best intentions in the world, somebody always ends up with a safe falling on their head. I'm the world's biggest authority on turning sugar to shit. It's such a curse that it's almost like a talent."

I saw him trying to get in a word, but I wouldn't let him. "No, no, it's true, Andre. If I hadn't hired that oily little guy he'd be alive today."

"There's no way on earth for you to know that," he protested, trying mightily to keep his tone even. "Gigi was a petty criminal. Maybe even not so petty. That's how he made his living. Who did he associate with: pimps, whores, pickpockets. His death could have had nothing to do with you—I mean us. Hell, maybe it didn't even have anything to do with him. I mean, look where he was hanging out. He could've just been mugged and tried to fight back. Being in the wrong place at the wrong time—that's how it is in every city in the world."

"Oh, come on, Andre. Do you really believe that?"

"I don't know what to believe, Nan. I don't know what happened to him any more than you do. I just know we didn't kill him. Maybe that bitch of his did it."

"Martine did not kill that man," I proclaimed. "You saw her. You saw what she looked like. She came upon him the same way we did. And ran. The same way we did."

"All right, so she didn't do it. So she ran away. What do you think she's going to do now, accuse you? No. She wanted to get as far away from the scene as she could. People like Martine and Gigi don't go to the police. The police come to them."

"That's right! That's my point. And what's going to happen when they find her? She'll tell them about Viv. 'People like Martine' don't just grit their teeth and go off to jail. They start bargaining with the cops. They rat on their cohorts. Vivian and you and I will be implicated."

"Listen to yourself! We're not her motherfucking cohorts, Nan. And why should Martine end up in jail if she didn't kill the guy?"

"Why, why, why? Stop asking me that!" I shouted in frustration. "Why are you being so dense? Why do you refuse to see the connections between Vivian and all the crazy shit that's happened?"

"Because if there is a connection, it isn't crazy. There's a reason for it. And because I don't believe in karma. I don't believe in voodoo. I don't believe in curses. You're not a curse, Nan."

I started laughing grimly. "I'm what? A blessing?"

"Yeah. Or something like that. What else do you call it, what's happened between us?"

"Listen, Andre. I'm never going to be able to sort this out if we don't keep things separate."

"Separate?"

"Yes. Vivian. Missing. In trouble. And somehow—we don't know how, but somehow—mixed up in Gigi's killing. Rube Haskins a.k.a. Ez Whatever the fuck his name was. Martine. *All* that shit on one side. And on the other side, you . . . and me."

"I'm not keeping anything separate, Nan. I've had it with being separate. The last person who 'separated' from me left

COQ AU VIN 125

me with a lousy insurance policy and my dad's Al Green records."

"Please—*please*—" I jerked away from his embrace. "Let me think!"

"Think of what, more reasons to leave?" He grabbed me again and once again I twisted out of his grip.

He stepped off from me then and removed his spectacles. I stood there in silence watching him as he polished them deliberately, compulsively, finally abandoning them on the table.

"What if I can find her?" he said at last.

"Find who?"

"Vivian. What if I find her for you? Will you stay then?"

"How are you going to do that, Andre? We've been jumping through hoops trying to find her."

"Not the right ones, obviously. We didn't do it right."

"I don't want you going to the police, Andre. Don't do it. Do you hear me?"

"What if I find Martine? What if I make her talk—tell me who this pickpocket was who saw Vivian?"

I tried to answer him, but he wouldn't let me. "What if I figure out who killed Rube Haskins? What if I can get the answers to these things—even just one of them—would it be enough to make you stay? Say yes and I'll leave right now and I will find something for you. Will you give me just one more day and let me try?"

"Jesus Christ, Andre, it's two in the morning."

"Will you?"

"But—"

"Will . . . you . . . do it?"

"Yes, yes!" I shouted. "All right."

"All right," he echoed. "Just don't pull away from me again. Just don't, Nan." He gathered me to him, nearly crushing me.

"Andre, don't do it. What if something goes wrong?" I said. "If something happens to you, what'll I do, baby? I'll go crazy."

"Nothing's going to go wrong. Just stay here. Just wait. No plane reservations, no packing, no leaving. Wait here for me. Okay?"

I nodded yes. "Andre?"

"What?"

"Don't forget your glasses."

"Girl, now I *know* you out of your mind!"

"I know, I know," I said wearily. "Please, Aubrey, don't bust my chops over this anymore. I'm kind of at the end of my rope here. Wait. Hold on a minute. I'm getting a cigarette."

I pulled the pack of filtered Gauloises and a packet of matches from the kitchen counter and ran back to the telephone.

I hadn't even bothered to calculate what time it was in New York. Perhaps I had awakened her in the middle of the night. She didn't sound sleepy, though, and I didn't really care. I just knew I had to talk to her.

Just as Inspector Simard had done, she asked few questions, merely listened while I recapped my activities over here and my efforts to locate Vivian:

Taking a room at the low-rent hotel. Checking all the fleabags in town. Checking the hospitals and the morgue.

First the dueling banjos bit with Andre down in the métro, then making friends with him. The feeling that someone had been in my room. Searching Vivian's suitcase and finding the Ez photograph and the hundred dollar bill. Placing the ad in the *Trib*. The move to Andre's place and our playing on the street and at Bricktop's. Taking on Gigi Lacroix as a consultant. Martine's rap about the genius of Rube Haskins. The tip Gigi received about Viv. The Rube Haskins/Ez mystery. The visit to Simard. The discovery of Gigi's corpse. And finally, Andre running out into the night.

"Nanette, if I didn't know you for all these years, I wouldn't believe a word of this story," Aubrey said. "But 'cause I do, I know it's all true. Fact, you probably haven't even told me the worst of it yet. Goddammit. Other people just don't have your fucking life, girl."

Her voice had taken on that edge of maternal outrage that I both resented and craved. With Mom, I had always been so fundamentally secretive about my life that she didn't have a lot to bust my chops over. Aubrey, on the other hand, had plenty of ammunition. She not only knew in excruciating detail about all the messes I got myself into, she usually played a role in getting me out of them. Where I was a dedicated spendthrift, she was shrewd with her money. Where I tumbled time after time after time into these ensnarling, take-no-prisoners affairs with men, she was cool and guarded with her feelings, could play a man like a tin whistle, and was always the one to walk away first. My childhood friend Aubrey Davis, tough bitch that she was, was unfailingly there when I required a killer pair of high heels for the evening, a sympathetic ear for my man troubles, or simple forgiveness. In short, she had earned the motherly stance—outrage and all—she sometimes took toward me.

In a voice thick with intimidation she demanded, "And who is this Jamaican Negro you're living with, Nan?"

"He's *not* Jamaican. I said he had dreads. He's kind of a mulatto from Detroit and his folks are dead and—God, I wish I could tell you—I wish I could tell you everything about him." Yeah, yeah, I knew how sickening this kind of rhapsodizing could get. But I couldn't stop myself. "Like I said, I met him down in the subway. He saved me from these racist geeks. And he's just so young and sensitive and serious and I don't want to hurt him, Aubrey, I can't, I—oh, shit—I guess I love him," I said hopelessly.

She was silent for a minute, gathering her patience, I suppose, trying to calm down, trying not to treat me as the fool she knew me to be.

"What does he look like?" she asked sheepishly.

"Child, he's so gorgeous you could die."

The both of us laughed for a long time.

"I'm not lying, girl. He's got these beautiful bony wrists and fingers and these long arms like a Watusi."

"Like a what?"

"Never mind. Let me tell you about his mouth, Aubrey. At the edges it goes down, but then it goes up again, see, like a surprise. You know what I mean? And you know how some guys have a butt that starts right underneath their waist? His is like that. And his legs are so long, they're almost as pretty as yours. And he has these humongous feet that make me want to cry when I look down at them at night, they're so—so big and awkward and the back of his ankle is so thin you don't know how he can stand up on it."

"Nan!"

"I know, I know, I know."

"You have to pack up and get out of there, girl. You could end up being tapped for that pimp's murder. The police ain't gonna hear about finding your aunt Viv. Or about Andre's butt. What are y'all going to do if they point the finger at him? If the cops over there are like they are over here, they ain't gonna look no further than the first black man they can put their hands on. They'll put his long legs *under* the jail."

That one hadn't occurred to me yet.

Since we found Gigi, I had run a whole world of horrible possibilities through the washing machine of my paranoia. For reasons I couldn't begin to explain, I felt that instead of helping Vivian I was putting more heat on her. I didn't know how, I just knew the danger to her was growing.

But I hadn't thought of the danger to Andre—Andre, who had from the very beginning wanted nothing to do with Gigi. My God, I *was* doing it again: I was calling down death and destruction on those I loved.

"You're right, Aubrey," I said. "I know you're right. I told Andre it was time for me to go. That we had to give up on the Vivian thing. That I had to go home. But he won't hear it. He begged me to give him another day."

"Another day for what? What's he going to find out in a day that y'all couldn't find out in two weeks?"

"Nothing, obviously. I just couldn't bear him nagging me

anymore. See, for him it's not about finding Vivian. He wants me to stay here maybe permanently. He wants to—"

"What? What does he want?"

"I don't know. Get married, I think. Or something."

"You kidding."

"He's young, Aubrey."

"How young?"

"He was twenty-seven last month."

"That's only a year and half younger than you are, fool."

I nodded slowly, as if she were there in the room with me.

"Nan?"

"What?"

"You not going to marry that man. I know it's good, girl. But you are not marrying a Geechee street-violin-playing Negro from Detroit. It's stupid, Nan. I don't care how cute he is and I don't care how intelligent he is or what he does to you at night. He got his head up in the same cloud as you, Nanette. He'll never have no money, he can't take care of business, and he can't take care of you. And you belong back here."

I fell silent.

"Nan!"

"Yeah, I'm here."

"Start packing."

I began to cry, hiding it.

"I'm not playing, Nanette. Start packing."

"Right. Will you call Mom like I asked?"

"Yes, girl. Ima call her as soon as you hang up. And you gonna call me when you get a flight out."

CHAPTER 11

What'll I Do?

I fell asleep in my clothes. Everything—shoes, skirt, top, underwear.

I'd felt sorry for myself plenty of times before. I'd been in that valley of indecision and self-pity and regret more times than I cared to recall. It had never felt quite like this before.

It was a restless, heavy kind of sleep. Hideous dreams about everything from being lost in the play yard at age four, to facing my father with a D in my grade book, to my grandmother's ravaging cancer.

I had told Andre on that day I checked out of the hotel: I bonded with another man once in this same way—all at once, and right down to the bone. *It ended up terrible.* Be warned, young man. Black widow Nan will get you.

I heard his key in the door.

To hell with everything else. He was back.

He had been unable to find Martine, let alone Aunt Vivian.

Unable to come up with anything new. I knew that he wouldn't. You have to let yourself hope. But I knew he wouldn't. Still, he was safely back home. He looked like shit.

We cried in each other's arms. I don't even know if we knew why we were crying. And perhaps we weren't crying for the same reasons. In any case the tear fest seemed to both exhaust and reanimate us. At the end of it, he reached into his back pocket, extracted a palm-sized object of plastic, and tossed it on the table.

"What is that?" I asked.

"The total fruits of my labors," said Andre. "I asked a couple of the musicians I've met playing on the street to help me find Martine last night. We never did. But one of them found this in his girlfriend's apartment. It's a bootleg Rube Haskins tape. She bought it at a flea market."

That sent us not into tears but hysterical laughter. Laughter that threatened to revert back to tears.

"Play it, Andre. I want to know what kind of chops this son of the South had."

He shook his head. "In a while," he said, sounding like an old man. "Let's go to bed now. You get undressed."

Well, *quel* morning.

We made love until noon—dozing, waking, doing it again, falling off again, waking each other from bad dreams, kissing, promising, doing it again. Finally, he fell asleep still inside me.

The late afternoon bustle down in the street woke us. I'd never been so hungry in my life. I put on the coffee and Andre jumped into some clothes and went out to the market for food.

I bathed, set the table, changed the sheets, tidied the apartment, watered the plants, made a pot of coffee, drank it, and made another.

He'd been away for ninety minutes by then.

By the time another hour went by, I knew.

CHAPTER 12

Poor Butterfly

I forgot to comb my hair, I thought, absurdly.

I bet I look like Martine, I thought. Eyes like pinwheels. Breathing through my mouth and probably drooling.

Help me! I was screaming inside my skull. *Somebody help me!*

But of course I made no sound as I ran through the neighborhood. I was hoping for a miracle. Hoping I'd see him sitting in the café. Hoping he was waiting on line for a pound of ham at the open market. Hoping he had run into one of his musician acquaintances or was shooting the breeze with the guy in the wine store. Hoping, even, that he'd been hit by a motorcycle and been taken to the hospital with a nice, safe, lovely broken leg.

I ran blindly down into the métro and back out again.

I went back to the apartment, still running, still hoping, still screaming inside.

No Andre.

I couldn't catch my breath. "What'll I do baby, I'll go crazy," I wailed.

I was talking to myself.

I went on talking: "No—Don't go out again. Stay by the phone. No, use the phone. Call! Call somebody."

Inspector Simard didn't answer. Where the hell was he? In that stupid garden of his? Drinking wine out on the lawn as the sun went down? Having coffee with the postman in the town bar? I pictured his two lazy brown dogs looking up in boredom at the ringing telephone.

I went rummaging in the liquor cabinet, knocking over a couple of those goddamn useless little cordial glasses. All I could find was a bottle of Jamaican rum. I poured out a huge glass and gulped it. No cigarettes in the house. I pulled at my hair until my scalp ached.

Simard answered on the second try.

"Ah! *Salut*, mademoiselle. Are you well? I was thinking of you and your friend only last—"

I stopped him there and began to babble out the story in that kind of fractured French for which the Academie Française would have brought back the death penalty.

Gigi Lacroix no longer needed my discretion, my protection from the authorities. I told Simard what I'd omitted from my story before.

"That was not a very wise course to follow," he commented softly at the end of the tale.

A masterpiece of understatement.

And then he added, "It might have been better for you to have disclosed this to me during your visit."

I sighed into the receiver, not out of exasperation but grief. The sigh soon became a sob. I cried my heart out while he hung on at the other end, making no sound except to clear his throat periodically.

"Very well, very well then," he said at last. "Listen carefully, young one. The *sûreté* will not undertake a search for Monsieur Andre for at least another forty-eight hours. But you must get the wheels turning a great deal faster than that.

"I will give you the name of a lieutenant at the Quai des Orfèvres. He will contact you later, after I've had a chance to locate and speak to him. But first, go to your embassy. Do it right away. It does not matter what you tell the consul about how your friend came to be missing. The authorities are accustomed to dealing with young people in trouble. Tell them . . . Well, you are obviously adept at inventing things. Or tell them the truth, if it appears warranted. The important thing is that you go to them now. *Entendu?*"

"Yes, sir," I said, sniveling.

"Go now," he said sternly, "but first, some other advice."

"Yes?"

"I know you are a brave, independent young person, and that you are trying to do the honorable thing. But I ask you this, mademoiselle: How good an actress are you? How good are you at being a Frenchwoman?"

"What do you mean?"

"Only this: It will not do to go to the embassy, and especially not to the Paris police, as a hysteric demanding action. Present yourself as a respectable young woman, one who has taken a misstep perhaps—but a *woman*, if you take my meaning. *Une femme française.* Cry discreetly, cross your legs demurely, show how distraught you are over the disappearance of the man you love. But do not become shrill in the face of their lassitude."

Got it. The basic damsel-in-distress riff. Get the men to do what you want. Could I pull it off? Here was yet another occasion for me to wish that I was Aubrey.

On the other hand, if I wasn't genuinely in distress right now, then what in God's name could distress possibly mean?

While Simard instructed me, I began undoing my jeans and searching the room frantically with my eyes. Where were my pantyhose?

"Inspector?" I said.

"*Oui?*"

"Do you think he's still alive? Do you think that's possible?"

He didn't hesitate at all. "Of course I do. You love him, *n'est-ce pas?*"

I knew fully how little logic there was in his enigmatic answer. Still, it made sense to me, and I had to hang on to it. I rang off.

But before I could take my femme act on the road, it became academic.

As I was wrestling horribly with the back zipper of my dress, the telephone rang. I pounced on it, thinking, Thank you, God/Allah/Siva/Sojourner Truth. I'd rather take my chances with Simard's contact at the police department than face an unknown quantity like a white American diplomat— one who, for all I knew, might even turn out to be a woman.

"*Oui, allo!*" I called into the phone.

"Nan."

It was Andre.

I fell to the floor, receiver still in my hand.

"Nan?"

"It's me, sweetheart," I said, matching the grave hush in his voice. I willed my heart to stop pounding so loud. "Something's wrong, isn't it?"

"Yes."

"Are you okay, Andre? I mean, not hurt."

"Yes."

"And someone's there, right? Listening. Telling you what to say."

"Yes."

"What do they want?"

"I told—" He broke off with a sharp intake of breath.

"Andre!"

"It's all right. Just listen. You know how you told me once there used to be a rape crisis center where a friend of yours was a counselor? You remember where that was?"

"Yes, I remember."

"Don't say the name of the street," he cautioned. "Just come there. Now."

"All right. I'm coming."

"Wait a minute! Come alone, right?"

"Yes."

"And bring those papers from home—from New York, I mean. You know what papers I mean, don't you? Bring all of it. You have to bring all of it and you have to come alone, then we'll both be all right. I promise. It's not a setup, understand?"

"Okay," I said, understanding perfectly what he meant by "papers": the money I'd been sent over here to deliver. The money orders. Someone knew about my mission and was holding Andre until I turned over the money.

Of course, I thought, it had to be the Gigi/Martine underworld connection. I had been stupid enough to go to a petty crook for help, and now I was reaping the wages of that error.

Except I had not been stupid enough to tell them the reason I was looking for Vivian was to turn over an inheritance to her. I'd never said a word to Gigi or Martine or anyone but Inspector Simard about the ten thousand. Yet, somehow, they'd found out.

I was betting Gigi had been killed because of that money.

"Understand everything now?" Andre asked.

The answer to that one, obviously, was no. But that isn't what I said.

"Yes," is what I said, "I'm on the way." I started to ask once more if he was okay, but I realized I was speaking into dead air.

The street he would not let me name was a little cul-de-sac in the 11th, off the rue Chanzy. There is such a thing as the beaten path. There's off the beaten path. And then there is Cité Prost—that's the street Andre was talking about.

I had indeed once known someone who volunteered her time at a women's counseling center there. Andre and I had dropped another musician off in a cab one night and I had pointed the old building out to him.

"Kind of an isolated part of town for something like that, isn't it?" he had asked.

"If you think it's weird now, you should have seen it then," I countered. "When you went in for counseling, you were always looking over your shoulder to make sure somebody wasn't going to rape you."

There was still a slice of sunlight left when I emerged from the métro. The rosy horizon lit my way as I trotted along the avenue, looking for the sharp turn into Cité Prost.

I found it, made the turn, and then halted in my tracks. The grimy street hulked before me like a living presence, a fearsome thing with hollow eyes and wings.

Half the buildings on the street had been razed. Half of those remaining were in some stage of gentrifying refurbishment. Piled building bricks, wheelbarrows, and construction machinery cluttered the sidewalks.

The women's center was all boarded up. I stood on the pavement and waited, staring at the building. Was I expected to go *in* there? My heart froze in my chest. How was I going to get in? I looked around for the inevitable smelly *type* who would emerge from the shadows and take me around the back way. Who else would be inside? Homesteading junkies fixing by candlelight? Lady Martine in her stilettos, the ring leader of some murderous band of outsiders?

Where did they have Andre? The thought of him gagged and locked in a closet or in a corner with his wrists and ankles bound made me tremble. And though I tried willing myself not to think of the worst—that they had killed him as soon as he hung up, as soon as I'd agreed to bring the money—I was losing the battle.

What if they were watching me right now? Killing him right now?

The press of all those gruesome possibilities was too much. I began to rush toward the building. But a word spoken softly and carried on the mild air stopped me.

"Nan."

I whirled.

Not another soul on the street. I looked around frantically. Up at the bricked-in windows. Even to the branches of a yellowing plane tree. Where had that voice come from?

There was an old gray Volkswagen parked directly across from the center. I hadn't even noticed it before. I walked toward it, slowly. And then I began to cry, making no noise, just weeping silently, happy, grateful: that was Andre sitting behind the wheel. He lifted one hand slightly and beckoned me to him.

I ran to the driver's side and tried to open the door.

"Take it easy, Nan," he said tonelessly. "Go around to the other side and get in."

For a moment I couldn't move to obey him. I was too busy searching his face for bruises, checking his clothing for bloodstains. But then I saw him wince, and he repeated sharply, "Go around and get in, Nan."

I did it on the double.

"Don't turn around yet!" he barked when I had closed the door after me.

It soon became plain what his wincing was all about. There was a gun less than half an inch from the nape of his neck.

"I'm *okay*, Nan, just you be cool," he said desperately, seeing me seeing the black muzzle.

A "titter" came from the backseat then, no other word for it, really. Yeah, a titter—and the motherfucker was girlish as all get-out. Tinkling and merry, and perhaps tinged with madness.

"Yeah, he's *okay*," said the laugher. "And you know what, girl? I want to thank you for letting me borrow this pretty man of yours for the day. We had a lot of fun."

Andre's warnings be damned. I turned around and took a good look. A good hard look.

A silence had fallen in the car. It went on and on and on. I was the one to break it.

"Vivian," I said, "I hate you."

CHAPTER 13

You've Changed

I mean, Vivian, I hate what you're doing. Whatever that is."

"I swear to Jesus," she replied, "sometimes I barely know what I'm doing anymore."

"Here's a suggestion," I said acidly. "Get that gun away from Andre's head. Are you out of your mind!"

The thing was withdrawn and Andre let out an endless breath. I took his hand and held it for a long moment before turning back to my sweet old aunt, as Gigi had once called her.

"I'm not sure you heard me, Viv. I just asked you if you were out of your mind."

Vivian sighed heavily, then, as if she'd just had a hit of B_{12}, demanded breezily, "Where's that money, Nanny Lou? Pretty man here tells me my ship's come in. When I found out you were in Paris looking for me, I figured you'd brought some dough from home. But I never dreamed you were going to make me a rich bitch."

It was my turn to laugh gaily. "Just a minute here, Aunt Viv. Let me get something straight first, okay? You think you can frighten my mother half to death with your stupid telegrams, get me all the way over here, and then, like, *hide* from me—terrorize me—kidnap my fucking boyfriend and hold me up at gunpoint. Then you're gonna call me Nanny Lou, right? Like when you used to bounce me on your knee. Do I have all that right, Aunt Viv?"

"I'm something else, huh?" she said soberly.

Vivian leaned forward a bit. There was gray in her hair now and her eyes were dull, the coppery skin over her thin face not so taut anymore. But she was still my wild auntie. Great bones, high forehead, wide and noble nose with that sexy bump between the nostrils. Still a package of nervous energy and sharp angles. My dad's wayward sister. My baby-sitter and role model, whom I adored. Aunt Vivian. Armed kidnapper and holdup woman.

I couldn't take it in. "Why'd you do it? Why?"

"That makes no difference now. I know I scared you shitless and I'm sorry I had to do it this way. But I want that money, Nan. You give me that money and then you and your young man get on a plane and go home, you understand me? Get out of Paris. This has nothing to do with you and you're going to get burned bad if you stay here."

"Nothing to do with us?" Andre at last spoke up. "Lady, notice I'm not asking you if you're crazy. I already know the answer to that. You've been threatening to blow my head off for several hours now, and you can sit there and say it has nothing to do with us?"

She didn't answer him, head turned away.

"God damn!" he exploded. "I ought to come back there and snatch you—"

I managed to shush him with a hand to his face.

"Who was Ez?" I asked her point-blank.

Snap of the head. Her voice broke as she asked, "What?"

"Come on, Viv. You heard me. Who was Ez? The man who also called himself Little Rube Haskins. And what do you know about the way he died?"

"I'm not going to talk to you all about that. I told you, that's nothing to do with you!" She was gripping the back of my seat tightly as she spoke.

"You heard what Andre just said, Vivian. If it didn't have anything to do with us, we wouldn't be sitting here looking down the barrel of a gun. So cut the shit, auntie. I want to know what's going on here. I want some answers! Were you sleeping with that guy Haskins when you lived in Paris all those years ago? Did you set him up to be killed?" It frightened me to ask the next question, but I did it anyway: "Did you run him down yourself?"

Her fingers tightened on the old upholstery.

"Why did you run from your hotel and why did you make yourself so hard to find? Who told you I was looking for you?" I pressed.

No answer, of course. Just an awful grimace and her knuckles going white.

I began to scream out my questions then: "Did you know

a pimp named Gigi who was murdered the other day? Don't just sit there like a mummy, Vivian. You owe me some answers! And don't give me any more of that stupid shit about getting burned, okay? We're already burning."

"All right, Nan, that's enough!" She returned my nasty tone at equal volume. "Stop playing the tough guy, because it isn't going to work with me. There are much nastier guys than you after my ass. And they don't just want to make me apologize for not dropping a line every once in a while. They're trying to kill me."

"*Who!?*" Andre shouted before I got the chance to. "Who's trying to kill you? Jesus Christ, woman, why don't you just tell us what this is about?"

Vivian flinched at his tone. And then she almost smiled. "All right. Listen up, the both of you. I'm going to tell you as much as you need to know, and hope it's enough to convince you to get out of town." She turned those now-sad brown eyes on me.

"I had me a lot of men, Nan. A lot of friends and a lot of coke and a lot to drink—but mainly a lot of men. This one particular one," she said slowly, "your father used to call a cracker. To his face. He thought that was funny. But then, as you know, my brother never had much of a sense of humor.

"I don't know why, exactly, don't ask me to explain it, but this one I loved. Jerry Brainard was his name. I don't know if you remember him."

"Kind of," I said. "We found his picture in your album."

She nodded. "You're young, baby. Both of you are. You don't know yet what it does to you when somebody you thought loved you, turns around and puts a knife in you. I don't just mean leaving you. I don't mean hitting you, or fucking around on you, or anything like that. I mean when you love them enough to give them your eyes, and then they actually put you in a position where—where you're going to die. They could've saved you. They could've warned you. But it wasn't convenient for them. You just don't know what that kind of betrayal is like."

Oh, don't I now? I wanted to say. *You really should have dropped a line, auntie. I could have told you some story.*

I had to fight myself to keep from interrupting her, to tell her that, young or not, I'd had almost the identical experience with a man I thought I loved. But I couldn't go into that now. I had to hear *her* ghost story now.

"When we were living here in Paris, it was fabulous," Vivian said, coming alive again, for just a second. "I was over here—speaking French, girl! I had this fine man who was crazy about me and a lot of other men in love with me and all the fun in the world and the party never stopped. Just like back at home. Just like everywhere in those days. Your aunt Viv could hang with the best of them and drink most men under the table. I was bad, baby, I was out there."

"I know," I said.

"Well, the day came when the party *did* stop. Jerry screwed me royally. Took everything I had. But hey, those are the breaks, right? Somebody dogs you like that, it's cold, yeah, but you can walk away from that in one piece.

"No, that wasn't the worst of it by a long shot. See, there was this other fella who was crazy about me, too. He loved me, Nan. This Negro loved me in a way I couldn't begin to understand at the time. And I played him. I played him something shameless."

"You mean Ez. Rube Haskins."

"Yeah. Ez. A sweet little guy who was in way over his head and never knew shit from Shinola. I let him think I could have the same kind of feelings for him that he had for me. And I took him for a lot of money—everything he made from singing and all the front money this German company gave him to make this record. All to help Jerry. I'm not proud of it, Nan. I did a lot of stuff I never should have done—things you'd be ashamed to know about me—things that could have landed me in jail if I'd been caught—but I feel the worst about Little Rube.

"Anyway, what goes around comes around, like they say. I fucked over Ez, and Jerry did the same to me. He made off with more than a hundred and fifty thousand. Except—before Jerry left Paris—before he dumped me—Ez was—"

"He was run down by a car. Murdered," I supplied.

"Yes, that's right."

"Jerry killed him?"

She nodded. "Right. That piece of shit killed him. Wasn't enough that I had ripped him off and tore his heart out. Jerry had to kill him, the poor bastard. The cops looked into it, but they had no suspects. I figured it was only a matter of time before they'd hear something about the woman Ez had been keeping company with. They'd learn about me, come after me. What could I do? I felt horrible for the way it all came down. But it wasn't me who did the killing, and I didn't intend to get cracked for it. Sure, I was ashamed of myself, but I wanted to live. I left here on the run and never stopped running."

"Until you got to the next party," Andre said brutally.

Vivian shot him a bullet of a look. But she didn't deny his words. "That was all a long time ago," she continued. "I did what I had to do to survive. A lot of the stuff I did wasn't very nice. Wasn't the kind of news my family would appreciate hearing. But I never forgot Ez, I never forgot Jerry, and I never forgave.

"I'm about played out now, Nan. Look at me. Do I look like I'm still a party girl? You think all the pretty men still want me? Think anybody wants to use my picture to try and sell nylons or a pack of cigarettes? I don't think so.

"But now I see my chance to get even with Jerry Brainard. To even the score—for me and for Ez. A couple of months ago I heard through some people I know that Jerry was living in Paris again. I decided to come over here and see him, see him one more time—and kill him. I've got to kill him, understand, because he's still at it. Even after all this time he's still trying to bury me."

And Daddy had once voiced the fear that "maybe" Vivian was "accepting money from men." I had to laugh at the memory.

My fabulous aunt Vivian. Next time I guess I should be a little more careful about choosing a role model.

I shook my head. "You can't do it, Viv," I said sadly. "You *can't* get even."

"Watch me," she said, then corrected herself: "No, don't watch me. That's what I'm trying to tell you and this boy. Get out of here so you don't have to watch me. So none of it touches you."

Too late for that.

"What did you mean—that thing about burying you? You mean Brainard knows you're in Paris and coming after him?"

"Yeah, he knows all right. A piece of scum he sent after me almost killed me one night. If I hadn't been carrying a can of Mace, I wouldn't be here talking to you now. I spotted the same guy hanging around my hotel, waiting for a rematch. Oh yeah, Jerry knows I'm here all right.

"Then, a couple of weeks ago he killed a woman. Or had her killed. A white girl who was working for him. And now the son of a bitch is trying to frame me for it. He's been slowly, steadily turning the cops on to me. He left things I had in my suitcase at the hotel near that girl's body—some old scarf of mine. It looks like the candlestick or whatever it was he used to bash in her skull was mine, too. I can't re-member half of what I had in that bag. He's playing some kind of game with me, that old Satan. But he's not going to win. I'm going to get him first, and after that—whatever hap-pens, happens. If I make it out of town, fine. If I don't, fine. But I don't want you here. I don't want you to have to deal with the fallout."

I went back to that morning when Andre and I sat on the hotel bed amid the breakfast dishes, reading about Mary Polk's murder in the morning paper. I recalled the cold ripple that had gone up my back.

Thank God, I had thought then, thank God it isn't Viv lying dead in that alley. I had tossed the newspaper aside and never spoke of the story again. But that killing had worried me, even then. Maybe it was something as ethereal as that little square of fabric on the ground, the one that had indeed been Vivian's Scout bandanna. I don't know. But something had made me fear the murder was no out-of-the-blue occurrence, a tragedy unconnected to our lives. I felt somehow that it did have something to do with us—with Vivian and me. And that it was going to come back on us one day.

"Back up a minute," Andre was saying to Vivian, trying to sound soothing. I knew what he was going to ask her, 'cause I had the same question for her on the tip of my tongue. "What kind of work did the white woman do for him?"

Vivian snorted. "Work? You work for Jerry and Jerry works you. He's been into so many different scams and businesses. He moved dirty money for a while. Computer secrets. Drugs. I don't know what that chick was doing for him. It could have been any one of a hundred things."

"What a sterling fellow you gave your heart to, Viv," I commented. "Did you ever help him in any of his businesses when you were with him? Did he work you?"

Her stiff posture and the way she bit off the words she was about to utter gave me my answer.

My role model had done a bit of everything, it seemed. That pickpocket, whoever he was, the one who made the cryptic remark to Gigi about Viv being up to her old tricks? Guess he hadn't lied either. I no longer wanted to know exactly what he meant by the remark. It didn't matter anymore.

What mattered was shutting my aunt down before she blew away this Satan of an ex-husband and spent what was

left of her life in prison. Hell, after all my contortions to keep
the authorities out of her business, I now realized she would
be better off just telling the police that Brainard had killed
Rube Haskins. If they reopened the case and could prove
that, she'd have her revenge. If the law in France worked the
same way it did in the States, there was no statute of limita-
tions on murder. They could, theoretically, nab you a hundred
years after the fact.

Inspector Simard would help us, I was certain, advise us.
Viv had done an awful thing beating Haskins out of his
money, but he was in no position to bring charges against her
for that. And most important, she had nothing to do with the
murder.

Now, how was I going to get her to see it that way?

I had had a lot of men, too.

I was going to be thirty in another year and a half. I had
lived in Europe. Seen a bit of the world. I'd done my share of
dumb things, and God knows I play fast and loose with the
truth when it suits my purposes. But I tell myself that I still
have a fairly good heart; at any rate, whatever there is in my
heart, it ain't larceny. I have a salty tongue sometimes, I'm
told. But I'm not a cynic, either. Something beautiful, new, intriguing, sexy presents itself to me, my first instinct is to say
yes rather than no.

I had always thought Viv had a lot to do with me being that
way. That my determination to be *out there*, as she put it, was
due to her influence. Now I wasn't so sure. I just knew she was
family, she was in deep shit, and I had to help her.

"I want my money, Nan."

"Okay," I said, stalling. "Tell us where Jerry is now. Do you know where to find him?"

"I know—now I do. But I'm not telling you. How stupid do you think I am, Nanette?"

"Honestly, Viv? I don't know how stupid you are. Excuse me for pointing it out, but you're about to embark on one of the stupidest-ass mistakes I've ever heard of in my life. You've had it bad for a long time, it sounds like. But now you've got ten grand, like a gift from God, and all you can think to do is go to prison for murder. Why don't you rat Jerry out to the cops and then go get yourself a room at the Ritz and start living? Fuck this revenge thing."

"I have my own reasons for doing it this way," she said icily. "Hand over that money."

"All right. Just a minute. Just answer one thing more."

"What?"

"Why on earth did you write home to Mom asking for help—telling her you were broke and stranded?"

"Andre asked me the same thing," she said impatiently. "I already told him. I *was* broke. But I didn't write jack to your mother. I don't know what the hell you all are talking about."

"Then it had to be Jerry who sent the card and the telegram," Andre reasoned.

"That's right," I echoed. "He's been setting you up for something for a while now, Vivian. He's just playing with you. He must've known where you were long before you knew where he was. Why don't you face the fact you're not going to win this game with him? He's going to—"

"I'm through talking, Nan. Give me those checks."

"Vivian, you're not going to put that gun on us again. You're not going to take this all the way there— Oh. I guess you are."

"You think I want to, girl? You're making me do it!" she shrieked. "Just give me the money and stop asking questions!"

I did as she asked.

"All right, Andre," she instructed, "leave the keys and get out."

Frantic, he began to splutter: Where was she taking me? Why couldn't he go, too? If she was going to commit murder, that was her business, but how could she do this to me, her own flesh and blood? Why was she taking me down with her?

"Just . . . get . . . the . . . fuck . . . out. Nan's not going anywhere with me. She's getting out, too."

I climbed out wearily and joined Andre on the sidewalk, Vivian's gun trained on his heart.

"The two of you, get over there in the doorway of that old building. And don't move until I drive away."

"One last time, Viv—" I began to beg.

"I told you, Nanette. I'm through talking. Move!"

We backed over to the abandoned women's center.

"Forget it," I heard Andre say as I craned my neck to read the back license plate. "She's covered up the back one. I never got a look at the front."

We heard the engine turn over.

"You're on the way to the guillotine, Viv," I suddenly shouted across to her. "What do you need that money for?"

Her face appeared for a moment in the window on the passenger side. "I need to buy a gun," she shouted back.

Andre and I looked at each other in puzzlement.

"Here, baby!" she called, sounding young and merry again. "Go play with your toys."

A second later we heard the dull clatter of a metal object hitting the pavement. Then the car zoomed off.

I ran over and picked up the weapon, which was, despite its weight, nothing more than a prop—like she'd said, a toy.

The Volkswagen was nowhere in sight. No, it wouldn't be. I recalled how Viv had this one boyfriend whose car she would borrow sometimes, a cute red convertible. She drove incredibly fast, like a demon. Cut quite a figure behind the wheel with her pretty hair blowing against the wind.

CHAPTER 14

Do Nothing Till You Hear From Me

The *gardien* for the apartment building told us a police detective had come by to see me. He had left his card and asked me to phone him at the station the moment I got back.

I put the card in my pocket and followed Andre up the stairs and into the apartment.

So my big, strong stud—the love of my life—had been held hostage for five hours by an unarmed hundred-and-five-pound middle-aged lady.

I wanted to yell at him. Ridicule him. Slap him silly. Call him a sissy and an idiot.

I also wanted to laugh.

But I didn't do any of that. I was too tired. And too grateful he was alive. And too mad at Vivian.

I borrowed another phrase from the late Gigi Lacroix. "So you thought you were looking up the ass of death, huh?" I asked Andre. "What was going through your mind? Were you praying? Did you curse the day you met me?"

"Praying that her finger didn't slip," he said quietly. "And I cursed all right. But not you. Your aunt—" The words seemed to fail him there. "God, that bitch is crazy."

He collapsed into the nearest chair and I poured him a stiff drink of the rum I had been guzzling a few hours earlier.

"I don't suppose there's anything to smoke in the house," he asked leadenly.

"I ran out of Gauloises last night."

"No, Nan. I mean something to *smoke*. If ever two people in the world deserved to get high, it's us."

I walked away from him and settled in the chair on the other side of the room. "Listen," I said, "I know what you must be thinking."

"What do you mean? Thinking about what?"

"About Vivian. Deciding what to do."

"Do?"

"Yes. I know you've had it. You're just grateful that you've still got a head on your body. All you want to do is wash your hands of Vivian. And I don't blame you, believe me."

"Wash *my* hands! Nan, she just blew us off. Like you told her, she kills that guy and her problems are just beginning. There's no decision for us to make except who to call first— the cops or the men with the white lab coats and the Thorazine. Vivian's not responsible anymore. She has to be stopped."

"I know that!" I said impatiently. "Yes, of course she has

to be stopped. But not by the police. I've got to get her out of here and back home where she can get some help."

"Don't you start with that shit again, Nanette. I'm telling you."

"Andre, what do you want me to do? Send a SWAT team after her? Do you want me to call these people and report she's running around with a real gun now?"

"Do *I* want you to? No. I want her in a straitjacket. And I want you to stop fucking around in this mess so we can live the rest of our lives."

"Andre, they'll cut her down without blinking. She's not responsible anymore. You said it yourself. She's nuts."

"I'm not going to argue with you about this, Nan. Call that detective. Or call Simard. Just do it. But you can't go around like the angel of justice, saving the day for everybody—for your mother, for Vivian, for this bastard Jerry, for dead people even. You got your hands full just barely keeping yourself in one piece—and I mean just."

"Well, thank you so much, Andre. I'm an incompetent, right? And an egomaniac along with it."

"I give up." He dismissed me with a gesture of disgust.

"What—I'm supposed to talk to the hand now?"

He turned his back on me and snapped on the stereo with a violent push of the button. I guess he just wanted to tune me out. A minute later I heard what he was tuning in: the whiny twang of a solo guitar. Startled by the deafening volume, I jumped.

Andre was playing the Rube Haskins cassette he had thrown across the room early that morning. That was some twelve or thirteen hours ago. The morning seemed like a life-time ago.

I went over to the refrigerator and began searching for food I knew damn well we didn't have.

Plunk plunk splunk! Plunk plunk splunk! went the insistent guitar. I heard Little Rube's voice then. A dusty, pain-filled tremolo telling about the blood-drenched beauty of the South, and how writing these songs had been his way of surviving it. There followed some familiar-sounding blues licks, and then his slave's wail. No doubt he was now performing Martine's fave: "The Field Hand's Prayer."

"Turn it down just a little," I said in the middle of a lively walking blues with barbed lyrics about King Cotton.

Andre was making no move to adjust the earsplitting level.

"Hey, man, did you hear what I said?" I asked belligerently. "Turn that down!"

Andre did not heed me and did not answer. Still furious at me, I supposed.

Halfway through the next selection, he ran over to me and grabbed my elbow. "Listen!" he exhorted, eyes blazing.

"No," I said wearily. "No more talking, no more fighting. I can't stand it anymore. Just give me a minute before I sic the dogs on Vivian. I'll call that cop, okay? I'll turn her in. Will that make you happy, Andre?"

"No no no! Not that. *Listen!*"

I did, for another ten minutes. It was just more of the same.

Haskins talking for a few minutes about the horrors of life on the chain gang, telling a hair-raising anecdote about the circumstances that led him to write one song or another. Then another tune. Some nice fretwork here and there. A good voice but hardly a riveting delivery. It was true that I didn't have a trained ear for the blues or folk music. I thought the world of Muddy Waters and Bessie Smith, Bobby Blue Bland and Charles Brown and quite a few others, but didn't fancy myself as any kind of expert about the bedrock blues. I worshiped the bebop deities and their inheritors, and so to that extent I knew the blues.

To me, Rube Haskins just wasn't that special. He sounded like a competent musician showing off his stuff. But without any defining style.

In addition to that, the background noises—after all, this was an amateur, bootleg tape—were driving me crazy.

I sighed loudly and then began literally to plead with Andre to turn the tape off.

After he complied, he gave out with an eerie cry of triumph. "I knew it!" he shouted. "I knew it!"

"Excuse me?"

"Nan, Little Rube Haskins is Little Rube Nothing."

"Well, that's a little cold, Andre. I don't think he's so bad."

"No, of course he's not. He isn't bad. He's nothing."

"Explain, please, Professor. You've lost me here."

"You must have been asleep that day in class. That day when the music teacher lectured about the various trips the scholars made down south to record indigenous blues artists. It started even before the twenties, and people did it on and off for the next half century. Most of the stuff on this tape has been lifted from the old cylinders those researchers made.

Half the famous blues artists who ever existed were first recorded on those field trips. The Library of Congress gathered hundreds of hours of it. There were even some commercial records issued."

"What!"

"Yes, yes. I'm telling you, Rube Haskins did not write that stuff. He stole it—or coopted it—or whatever you want to call it. I recognize some of the protest stuff this guy Gellert recorded in the thirties. Some of the words have been switched around. Some of the dialect has been cleaned up. But that's what this is. Don't you remember? John and Alan Lomax, these two Southerners—father and son—"

"Oh my Lord—yes! And the venerable Zora Neale Hurston took part in it, too," I interrupted. "I'm remembering it now. And for your information, I might have dozed off once in a while in ethnic studies, but I never fell asleep in music class, mister."

Andre was almost drooling by that time. "If I ever have the misfortune of seeing that lowlife bitch Martine again, her ass is mine," he said.

If I was remembering the story right, they would sometimes go into the prisons and record these black men singing their chain gang blues. Unbidden, the image of a rickety jailhouse in the Mississippi sun sprang into my head. What Andre had said about the future blues stars first being recorded as part of an anthropological study might be true. But what about all those anonymous men and women—musicians—nobody had ever heard of before, and never heard of again? Rube Haskins had ripped them off. The sweet country boy who didn't know shit from Shinola knew enough to do that. I found I was oddly disappointed in Little Rube. I must have needed to believe in his purity. I was truly shocked that he was turning out to be as dishonest as Vivian was.

"You know that's how Leadbelly was discovered, don't you?" Andre was saying. "Terry and McGhee, too."

"Right, right," I answered, distracted, fretting.

Andre was giving me the capsule version of the life of Sippie Wallace now. I liked her, too, but I wasn't concentrating. I began to pace furiously while he alternately pontificated and sadistically, scatologically set out what he'd liked to do to Martine and every condescending, ignorant black-music manqué like her.

"Andre?"

"Huh?"

"Shut up."

"Huh?"

"I've got to make a call."

"Inspector Simard? It's Nan Hayes."

"*Oui.* What has happened? Did you see my young friend from the prefecture?"

"I'll tell you about that in a minute," I said. "First of all, Andre is safe. He's here, with me."

"I am relieved."

"Yes. Me, too. Now I have to ask you something else. I know it sounds strange, but please just tell me. It's important."

"If I can, young one. What is it?"

"Do you recall, Inspector, when you were working the

Rube Haskins case, if there was ever any mention of the name Jerry Brainard?"

There was a long silence. When at last he answered *non,* it seemed to be with great hesitation; that one-word answer was heavy with meaning.

"Why did you say it that way, Monsieur Simard? Please tell me. Do you recognize the name or not?"

"Actually, yes, I do."

"You mean he was questioned in the murder investigation?"

"No, never. I know that name for quite a different reason. Brainard was well known to the police. He was suspected of counterfeiting as well as several other crimes, large and small. But we were unable to put him away. He associated with a host of known criminals, but we were never able to catch him at anything. He cut a path between America and Paris, Toulouse, Marseilles for years. But he was uncommonly careful. Tell me why you are asking about this man."

"Because my aunt—because Andre and I know now that he was my aunt's husband. Vivian and Brainard scammed Haskins out of all the money he had. Then Brainard deserted her. And listen to this: he's the one who killed Rube Haskins."

"*Comment?* He did what?"

"It's true, Inspector. And now we've got to do something before he ruins another life—causes another death."

"But how did you . . . Are you certain about this?" Simard asked doubtfully.

"Well, yes. And no. I mean—please tell me, what are you holding back?"

"Mademoiselle Hayes, Brainard escaped punishment for many years. But I don't see how he could cause ruin to anyone at this time, or ever again. He was murdered only last month."

Another one! How many blows to the head was I expected to sustain in one twenty-four-hour period?

"But that can't be," I insisted. "It can't."

I was convinced he had made a mistake. Vivian had just told us she'd been in Paris for a couple of months. If that was true, she had to know Jerry had been murdered. How could she not know? She had distinctly said she knew where Jerry Brainard was right now—that she was going to get him as soon as she obtained a weapon. It meant she was chasing a dead man. Taking her revenge on a dead man.

"Are you sure it was the same Jerry Brainard who was killed?" I asked.

The inspector answered huffily, "I am no longer with the department, but I can still read the newspapers. It was there for anyone to see."

I hung on to the receiver a long time, trying to digest this latest news, my mind racing as it grabbed hold and then let go of one slippery fact after another; as I tried to sort out the sane from the insane; figure out who was crazy and who was merely a liar.

"What's he saying? *What's he saying?*"

I batted Andre away from me.

"Hello—Mademoiselle?" the inspector called.

"Yes, yes," I snapped, rude as could be. "I have to go now."

"*Ne quittez pas, mademoiselle!* Don't hang up yet! Have you seen my friend from the department? If you know anything about this murder, you must tell him."

"Yes, yes, yes. I'm going to see him right now," I said and hung up.

"What do you mean, you feel like a drink?"

"Just that, Andre. Let's go get a drink. Please, let's just go *now!*"

"Nanette, you must have caught something from Vivian. She's talking about killing a man she must know is already dead. And you—with the French police looking for us and Vivian out there with a weapon—you want to go have a nice drink somewhere."

"You got it. No more questions now, lamb-pie. Move it."

CHAPTER 15

Wham Bebop Boom Bam

I don't get it," I muttered, looking around. "Where is everybody?"

Jacques waved at us. He was the assistant manager at Bricktop's.

"*Ca va?*" he asked.

"*Oui*, I'm fine, Jacques. How come the place is so empty tonight?"

"It's Tuesday," he explained.

"Yeah, so what?"

"Everyone goes to Parker's on Tuesday. Even Monsieur Melon. Tuesday is new talent night over there. Monsieur Melon never misses new talent night at Parker's. He finds the best young musicians there and asks them to perform here. Just like you and Andre."

✳   ✳   ✳

"You need help, Nan. You've lost your mind, do you know that?"

Andre was speaking through a mouthful of the chestnut crêpe that he had grabbed on the run from Bricktop's to the métro.

Parker's was back in the 5th, not ten minutes away from our place on the rue Christine.

"I can't explain it yet," I kept telling Andre. Not *all* of it. Because a couple of pieces were still missing. And without those pieces, the rest was—well, inexplicable. The important thing was to get to Parker's right away, to act now, before something irreversible happened.

When we strode through the double doors of the impeccably smoky, low-lit club, I may have looked sure of myself. I wasn't. In truth, I didn't know what was going to happen—or even *if*. Maybe Andre was right and I was loco, tripping again. But what if the evil if's stirring around up there in my brain were all true? I had to do something. This was my last chance.

A girl singer in Carmen McRae capri pants and button-down white shirt was just finishing the last chorus of "The Devil and the Deep Blue Sea."

The emcee announced intermission and a curtain of conversational babble descended, almost covering the taped music (Wayne Shorter, live, 1964) they had begun to pipe in. The voguing, profiling, and table-hopping started then. Folks moving around, floating through the place like minnows. Black-clad Euros, white Yanks with black ladies, black Yanks with blondies, and a healthy measure of prosperous Japanese in drop-dead designer clothes. Not a bad-looking crowd.

With the flummoxed Andre trailing behind me, still regarding me as if he thought I needed electroshock therapy, I
made my way across the packed room to the brass-railed bar.
I began to scan the crowd. If there had been any doubt before,
now I knew Andre was freaked out, off his game, because I
spotted the celebrated American jazz musician at a table near
the stage before he did.

"What are you looking at, Nan?"

"Not 'at.' 'For.'"

"Okay. What are you looking for?"

"I'm not sure. Let's get a drink."

We ordered and I continued to look around.

"Comfortable now?" Andre was patronizing me, attempt-
ing to push me down on a barstool, a controlling hand in the
small of my back.

I didn't bother to answer. I just nodded, craning my neck
to take in every corner of the room.

"Boy oh boy, I hope Satchmo answers my letter," Andre
said, testing me to see whether I was paying any attention to
him.

I laughed and took his hand and kissed it quickly, then returned it to him.

"Who's this on the tape now," I asked, "doing 'High Fly'?"

"Jaki Byard. Like you don't know."

Andre downed a good half of his wine along with a fistful
of cashews. "I never liked that guy, you know?" he said in a
confessional tone, nodding discreetly toward the famous musician. "I always felt bad about it, not liking him, I mean. But
I just don't. He's a smug little prick."

"Right," I said. "I'll tell you later what David Murray said about him."

Well, this was good. Andre was getting distracted from what he considered my mental breakdown. He was also getting a little drunk. Understandable, since he hadn't eaten in days. I was fighting a hunger headache of my own. He polished off the nuts and then dug in on the basket of pretzels.

"There's that couple," Andre said, pointing to an elderly man and woman not far from us. "You know, they always give us a hundred francs at Bricktop's."

"Yes, they're nice people," I agreed, not looking.

"I wonder if I should try to interview them sometime. They're not black, but they are Americans who've been over here for something like forty years. Maybe they could fill in a few blanks for me. Maybe they knew some people I can't quite nail in that chapter on the fifties."

"Good idea," I said, still searching the room. I signaled the bartender for refills.

"I guess Jacques didn't lie about all the Bricktop people being here. Those actors who always come in late are here, too," Andre noted. One of the women in the troupe was waving at us—well, at Andre. I knew what that was about. *In your dreams, bitch.*

"I bet I know what all this is about, Nan," he said a few minutes later. He was grinning like a Cheshire.

"What?" I said.

"This is some kind of complicated trick you're pulling. A surprise. For me. Somebody is about to walk in here—somebody who's so famous and so great that it's going to knock me off this chair. And you knew all along they were coming. The scene with Jacques was just part of the plan. You knew everybody'd be over here tonight because whoever's coming is going to be here tonight. I'm the only one out of the loop. Isn't that it? Some eminence is just about to walk in, and I'm going to be totally knocked out. Right?"

I looked at him. Be careful what you wish for, is what I was thinking. "Sweetie," I said, "I wish that was true."

"Then what the fuck is it, Nan? You expecting somebody from your wild past?"

"Just be patient a little longer," I begged. "Hang in there. I almost have it figured out, Andre. Have some more wine."

"No problem if you're looking for Morris," he said. "There he is—over there."

Yes. On the far side of the room Melon was holding court, as usual, the center of attention in his fraying London-tailored jacket. He and four other people were hunched around a little pin dot of a table and the old man was serving up some obviously tasty star-filled gossip. And, like always, the drinks were flowing nonstop. Lots of raucous laughter. Looked like a good time was being had by all.

Andre knocked off the guessing game for a while and began to weave this elaborate plan for making us and a number of his street music buddies famous. Something about an album featuring a miscellany of street performers playing all kinds of music. What was it he wanted to call it—*Street Smart, Street of Dreams*—something. Not a bad idea, I guess, unless somebody had already thought of it. I nodded my "that's nice, dear" approval.

"See, this wouldn't be so bad if I really was a legal resident."

"What wouldn't be so bad?" I asked.

"Your insanity. They've got socialized medicine here, you know. We could have a shotgun wedding and I could check you directly into the clinic. Ah, Jesus, Nan, I've had it. You tell me what's going on, and tell me right now."

"Okay," I said, "I'm going to try to. But keep looking around while I'm talking."

"Look around for what, girl?"

At that very moment, my eye had fallen on a female server. Not a young person like all the others. And not wearing the ubiquitous white apron. She was walking briskly across the length of the club, tray in hand.

"The waitress—" I said slowly. I broke off there.

"What waitress?"

I grabbed his head and turned it toward the woman.

"Forget her," he said. "Why don't you ask the bartender if you want a drink?"

"No! The waitress, Andre! That woman with the tray!"

I meant the one with the automatic weapon resting next to the highball glasses. Vivian still had nice taste. She had chosen something in understated gray—very sleek, very expensive looking, and definitely not a toy.

"That's Vivian! She's going to kill him!"

I leapt off the barstool and began to rush toward Morris Melon's table. "Stop her, Andre!" I screamed as I ran. "It's Vivian! Stop her!"

Viv let the glass-laden tray fall to the floor with a crash.

The important item on the tray, the gun, she was now hold-ing with both hands as she strode like the Jolly Green Giant, closer and closer to Melon.

He and his party were so high, and so wrapped up in their own fun, they had paid no attention to the shattering glass. But now, with screams breaking out all over the place as one by one the patrons spotted Viv and realized what was hap-pening, Melon was turning in the chair, bringing his chest full into Vivian's line of fire. He might as well have been wearing a bull's-eye on his breast.

Still a few feet away from him, I already had my arm ex-tended so as to grab the back of his collar and pull him to the floor.

Andre was closing in on Viv using the same M.O. I heard him call her name crazily. I know she must have heard him. But she never broke stride.

The old man had bounded out of his chair before I could reach him. The others in his party were diving for cover—use-lessly. Those little tin café tables wouldn't have provided de-cent cover for a tadpole.

The first shot rang out then, roaring past the clumsily mov-ing Melon and exploding a glass-fronted cabinet.

Melon tried a serpentine footballer's move. Pitiful. Loping like an old dog. *Pitiful*—it was almost funny.

More screams. We were in it now.

But then, switching tactics, Melon suddenly turned back to face Vivian. He raised his arms, begging, as if a heartfelt plea was going to stop her next bullet.

Everyone seemed to freeze then, waiting for what would come next.

"Listen to me, Vivian!" Melon cried out. "I had to do it. Jerry showed up at my place. Told me he was broke, desperate. He had to have money, he said—eighty thousand dollars. I almost spat in his face. When you and Jerry took off with that hundred and fifty thousand dollars, I wanted to kill you—all of you. And now, twenty some years later, I'm supposed to bail him out of whatever trouble he's in? I laughed at him. Where was I going to get it anyway? I'd have to sell Bricktop's to raise that kind of money. But he didn't care. You know what he was like—you of all people. He said if I didn't come up with the cash, he'd start making calls— and not just to the police—he said that he'd tell—everything. I'm too old to lose everything again, Vivian. I *had* to kill him."

Vivian broke into hideous laughter. "So you had to. So what? What do I care about that? I'm glad you killed the son of a bitch. But you know this ain't about Jerry Brainard, Morris. You are *not* going to hell thinking that."

He swallowed with great effort and his eyes went neon.

"No," she stated simply. "Not for Jerry. This is for the country nigger. Isn't that what you always called him?"

Whang! went the next shot, into the amp up on stage. That caused a sort of Vietnam-movie boom that seemed to shake the club to its foundation. The people rolling around on the floor were now trying to cover their ears as well as their asses.

Melon limped on. Looking for shelter. Hollering.

Before she got off the third shot, Andre was on her. They twisted and lurched together, both of them keening and cussing as they struggled for the gun.

As I took the first step toward them, the gun began to splutter madly. I ducked, then began to crawl toward them through the bedlam.

Another burst of bullets. And then I heard Andre's roar of shocked pain.

I stood up just in time to see him go down, blood on his shirtfront.

I tried to rush Vivian, but it was no good. With a clear field now, she was aiming at Morris Melon's back, and she sent out a long, clean volley straight into him. He crumpled at the mouth of the small kitchen.

What the hell did I think I was doing? I went for her, screeching, my hands out like cat's claws.

"Get back!" she commanded, the gun now on me. "It's over, Nan. Get back!" She was shaking so hard I almost took the gamble of reaching for the weapon.

Over. How right she was.

I heard myself repeat the words I had uttered to her in the Volkswagen: "I hate you, Vivian."

Through a flood of tears she tried to say something.

I heard Andre moan deeply then, and fell on my knees beside him. When I looked up again, Vivian was disappearing through the front doors.

While the crowd scattered like frightened cockroaches, I covered Andre with my body, begging no one in particular to get help, and to let him live.

A minute or two later I heard a muffled explosion outside the walls of the café. A single burst of gunfire.

Yeah. I knew that was coming, too.

How else could something like this end?

CHAPTER 16

I Want to Talk About You

I had to go. Soon. Vivian was rotting in the municipal hospital.

Luckily, I was free to suffer the agony of all the hard decisions I had to make from the relative luxury of the rue Christine. Thanks to Monsieur Simard's friend in the department, I wasn't in a jail cell on an obstruction charge.

My last look at my once-beloved aunt was a horror show in itself. She lay all curled into herself on the stones out behind the kitchen of Parker's. Most of her face was gone. Deal with that. I'd never seen anything worse. Yet all I could think was: My God, how little she looks—she must be so lonely. But, touch her? No. Nuh-uh. She was family, my father's flesh and blood; she and I had loved each other once; and I knew I'd forgive her someday for all the pain and mayhem she had caused. But I would not touch her. I know I should have found some way to say good-bye to her. I guess I could have prayed over her, or something, but I didn't. I was stupefied by then and I had to get to the hospital to be with Andre.

They found a letter addressed to me in Viv's skirt pocket. But not the ten thousand dollars. The message, written on the back of a café menu, was less a suicide note than a cryptic, telegraphic kind of poem:

Nanette—
Forgive all the lies. But that's what liars do. So now I've got only one truth to give you. Six months ago. In Chicago. Down and out. As usual. Trying to figure a way out. As usual. I've got a job not worth having and a man not worth the trouble—but a damn sight better than me. They tell me over at the clinic I got cancer and nothing they can do about it. Nothing I can do rather.

A lot of thinking about it all. Everything I did and everything I didn't do. My father. Your father. Jerry and the rest of the stupid parade. Out of all of them, only one really loved me. And that was the one I betrayed. He never did make up his mind what side of the fence he should be playing on. But that didn't matter. I always knew he loved me. Traveling Viv, always on the move. I say to myself, Girl, it's time for one last trip before Miss Cancer comes by for tea. Time to make amends.

You'll never look up to me again baby. But please don't look down on me either. I love you Nan and I'm sorry.

One of our street musician acquaintances had brought a keyboard by the apartment. Andre sat up in bed for hours on

end picking out tunes on it with one hand. He was going to
be just fine. Andre did not appreciate being told that his
wound was not particularly "serious," and in his place neither
would I. After all, getting *shot* is by definition serious when it's
your body the bullet has ripped through. But he did need to
let the wound near his left nipple heal. Playing the violin
would have to wait for at least a month. There was no reason
he couldn't go outside if he took it easy, though . . . walk, sit
in the café. He just didn't want to.

I fed him soup and gave him his antibiotics and, as if I
weren't already guilty enough, broke his heart all over again
every time we argued about me going back to New York. That
argument seemed to take up about twenty out of every
twenty-four hours. In the heat of the moment he called me a
few names I knew he didn't mean, and so I never responded
in kind.

"Look, Andre! I know you're deep into being Mr. Black
Paris Exile. But for god's sake, baby, even Sidney Bechet came
home once in a while—didn't he?"

"Stop calling it home, Nan."

"But it is!"

"Bullshit. Home is someplace where you belong. Where
you're wanted, and respected, and loved. Unconditionally.
Home is where there's a place for you."

"I have a place for you, idiot. I have a home for you. We
can work, Andre. We can get back here."

"To visit, you mean." He said it as though there was spoiled
milk in his mouth. "Dabble, you mean. That's not me,

Nanette. I'm not into vacationing. I want to belong. I'm for real."

"And I'm not? Just because I can see it's my place to take Viv's body home—be with my parents over this. I not only let her die alone, I threw away ten thousand dollars, man! I couldn't turn away from Viv while she was alive, and I can't turn away now."

"But from me you can. Right?"

"But I don't want to, Andre. I don't want to."

"Well, you have to. Understand that. You have to either turn away from her or turn away from me."

After a while he just stopped talking. He put on a pair of blue-tinted wire-rim shades that just covered his eyeballs, and sat there looking like a banjie-boy CIA operative.

I tried to play it for laughs. I tried reasoning with him. I tried to play it from every angle in the book. But he wasn't having it. I was "leaving him," that's how he saw it. "Leaving. Period." The silent treatment became his way of leaving me before I left him.

I knew how miserable he was. Because I knew how miserable I was.

When Inspector Simard phoned to say he was in Paris and wanted us to join him for lunch, I begged Andre to get dressed and come. But he wouldn't budge.

"I'm bringing back some ice cream for you," I told him as I slipped on my shoes and picked up the folding umbrella. "What flavor do you want? Pistachio?"

No answer.

"Come on, sweetheart. Please come. Simard wants to see you. He asked for you especially."

Nothing.

"You really hate me now, huh, Geechee? Okay. Pistachio it is."

Ile St. Louis in the rain. Notre Dame hanging behind me in the mist like the fingers of an old hand pointing blackly up at God. There was a time when that would have given the old tear ducts a workout. All out of tears now. Well, there would be plenty of time for that later. Never made love with Andre while it was raining. How could that be?

Simard looked very snappy in his dark suit. He stood as I approached the table, took my hands into his, looked into my eyes for a long time. For a minute there I thought he might kiss me. But no, he was an elderly man who had seen me only twice in his life and that Gallic sense of reserve was too strong. Still, I took note of the kindness in his eyes and was grateful for it.

I extended a fake apology on Andre's behalf for his absence, and the meal commenced. The inspector of course did all the ordering. The food was beautiful and we put off talking about the very reason he and I had ever crossed paths until the waiter was clearing away the dishes.

"So," he said, "I have seen a copy of the letter your aunt left for you. The anguish in it was painfully apparent. It must have been heartbreaking for you to read."

I nodded.

"At any rate, the autopsy has confirmed what she told you.

She was indeed gravely ill. There was an inoperable cancer of the pancreas. One of the worst sorts, I'm told." He stopped there, but a minute later added, "I've always said, when the day comes that I'm given a similar diagnosis, I will most certainly consider her way of . . ."

"Going out," I said, in English. "Yes, me too, I think. But in a much quieter way."

I took a long drink from my—what?—third glass of wine. "It's been mighty quiet lately in the apartment. I've had plenty of time these past few days to try out a lot of answers to everything that happened.

"When Vivian was holding Andre and me in that car, she told us a series of lies. But, in her own crazy way, she was telling the truth at the same time. What I mean is, she laid out the cast of characters, and she provided a list of their actions—their betrayals, if you will. What I had to do was juggle the players—switch the names and faces and match them with the crimes committed.

"I think I know what happened to all the players, including my aunt. I don't claim it's the whole story, but it's close enough to explain almost everything—almost."

"Please," Simard said. "I am eager to hear it."

I began. "The time is more than twenty years ago. Vivian is young and gorgeous, and all the players are having the time of their lives. Americans in Paris. Vivian, Jerry, Morris Melon, and Ez. Morris Melon and Ez hit on a scam to make money. Surely Melon was the mastermind for the scheme. Vivian may or may not have been in on the planning of the scam. I say she wasn't; I say Ez was indiscreet and leaked to her what

Melon and he were planning to do. That would be perfectly understandable, because Ez was flipping from Morris Melon's bed to Vivian's. Unable to decide which side of the fence he was playing, in Vivian's words. Let's say that little Ez was quite drunk with being desired by this sexy lady *and* this very smart, sophisticated, charismatic older man.

"So now Vivian knows about the scheme. And she tells Jerry about it. Jerry takes it all in, and bides his time to see if Ez and Melon can really pull such a thing off.

"Well, what do you know? It appears to be working. Ez is posing as this blues singer and songwriter from the South with the disingenuous moniker of Little Rube Haskins. He's making a splash in Europe with his songs. Except they aren't his songs. They're tunes stolen from old compilations of folk music gathered by historians nearly half a century before.

"Now, Inspector, here I have to add a footnote to this story that jumps from the present to the past and back again. My friend Andre is a kind of walking archive. Never forgets a thing. But for some reason his memory betrayed him when it came to Morris Melon. Andre knew that he'd heard Melon's name in connection to some kind of scholarship related to the migration of blacks from the South to the North. But he had the story just a little bit wrong. Melon was a scholar all right, a sociologist, but his great interest was in music, and he had taken part in one of the song-gathering missions to the South in the 1940s. I've also had time to make a phone call to a music critic friend back in New York. He found Melon's name and even his photograph in the literature accompanying some of the old recordings. Melon himself had some musical talent, and it was easy for him to take those songs and rework the tunes and lyrics. He and Ez would have been exposed in no time back in the States, but over here it was a different story.

"So, to pick up with the Ez and Vivian story, it seems he's decided at last which side of the fence he wants. He's now head over heels in love with her. And she makes him think she loves him, too. But she's married to Jerry Brainard."

"Not really," Simard said, shaking his head. "No record of a marriage between them has ever surfaced."

"I see. Yet another one of Vivian's lies. Well, no matter. Married or not, she wasn't planning to leave Jerry. And, probably at Jerry's direction, she played Ez for everything he was worth and got her hands on his money. She cleans him out, gets the money to Jerry, and then, in keeping with the plans that she and Jerry have made, she runs.

"Vivian waits for Jerry. And waits. But he doesn't show and he doesn't send for her. Slowly it begins to dawn on her that he never will. Meanwhile, poor Ez is brutally murdered. Vivian hears about it. She thinks that Jerry ran out on her *and* killed Little Rube.

"Now you come onstage, Inspector. You take the murder seriously, pursue what leads you have. But, unfortunately, the police never catch the killer.

"The one and only winner in this story: Jerry Brainard. The murdering bastard has double-crossed everyone. Vivian and Melon can do nothing. For obvious reasons, they can't tell the authorities, or anyone else, a thing. Besides that, they don't even know where the hell Jerry is.

"Curtain on the Little Rube Haskins story. No recordings exist to carry on his legend. A few people know who he was, but in general he's merely a footnote to a footnote in music history.

"The years pass. Morris Melon becomes a kind of elder statesman of the smart black set in Paris. Mister Bon Vivant. It's like he got a second chance. Life didn't turn out so bad for him after all.

"Jerry Brainard, according to you, Monsieur Simard, becomes a career criminal, if not a terribly successful one. A little hijacking, a little smuggling, maybe a gofer for some of the more powerful criminals. Still, he manages to stay out of prison.

"Vivian gets on with her life, too. If we buy her story, she's been bumming around for the past fifteen years or so and the party, as she said, is finally over. Vivian is now older, and bitter, and sick. She hears that Jerry Brainard, the man who used her and deserted her, is living in Paris. And knowing she's going to die soon, she decides to exact a belated revenge, not just for herself but for Ez. Somehow she scrapes together the money to get here.

"Only Brainard always seems to be a few steps ahead of her. He seems to know where to find her before she knows where to find him. When someone comes around to her hotel to try to kill her, she assumes it was Jerry who sent him. She's so spooked that she never returns to her room. Finally, Viv is horrified when Brainard kills a woman, one of his criminal colleagues, and implicates her in the murder. It appears that Jerry is systematically planting evidence against her. She's in a rage now. She's going to get him if it's the last thing she ever does in this world.

"Then something truly unexpected happens. One day Vivian hears from one of her low-life sources that a young woman who claims to be her niece from New York is looking for her. She wants to know what on earth I'm doing here, why I'm trying to find her. Maybe it's a trap. But just maybe the family's worried about her and I've been sent to bail her out— which of course happened to be exactly right. But she can't just walk up to me and Andre. She's in danger, she's being hunted. So she stakes us out. She stalks us for a while.

"Viv is broke by now, desperate. Her last few dollars are back at the hotel, and she can't go back there. But if I do happen to have money for her, she wants it. No conditions. No questions asked. When she gets the opportunity, she forces Andre at gunpoint into this old heap she's gotten from god knows who or where. She makes him tell her about my mission here, and then holds the gun on him while he calls me to come and ransom him back.

"Big confession in the back seat of the Volkswagen. Big lies, rather. But are they?"

"Now," he said, lighting my cigarette as well as his own, "I think I see where you are going with this story. What your aunt told you in the car was both true and false. She did indeed intend to kill this man from her past. To obtain her revenge. But by the time of her confession to you, this man was no longer Jerry Brainard. She was planning to kill Monsieur Melon."

"That's right, Inspector. Melon was her target. And she was his!

"Vivian gets over here, intent on killing Jerry, but before she can do much of anything, Jerry is murdered. And it is that murder that leads to the subsequent revelation of who murdered Rube Haskins.

"Viv figures out that it was Morris Melon who killed Jerry Brainard, or had him killed. And suddenly she knows—it was Melon who murdered Ez, too. As you pointed out, there was hatred and passion behind that crime. Who would strike the victim like that and then run over him again and again until there was nothing left—Jerry? No. He was obviously no prize in the morality department. But Vivian's affair with Ez meant nothing to him. But Morris Melon? Not only didn't he get his share of the money from Ez, he was spurned by him as a lover as well. My God, I would think that if Melon could have gotten his hands on Vivian he'd have killed her as well."

"Melon," he confirmed. "Of course, Melon. But how did your aunt come so quickly to the conclusion that Monsieur Melon was Jerry Brainard's murderer?"

"It was the Mary Polk murder that convinced her. She read, just as Andre and I did, that the police had questioned and released a small-time criminal named Gigi Lacroix. One of the papers carried a photograph of him. Vivian recognized him immediately as the man who tried to kill her that day in the hotel. She assumed when Gigi first attacked her that he was Jerry's goon. But by the time of the Mary Polk murder, Jerry was already dead. She knew that it had to be Morris Melon who was after her; that Gigi worked for him, not Jerry. From there, it wasn't much of a leap to realize Morris Melon was responsible for Ez's death, too. And so it was still payback time, but not for Jerry. For Melon.

"But of course Nanette and her young man Andre don't know any of that. They walk right into the old man's net. He befriends them, sets them up with a part-time gig in his place, where he can track their progress just by keeping his ears open.

"And who has little Nanette enlisted to help find her aunt? A small-time criminal who knows a little bit about a lot of things. Gigi Lacroix. The very hood who works as a strong-arm man, snitch, or whatever, for Morris Melon.

"Lacroix appreciated so many of life's little ironies. He was taking money from me for the same service that Melon was paying him for—finding Vivian. 'Just string her along,' Melon probably told him. 'Take the money she gives you and tell her as little as possible.'

"There was more irony than I knew what to do with, Inspector. For instance—yes, somebody was framing her with those items from her suitcase, but it wasn't Jerry; it was Morris Melon. His man Gigi must have gotten his hands on Viv's address book. Melon sent that telegram asking for money, hoping somebody from the family would come over here and flush Vivian out. It was just a long shot for him. Little did he know, I actually did have a jackpot for her.

"And then there was all Viv's talk about betrayal. But the terrible betrayal wasn't Jerry's betrayal of her; it was her betrayal of Ez. She put the knife in Ez. On and on."

Simard was doing his duty as taster as the waiter opened

yet another bottle of wine. He nodded his approval and our glasses were filled. We drank in silence for a time.

"I know how useless hindsight is," I commented later. "But, thinking back on everything, I realize how plain some of these things should have been to me. Staring me in the face, almost. Once Andre played that cassette, the apples weren't just falling off the branches, they were practically jumping into the basket.

"But they were all jumbled together, see. I couldn't untangle all the parts of Vivian's story yet. It was impossible to sort out fact from fantasy, or just plain lies. But I knew Melon had to be at the center of everything. Old Satan.

"*Big* mistake, my not picking up on that one. Should have known immediately that day in the Volkswagen that when Vivian used that strange phrase she was referring to Melon and not Jerry. But, you know, here's the thing about Old Satan Melon: it's as if he made the decision to be as evil as he possibly could be. He made himself into a Satan. I mean, he must have started out on the side of the angels, and then, once he slipped—pulled that fraud with Rube Haskins—he figured he had to go all the way to the other end of morality—to being a devil. I remember how he talked about the blessedness of black people from the country. *Grace* was the word he used. When he hatched that scheme, it was like he was stealing the grace from his people and renouncing his own blessedness. He must have been so profoundly ashamed of what he'd done that he had to kill everyone who knew about it. He wasn't just killing people, he was killing his shame. First Ez. Then Jerry. Mary Polk. Then Vivian, very nearly. And finally Gigi, who had been Melon's hired assassin."

"Yes," Simard said. "In light of what your aunt said, Melon surely dispatched Lacroix to kill her. But as for the others? Open to question, I would say. With a little planning, Monsieur Melon might very well have personally carried out the murders of Mary Polk and Brainard. And he no doubt killed Lacroix. There is a very likely scenario based on what you reported to the police: The night of Gigi's death, Monsieur Melon was ill, or pretended to be ill with a hangover. He retired to his private office to sleep. But, while you and Andre and the others performed, he simply made the short walk to the métro, joined Lacroix in the square, sat quite close to him as they talked, and soundlessly drove the knife into his body. He returned to Bricktop's, slipped in by the back entrance, and no one was any the wiser."

"Right. That is how I'd figure it."

"As to why he felt he must get rid of Lacroix at that moment? We cannot be certain. Either Lacroix simply knew too much about his deeds, or Melon suspected that Lacroix was on the verge of trying to sell you some real information for a change— something that was much too dangerous for you to know."

"The thing is, Inspector, what made him start down that road in the first place? All the way back to the scam with Ez, I mean. What kind of pressure could have caused Morris Melon to sell out his principles so completely?

"In fact, that's what I can't figure out about all the people in this singular group of—I don't know what to call them— displaced persons—expatriates. For the moment let's call them that. Why did they do those stupid, stupid things? What sort of forces, mysteries, were driving them?

"I asked my aunt a question as she was driving away. 'What do you need that money for?' Viv knew she didn't have a chance of getting away after killing Melon. She didn't answer me then, and now those money orders have vanished. What did she do with them? What? God knows, I'd love to be able to answer that question when my mother asks it.

"As for Jerry Brainard, you know what I'm starting to believe about him, Inspector? Bad guy that he was? That he once cared for Vivian almost as much as she did for him. That he was a weak guy, always in trouble, always in debt, and he talked her into getting that money from Ez because right then it was the simplest way to get what he needed. I wonder if he didn't eventually realize he'd have been better off staying with Viv and working for a living like everybody else."

Simard smiled ruefully. "And what about Haskins?" he said. "What was, in your estimation, his driving need?"

"His need was for Vivian, I suppose. Poor bastard."

"Poor bastard," the inspector echoed. "You've cast a very forgiving eye on all the players in your little drama, you know. Mysteries or no mysteries, I could never look at them with the kind of pity you do. But, tell me this: are you purposely leaving one character out of this complicated tale of expatriates?"

"Who would that be?"

"Yourself, my friend."

Me? Sure, I could toss around some ideas about what drives me. But I did much better speculating, piecing together the motivations of four dead people. Who weren't around to tell me I was full of shit.

I merely shrugged.

We'd been lunching for three and a half hours. I had to get back to the rue Christine.

"I take it," Monsieur Simard said as I walked him to his taxi, "that you and Andre . . ." He allowed his voice to simply drop off the cliff there.

I shook my head, not trusting myself to speak.

"Ah." That was all he said. But the word seemed to come from his chest.

"Nanette," he said a few minutes later. It startled me. It was the first time he had called me by my first name.

"*Oui?*"

"You loved your aunt, did you not? And you believe that, despite the unhappy turn her life took, she loved you as well?"

I nodded.

"I think, Nanette, you must accept that everyone is entitled to his mysteries. But perhaps there is a very practical answer to what Vivian did with the bulk of that ten thousand dollars."

I looked at him expectantly.

"If Rube Haskins was so completely taken in by her, he probably told her who he really was. She may have known his real name, where he was born, everything."

"Yes, that makes sense."

"What was that phrase you used . . . payback? Too little, and too late. But a kind of payback." He continued to look benignly at me.

"What is it you're not telling me, Monsieur Simard?"

"The clerk who sold postage to your aunt remembered her because she looked ill. As if she had a fever. After she left you and Andre standing in Cité Prost, your aunt Vivian sent a large envelope by air to the United States. That is all the young lady at the post office recalled."

Ah. So maybe Vivian had made a last-ditch attempt to redress the wrong she had done Ez. She had sent her inheritance to his family.

I kissed the inspector then. I couldn't help myself. "I'll write to you," I said.

"Excellent. I haven't had a good letter in ten years."

"And will you?" I asked.

"The minute anything interesting occurs."

I forgot the ice cream.

Just as well.

Andre was gone.

Nan:

Go. Leave keys downstairs. Go Go I won't come back till you do.

I packed in a hurry, to say the least, so I'm sure I must have left something behind. If so, I didn't do it on purpose. Believe me.

Yes, I thought, there was another cue I hadn't picked up on. Before I left the apartment to join Simard, Andre was playing around with that keyboard. He was playing at something kitschy—Viennese—something like "Fascination." But, as I descended the stairs, I could have sworn I heard the opening notes to Gordon Jenkins's "Good-bye."

CHAPTER 17

Parting Is Not Good-bye

I wrote a note, too. On the back of the one he'd left for me. But in the end I didn't leave it.

I had it in my purse.

What am I doing here?

I belonged with Andre, didn't I? He was the one who was so caught up with "belonging" to a place. Not me, not any-more. I was beginning to accept that I'd always be a little bit on the periphery. Fuck the *place*—it was Andre I belonged with, no? So what was I doing up above the world, heading back to America? Alone.

You're taking Vivian's body home. That's what you're doing. Her brother is going to bury her, and maybe you along with her.

To repeat, I belonged with Andre, didn't I? Here was a man who had not only pledged the rest of his life to me. Not only could play "Billie's Bounce" on the violin. Not only showed a willingness to face down my shitty karma. He loved me enough to take a bullet that by all rights should have been mine.

"*Madame?*" I heard a soft voice say.

The flight was only half full. The attendant with the chignon wouldn't leave me alone. I had already declined the game hen dinner, smoked salmon, honey peanuts, champagne, the current issue of *Paris Vogue*, and the in-flight Julia Roberts movie. With each offer I turned my puffy, ugly old face to her and tried to answer in the fewest polite French words possible.

I had downed an ocean of black coffee since boarding the plane.

The poison gas began to rise again in my stomach as I had another flashback of Vivian lying in that alley with the back of her head blown off.

I turned on the overhead light to help chase the image away.

I lived too much in the past. That was my trouble. That's what the music was about, when you really got down to it. It wasn't just what I did for a half-assed living, what I respected and loved. It was my escape from the world as presently constituted.

Worse, it wasn't even *my* past. All my life it seems I've been caught up with the people, the music, and the feel of life at another time, a time at least three generations removed from my own. Here you are, little Nanette, it's 1969 and here's the gift of life. Welcome to the world, dear. What are you going to be, a postal worker, a bank manager—you know, they let us do that kind of thing now—or a computer whiz? *Me? Thanks, but no thanks. I'd rather be Mary Lou Williams. Ivy Anderson?*

Or, yeah, how about Sonny Rollins? I could never get with the music I was supposed to like. Nor the kind of man I was supposed to like. Nor the kind of ambitions that were supposed to drive me forward. I don't give a damn about the things that excite or tie up the folks drinking shooters on the Upper West Side or hanging with Spike in Fort Greene.

Yes, through the music of the past I had, like Andre, found a way to honor my forefathers. But I knew there was something terribly dishonest about the way I lived. It wasn't just living in a fantasy world, it wasn't just being phony—it was wrong. It's wrong not to live in the here and now. It's cowardly and pious and arrogant and wrong.

And the other kids just don't like me.

If I played my cards right I could spend the whole flight beating up on myself. I think it must have been Ernestine, that voice in my ear, that was telling me: *If you feel this awful, you must deserve it.*

Pictures of Andre were now interspersed with the memories of Vivian. Those big feet of his, and the way he moved, and that hollow place in his lower back. The day he took me on that breathless guided tour, the same day we first went to Bricktop's. Teasing him then, I said he was crazy—that his devotion to the past had crazed him. Well, maybe that was no joke; maybe he *was* crazy, crazy for real. And, finally, those cold blue killer-for-hire shades that had obscured his eyes, hidden him, taken him from me during the last days we had together.

Belong with him? said Ernestine scornfully. *You'll never see him again.*

It wasn't fair, it wasn't fair.

I dug a few paper napkins out of the seat-back pocket and dabbed at my eyes.

Would Andre continue to live and work in Paris, stay on in France forever? He sure had the talent and the determination. I had no doubt he would do our forebears proud, the obscure ones along with the famous. All those black people with a hyperdeveloped sense of the romantic which takes them to faraway places, out of the here and now they were born to endure in America. Maybe someday, as maturity softened his contempt, he'd be able to view Little Rube Haskins in a more sympathetic light. And Morris Melon. And me. All us permanent strangers.

Sure, Andre would distinguish himself in print or as a venerable lecturer or an acclaimed performer. He'd get—I made myself say it—get married, become a French citizen, like he wanted, and grow into his Inspector Simard role. A stone cottage in the provinces, two dogs—the whole bit. *Un homme français.*

The aircraft shimmied a little and then the pilot's reassuring baritone issued from the loudspeaker. In a nutshell: *Go back to sleep, it's going to be okay.*

Would I ever see Paris again? Probably. It was unbearable to think of dying without seeing those lights once more. Would I ever cry again as I drove past the Arc de Triomphe or walked in the Bois du Boulogne? Maybe. Would I ever again feel that the city belonged to me, and I to it? Like I wasn't just another savvy tourist, or even a starry-eyed expatriate, but the genuine article—*une femme française.*

No.